ARE WE HUMAN?

Melanie Martin & Leah O'Shaughnessy

Examcraft Group

Published by

Examcraft Group

89F Lagan Road, Dublin Industrial Estate, Glasnevin, Dublin 11

© 2024 Examcraft Group

ISBN: 978-1-907330-91-9

Disclaimer
The stories in this book are personal accounts as the contributors have experienced them. We have chosen to take their accounts at face value and meet them with compassion. Due to the nature of borders and countries, we cannot verify all claims or statements made within these personal accounts.

Images from Freepik, Shutterstock, Sudanese Documents Library, Offalyexpress.ie and personal archives.

This book is dedicated to Ashwak and to all those who have lost loved ones due to war, displacement, violence and poverty.

"THE TRUE MEASURE OF ANY SOCIETY
CAN BE FOUND IN HOW IT TREATS ITS
MOST VULNERABLE MEMBERS."

Mahatma Gandhi

ACKNOWLEDGEMENTS

We extend our heartfelt thanks to all who supported the creation of this book. As the saying goes, "It takes a village," and without the generosity of so many, we would not have made the connections that shaped this project. Special thanks to Shaykh Dr. Umar Al-Qadri, Joe Mason, Ciara McCluskey and Gary Parsons for their vital support.

Most importantly, we are deeply grateful to the book's contributors, whose vulnerability, bravery and strength have been truly inspiring. Their willingness to share their personal stories, insights and experiences has enriched this work in ways we could never have achieved without them. Their authenticity and diverse perspectives are the heart of this book, and their courage in the face of adversity has been a source of profound inspiration.

We also thank our families and friends, whose unwavering belief in us and constant encouragement provided the foundation for this journey. Your support kept us going every step of the way.

We are profoundly grateful to Philip O'Callaghan, Managing Director of Examcraft, for agreeing to publish *Are We Human?* and for his guidance, insights and tireless efforts in refining and perfecting this book. Philip's vision and trust made this project possible. His steadfast support, encouragement and belief in our abilities motivated us throughout. His leadership and commitment to addressing injustice, alongside Examcraft Group's innovative approach to education, have been truly inspiring.

To the entire Examcraft Group team, thank you for embracing this project with such heart. To our graphic design team, Renato da Cunha and Ana Carolina Amaral Fernandes – Ana, your heart, professionalism and boundless talent are truly exceptional. Your ability to bring our vision to life has been invaluable. Our editors, Stephanie Campion and Emma Sherry, your attention to detail and guidance have been indispensable.

A special thank you to Stephen King, Richie Delea and Henrique Fernandes for dedicating your time to film and edit. We also extend our thanks to Smartsite Media and Plunkett PR.

Lastly, to our readers, thank you for taking the time to engage with this book. Share it with a friend, and let its insights enrich your perspectives and conversations.

In Ireland, we are witnessing a rise in anti-immigration rhetoric and increasing hostility towards refugees and migrants. Through the sharing of stories, *Are We Human?* hopes to stir people's compassion and understanding and bring to light a voice that has been lost in the current climate.

Divisive rhetoric has resulted in an "us and them" attitude and an ill-informed hatred directed at the wrong people. At what point have we forgotten that no one has a say in where they are born or the conditions in which they must live? No one chooses war or poverty or to have their human rights abused. Yet we live in a world surrounded by war, poverty and human rights abuses. This book holds space for the voices of those who dare to leave; it reminds us that those who seek asylum and a better life are brave people.

The stories shared in these pages are a testament to the resilience of the human spirit, to the hope we hold and to the universal quest for a better life. They compel us to see beyond the labels – Asylum Seeker, Refugee, Migrant – beyond the statistics and headlines and the harmful comments online, instead urging us to recognise human beings. Each story reminds us of our shared vulnerabilities and aspirations. We should welcome these talented people, who have come looking for a better life.

This work challenges us to reflect on the conditions that force people to leave their homes. It compels us to ask difficult questions about justice, equality and human rights. We hear not just about the treacherous journeys but also about why staying was no longer an option.

This book is not just a collection of stories; it is a call to action. It serves as an easy-to-digest educational tool, shedding light on the complex human rights issues that persist globally. Through links to documentaries, reports and artistic expressions, it offers a multifaceted approach to learning and advocacy. It does not contain everything but provides a snapshot to help you know more.

The question "Are we human?" strikes at the core of our collective consciousness. At its heart, the title of this book came from the harrowing realisation that depending on where you are born in the world, the value of a life is measured differently. Each person within these pages has their own journey and has had to push boundaries to ensure their basic human rights were met: the right to freedom of expression, to safety, to live a life free from prejudice and discrimination. Ultimately, it leads us to an undeniable truth: regardless of nationality, race, ethnicity, age, gender or circumstance,

WE ARE ALL HUMAN.

Mary Robinson
Former President of Ireland, former UN High Commissioner for Human Rights and Chair of the Elders

CONTENTS

This book was born in response to the shifting landscape in Ireland, where a rise in anti-immigration rhetoric has led to a divide that is far removed from the values that define the Irish spirit. What began as a collection of stories has evolved into a passion project and a truly eye-opening experience.

As co-authors, we share a profound commitment to social justice and a genuine love for people. In the year leading up to this book, Ireland's political and social climate had changed drastically. For many, witnessing the growing hatred and rising racism has been overwhelming. An increase in immigration is being falsely blamed as the sole cause of the housing crisis. This suggestion forces people to take sides, as if supporting immigrants means opposing solutions to the housing issue, when in reality both can and must be addressed together. We recognise the suffering on all sides.

With this book, we urge readers to remember our shared humanity, and that to give to one is not to take from another.

Our reason for creating this book is to remind people that we are all human – Irish citizens, refugees and asylum seekers alike. We all seek the same things: safety, peace, security, a home. Over the past year, a vocal minority has emerged, intent on painting refugees as "other." Yet the harsh truth is that the only difference between us and a refugee is luck – that we were born here and not elsewhere.

We couldn't sit idly by and watch the dehumanisation of a minority group. We felt a deep need to remind everyone that these men, women and children have their own stories to tell, their own struggles, successes, fears and dreams. Most of them never wanted to leave their homes and families; they have been thrust into situations they never wished to face, often alone, without the language or any certainty of their safety.

A thought that distresses us is someone who is forced to flee their home being greeted by racism, discrimination or violence in a place they hoped would give them sanctuary, when all they wanted was a fair chance at life.

Let us never forget the 2015 photograph of two-year-old Alan Kurdi, washed ashore after the boat carrying him and his family capsized in the Mediterranean.

That little boy, lying lifeless on the beach – someone's child – deserved so much more. His mother and brother also drowned. If a mother was willing to risk everything to escape with her children, we can only imagine how dangerous it was to stay.

How can we see refugees living in tents in our own country and reduce them to mere threats, as if they are here just to take jobs or resources? We have lost sight of the fact that every refugee was once a child like Alan, with dreams and a future. Now more than ever, we need to remember that compassion must be the backbone of our society.

On the following pages, you will meet some of the bravest people we've been fortunate enough to encounter. Taking the time to read their stories of hardship and resilience brings the realisation that if more people – especially those who shout hate – understood their struggles, there might be more compassion in the world. And maybe these individuals would no longer be seen as "immigrants" but simply as human beings.

KEY DEFINITIONS

Asylum seeker

A person who has left their country and is seeking protection from persecution and serious human rights violations in another country, but who has not yet been legally recognised as a refugee and is waiting to receive a decision on their asylum claim (Amnesty International)

Displaced person

A person who has been forced to leave their home, typically because of war, persecution or natural disaster

Migrant

A person who moves to another country, especially to find work or better living conditions

Refugee

A person who has been forced to leave a country because of war or for religious or political reasons (UNHCR)

THE COMPASSION
OF STRANGERS

Compassion means showing care and concern for the suffering of others. On the pages that follow, we will see that the compassion of strangers has been a source of support and hope to refugees as they navigate their new life in Ireland.

You will read about Irish people who have demonstrated the extraordinary power of human kindness, illustrating how simple acts of empathy and generosity can transform people's lives in the most profound ways. A friend when they had no one, someone to fill out a form when they didn't have enough English, someone to visit their children or to stand with them when they are given an award.

Throughout history, Ireland and its people have been known for their warmth, hospitality, empathy, humour and solidarity. The Irish tradition of welcoming the stranger, extending a hand to those in need and standing together in times of adversity can be seen today in the thousands who march for justice or who volunteer their time. But much more than this, it is in their simple acts of kindness as evidenced in the stories that follow. These strangers did not simply offer aid, they offered friendship, a sense of belonging and a reassurance that even in the darkest of times, humanity can prevail.

Four such individuals, whose names are synonymous with kindness and connection, accompany these stories: Joe, Niamh, Ciara and Mary. Their actions and their relationships with the refugees they support are a living example of the good that can arise from compassion. Their lives intersected with those of the refugees, not by mere chance but through a profound sense of shared humanity.

They represent a broader community that stands for justice, showing that when we reach out to others in their time of need, we not only save them but also enrich our own lives.

Their story serves as a powerful reminder that as a nation of emigrants ourselves, kindness knows no borders.

"OUR WORLD IS ONE,
AND IN STANDING WITH
REFUGEES, WE ACKNOWLEDGE
OUR SHARED HUMANITY."

DESMOND TUTU

Khalid is a proud father to Ali and Sara. He holds a master's in Physics and
has studied multimedia. He is an entrepreneur and successfully ran his own
family business in Gaza, along with his wife, Ashwak.

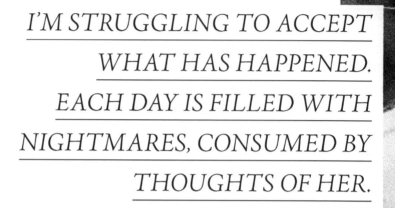

I'M STRUGGLING TO ACCEPT
WHAT HAS HAPPENED.
EACH DAY IS FILLED WITH
NIGHTMARES, CONSUMED BY
THOUGHTS OF HER.

KHALID

I am Khalid. I am 31 years old. I was born in Belfast, while my father was studying there. My father is a Professor of Physics and the Dean of the Faculty of Science at Al Aqsa University. In Belfast, he completed his master's and PhD in Physics at Queen's University.

When I was 8, my family moved back to Gaza, our hometown, where I shared life with my three brothers. Life in Gaza has been far from easy. Over the past 15 years, I have lived through five wars, not to mention numerous other hardships. Out of my 31 years, Gaza has been under siege for nearly 17. Every basic human right in Gaza was a challenge. Choosing a career, finding a job, deciding to get married or making any significant life decision was incredibly difficult.

After finishing high school, I studied physics like my father – a subject I am passionate about – and completed my master's degree. In 2018, I married my lovely wife, Ashwak, who was an engineer with a master's degree in Engineering Project Management. We went on to have two adorable children, Ali, now 4, and Sara, 18 months.

Khalid's family: Ashwak, Ali and Sara

My story may seem unbelievable, but I will try to tell it.

In 2017, getting engaged was a significant achievement. Unlike many other places, in Gaza, you have to have a job to support your family before getting married. During my engagement to Ashwak, I received a scholarship to study at Glasgow University. Of my generation in Gaza, about 95% of people know little about the world outside. They have never had the chance to meet new people or travel. The prospect of going to Scotland and experiencing life beyond the borders of Gaza was thrilling. However, despite being ready to accept the scholarship, the strict border control meant that I missed out on this opportunity. I had been on the list to leave for a year, but the Israeli authorities would not allow me to go.

My wife Ashwak and I had a wonderful life together. Marrying her was a dream come true. I have a very close relationship with her family; they are like my own. Our fathers are close friends. We got married a year and a half after we started dating, and it was the best day of my life.

I worked in many areas and had big dreams, as did my wife. She meant the world to me and I loved her more than anything. In 2021, I started a business with my friend Refaat, designing websites and managing projects. We worked

3

with clients in the Gulf region, including Saudi Arabia and the Emirates. We used our portfolio to secure online work, because finding a job in our field in Gaza was impossible. Unemployment there is over 50%.

Refaat is more like a brother to me; we share everything. We even had our children at the same time (two each). I am from Khan Younis in the south, but when I got married, I moved to Gaza City in the north. Whenever I visited my hometown and needed anything, I could go to Refaat's home and walk straight in, as if it was my own home. Such was our bond.

In 2021, my wife and I ventured into the food industry together. We hoped to make our business a success and ultimately, leave Gaza to start a new life in Ireland. As I was born in Belfast, I qualified for Irish citizenship. Our business was our greatest achievement. We did everything to ensure its success, from perfecting our products to the branding and packaging. We sold everything we had to start the business and borrowed money from family and friends. We initially worked from home, creating recipes. After three months, we rented a place and started producing various foods like hummus. I worked 20 hours a day, handling everything from design to operating the machines.

One of the biggest challenges in Gaza is sourcing equipment. Gaza is a very small place, with about two and a half million people living in an area roughly the size of Dublin. Israel controls the border and all imports, making it difficult to bring anything in. I had to modify what we already had, but we managed to distribute our products to markets.

My wife sold all her jewellery and put everything into the business. Unfortunately, in 2021, another war broke out and we lost electricity. Without electricity – controlled entirely by Israel – the food would perish and we couldn't afford a generator. We started losing produce daily and eventually lost everything. The loss was devastating. My wife tried to reassure me, saying we could start the same business in Ireland. I was depressed for a long time. Business failure was a turning point in our lives.

At the time I married, I was also running a YouTube channel with a friend; it had 5,500 subscribers. Some videos went viral and I made about US$4,000, which had helped me to get married. When the business failed, I had to search for work elsewhere. I never wanted to leave my family in Gaza, but I knew I had to provide for them. When I travelled to Turkey, people couldn't believe it, because it's so hard to get out of Gaza. It was only because I have an Irish passport. Most can't leave without a reason or a visa. Even with a visa, it's extremely difficult.

Initially, I didn't want to leave my family. My father wanted me to stay, but I couldn't bear the situation in Gaza. I went to Turkey twice, planning to work with my cousins, who export goods to Gaza. The first time, I stayed only three months. Initially, I was learning how everything worked in the markets.

During this time, I found out my wife was pregnant with our second child, Sara. The pregnancy was very tough on her. As with her previous pregnancy, she couldn't eat anything and was so ill that she had to be on a drip all day. When she had been pregnant with our son, Ali, I cared for her and I would stay by her side the whole night. When she moved, the drip would sometimes fall out and I would fix it and place it back in her arm. I couldn't be away from her when she was suffering, so I returned to Gaza and stayed with her until she had Sara.

After Sara was born, Refaat and I went to Saudi Arabia to take up some graphic design work we had been offered. Although he didn't have an Irish passport, there is a special time of the year when Palestinians can apply to leave if they are planning to perform Umrah during Ramadan. Refaat had to go through several steps to obtain the necessary visa and make travel arrangements, but he eventually joined me in Saudi Arabia.

Everything began to change in 2023 after the events of 7 October. I was in Saudi Arabia and started to worry about my family. During this time, a man called Fred contacted me. I didn't know him very well. He was a 70-year-old American lawyer, who had been in Gaza two weeks prior, providing training for young female lawyers. He had met my wife, while she was working as a project coordinator at the University College of Applied Sciences in Gaza, where the training took place.

Fred advised us to find any chance to leave Gaza, supporting our own idea of Ireland as a destination. After the events of 7 October, he urged us again. If it wasn't for Fred, we wouldn't have known that leaving was a real possibility. Fred guided us, advising us to go to the Irish embassy in Riyadh. However, the embassy informed us that Ashwak's passport had expired. We reached out to the Irish Foreign Affairs office and they issued a new passport for her, which was

Khalid and Refaat | *Refaat's children: Ameer (2) and Nagham (4)*

waiting in Egypt. They also issued permission for her to cross the border, as well as emergency travel documents for the children, who didn't have Irish passports. After a few days, I was waiting for the Rafah border to open so that my wife and children could get out, but it remained closed for the first month.

During this time, Fred advised me to stay where I was, because it would be easier to get my family out if I was already outside of Palestine and had access to the embassy in Saudi Arabia. However, I was planning to return to Gaza before Ali's birthday on 22 November. I had bought many gifts and toys for him and makeup for my wife. I was excited to be going home.

Before I had the chance to return, my friend Refaat had already gone back to his wife and family. He had decided to move his family to Rafah, believing it to be safer. On 11 October, before journeying to Rafah, Refaat decided to take a nap. He left his children playing in their backyard with his father and his wife, Rawan, 29. While he slept, an airstrike hit and he woke up to find his children, his wife and his sister Ola, who was very close to us, all dead. His father was seriously injured and later died in hospital.

Refaat's extended family lived downstairs and he lived upstairs. His uncle's wife and her daughter, along with the daughter's two children, were also killed in the strike. This was our first tragic event in the war. I was devastated and couldn't believe his children were gone. They were the same age as mine. I couldn't work for a week, overwhelmed with grief.

Refaat blamed himself for their deaths, thinking if he had left earlier, they might still be alive. His children were his whole life and he still struggles with their loss. He and his remaining family members are now sheltering on the streets of Rafah, struggling to find clean water and food. I worry about his mental health and contact him whenever I can. His suffering breaks my heart.

Eid is an important time of celebration in our faith. Recently, Refaat and his remaining family returned to Khan Younis for the first time in five months to pay respect to their loved ones. However, they found that the graves had been dug up, leaving nothing but holes in the ground. Refaat has nothing left of his family to visit, not even their graves.

At that point in my life, I didn't expect anything worse could happen.

Ashwak and I used to live in an apartment in Gaza City. When the war started on 7 October, she left for her family's place. Initially, she sought safety and shelter there, but there was none. After a few days, they moved to al-Quds Hospital in the Tel al-Hawa area of Gaza City, the second-largest hospital in Gaza. The hospital was overcrowded and they were told they couldn't stay. So they left for Deir al-Balah, located in the middle of Gaza, and sought refuge at her uncle's place. He was a lawyer and had solar panels, so they were among the rare few who had electricity. I was in constant contact with Ashwak and things were becoming extremely dire.

On 22 October, they bombed her uncle's home. Miraculously, everyone survived. That same day, they went to my hometown of Khan Younis to stay with my family. My father had arranged a separate place for her family, but I insisted she stay with mine, because we had batteries to charge phones and run the internet router. I needed her to have access, in case the embassy called about the Rafah border. She agreed to stay with my family.

That night, after the bombing, was the most harrowing for her. She cried with me the whole night, saying, "I can't take this, the sound of the bombings. I can't get these things out of my head." She spoke about pulling the kids out from under the rubble. I stayed up all night, trying to comfort her, telling her, "Don't worry. Things will be okay." I stayed awake, offering what comfort I could, reassuring her that things would eventually improve. She finally found sleep around 5 am. When she woke, she mentioned feeling somewhat better. That was the last conversation between us, before I rested briefly and then left for work.

While at work, I received distressing news from Refaat, who was at the hospital with his father. He sent images of my injured children, Ali and Sara, informing me that our family home had been bombed.

Further communication from Refaat revealed the devastating loss: my mother had perished and my 21-year-old brother, Abdullah, was severely injured. My uncle, his wife and their two daughters, who lived next to us, were also killed. There were no bodies left, just parts. Most devastating of all, my wife was in intensive care, with 70% of her body burned, including her hair and face.

Months later, I learned the tragic sequence of events from Abdullah, who had survived his injuries. He was at home when it happened. My mother was making dinner in the kitchen and the children were playing. When the airstrike hit, my mother and the children fell from the third floor. My mother died instantly, while the children were gravely injured, initially presumed dead, as they were buried beneath the rubble. My cousin found Sara moving under the debris. She had severe burns and internal bleeding. Ali was also injured but in better condition than Sara. My wife remained upstairs, severely burned. Abdullah had also fallen from the third floor, breaking his neck and suffering burns.

Ashwak, while burning, had stripped off her clothes and covered herself. She made it to the ground floor and sat on the stairs. When the ambulance arrived, she was asking about the children, who were not found immediately. A cousin mistakenly said they were dead and, in shock, Ashwak went into a coma for five days. Despite the devastation, the knowledge that Ashwak had survived provided a glimmer of hope amid the overwhelming despair. Even though her injuries were severe, the doctors said she was in a stable condition. No one could have predicted what was to come.

My mind was consumed with thoughts of how I could help her – perhaps by taking her somewhere outside Gaza to seek medical care. I entertained the idea of plastic surgery and treatments to improve her condition. Fred offered his support, suggesting we journey to Ireland together to explore options for her care.

Like most couples, we'd had our share of fights over trivial matters, but I resolved never to argue with her again and to fulfil her every wish. While I felt that two children were enough, she had expressed a desire for more. I vividly recall promising myself to have ten children if we made it to Ireland together. Despite everything that had happened, a glimmer of optimism remained.

However, a few days later, tragedy struck again. I cannot pinpoint the exact date, but my cousins back in Gaza, along with cherished friends, suffered a devastating loss. My closest cousin and friend, someone I used to visit weekly, fell victim to a bombing. He, along with 37 others, lost his life, leaving behind a void in my heart. The routine Thursday gatherings for barbecues on his land, once symbolising camaraderie and joy, now haunt me with their absence. His

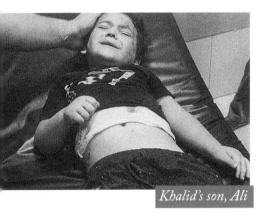

Khalid's son, Ali

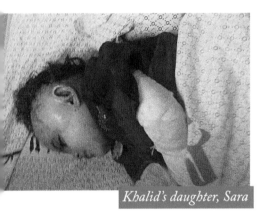

Khalid's daughter, Sara

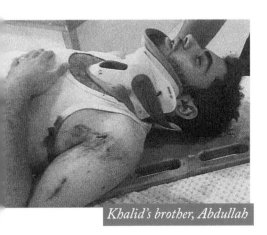

Khalid's brother, Abdullah

wife and two of his children perished alongside him, leaving their two younger ones orphaned, at just one and five years old. Their aunt, along with her husband and their five children also perished in the same bombing. The devastation was absolute, leaving almost no survivors.

On 1 November, while spending a fleeting moment of happiness in the park with a friend, I received a call from the hospital. It was my brother-in-law, urging me to speak with my wife. I was confused – she had been unresponsive since going into a coma. The call was horrifying, as I listened to her agonised screams. She had contracted a severe infection, her blood poisoned beyond recovery. Her passing, just ten minutes after our call, shattered me to the core – gut-wrenching news that no one should have to hear.

It was a day marred by the collective suffering of countless families in Gaza, enduring hardships that surpassed even my own. Following these tragedies, Fred extended an offer of support once more, again suggesting he and I journey to Ireland. I was afraid to take that step, as I had no friends or family there. Despite my initial reservations, the plight of my children spurred me to accept. Only one day after Ashwak's passing, I found myself at the airport. I met one of her friends, who graciously stayed by my side. I was in a terrible state, feeling as though I was slowly unravelling. I remained in the airport for about a day, waiting for my flight. However, it turned out to be overbooked and I was bumped to the next available flight. The entire time, tears streamed down my face uncontrollably.

It was during this tumultuous time that I met an Irish gentleman named Daithí. The way our paths crossed was unusual. Fred was trying to organise a place for me to stay in Dublin, as I had nowhere to go. He reached out to Dr Umar al-Qadri, an imam at a Dublin mosque. Dr Umar mentioned that he knew of an Irish teacher in Turkey. When Fred contacted this teacher, it turned out that we would be on the same flight to Ireland. On the flight, a fellow passenger noticed me in tears and offered his condolences, saying, "I'm so sorry for your loss." The man was Daithí, who happened to be the Irish teacher that Dr Umar spoke of.

Since then, Daithí has become a very close friend and is practically family now. We visit him regularly in Naas, spending at least every second weekend with him. He is an integral part of our lives. Daithí introduced me to Nicola and I ended up staying at her place for about two weeks. She's like a second mother to me and incredibly close to our family. I found solace in the warmth of these newfound friends, who opened their hearts and homes to me. Despite the overwhelming grief, their unwavering support and compassion infused my shattered existence with hope.

It was suggested that someone I knew should accompany Ali and Sara from Gaza. Mohammed, my brother-in-law, seemed the best fit, as he was unmarried and willing to leave. Initially, I asked Refaat if he would come with them, as I was concerned about his situation. But he refused, citing his commitment to his mother. So Mohammed stepped in. Unfortunately, when they reached the border, they were turned away without explanation. It was a confusing and stressful time, compounded by the lack of communication, as they had no internet access.

Then the Irish embassy called me to say that he should go to the border again. Without the internet or any other way of contacting Mohammed, I managed to give instructions to my cousins, uncertain if they would be able to reach him or if Mohammed and the children would reach the border. I remained in the dark until they finally arrived in Egypt.

Their eventual arrival in Ireland on 19 November was a turning point. Despite the challenging circumstances, migrating to Ireland was the best decision I ever made for my children's safety. It's not just about the children though; there's a deeper reason why I'm still here today. I was in a dark place, battling depression and contemplating drastic measures. However, upon arriving here, the people I encountered gave me hope. The children, of course, were my primary motivation, but the support and love from my new friends made me realise I couldn't give up. They've become more than family to me. The community here is truly amazing.

I also met a man named John, who visits from Kildare every two weeks to spend time with the children. They love him like they love me. He takes them out regularly and they've formed a bond with him, akin to family. John is a steadfast presence in our lives; he epitomises the kindness we have encountered in Ireland.

Amid the darkness, people like Christine also emerged as beacons of light, selflessly dedicating themselves to helping others. Their acts of kindness, ranging from providing shelter to distributing essentials, restored my faith in humanity. Their generosity extended to embracing my children, easing their transition and nurturing a sense of normality in all the chaos.

Yet, despite the outpouring of love and support, the pain of loss remains insurmountable. Nightmares plague my sleep and the absence of my beloved wife is a constant torment. I'm struggling to accept what has happened. Each day is filled with nightmares, consumed by thoughts of her. It's unbearable, especially at night when the world quiets down. But I can't cry all the time. During the day, I try to keep busy, but the nights are relentless with thoughts of her.

My son, just four years old, sometimes asks me about his mother. I'm at a loss for words. I sought guidance from a therapist, who advised me to tell him the truth, that she's gone. Attempting to explain this to him has been the hardest thing I've ever had to do. I try to make him understand that she won't be coming back, but it's beyond his comprehension. His struggle weighs heavily on my heart and pierces through the facade of strength I try to maintain.

At the moment, we live in emergency housing, surrounded by others sharing similar tales of loss and displacement. The solidarity among us offers solace. However, I fear for the plight of my father and brothers, Abdullah, 21, and Abdulrahman, 25, still trapped within Gaza's confines. Despite my efforts to secure their passage to Ireland, bureaucratic hurdles and geopolitical tensions prolong their suffering. My father never anticipated things would deteriorate to this extent. They live in tents near the sea and endure immense hardship following the loss of my mother and my brother, Majed, 29.

Khalid and Mohammed holding Khalid's children, Ali and Sara

Ashwak alongside Khalid's father and two brothers

Each time I speak with my father, I am overwhelmed by a sense of helplessness. Witnessing his grief over the loss of his wife and son is heart-wrenching, compounded by the daily suffering of my brother, Abdullah, who endures unimaginable pain in his neck, without access to adequate care. At the tender age of 21, he had been establishing his own small perfume business before tragedy struck. My other brother, Abdulrahman, a talented accountant, has aspirations of pursuing a master's degree. Not only do they face the devastating loss of loved ones, but also the displacement from their home and having to relocate several times in search of shelter. My father calls me incessantly, pleading for assistance. I submitted his application about five months ago and all the paperwork is in order. Even though my siblings have Irish citizenship, they're confined in Gaza.

My father's constant calls weigh heavily on me. "What have you done?" he implores. "Please, we need to leave. Please, get us out." His affection for my children is what pains him the most. When I took them away, it shattered him. While my children have everything they need, my father possesses only a passport and a document identical to what my wife was using to leave Gaza. He and my brothers await Israel's approval.

The atrocities inflicted upon civilians in Gaza, documented in harrowing detail, defy comprehension. Innocent lives are mercilessly extinguished, families torn apart and basic human rights violated with impunity. The international community's silence only compounds the anguish, leaving us to question our worth in a world indifferent to our suffering.

"NO ONE LEAVES HOME
UNLESS HOME IS THE
MOUTH OF A SHARK."

WARSAN SHIRE

Baraa is from Gaza and is 24 years old. He has studied media and photography. In Gaza, Baraa worked in his family's business, alongside his brother. He has a passion for videography and has worked with Irish artist Accidental Rapper to create video footage for music videos.

UNDER THE COVER OF DARKNESS, WE STARTED SWIMMING.

BARAA

My name is Baraa. I'm from Gaza, Palestine, and I'm 24 years old. Growing up, you could say we were a rich family, because we had everything we needed. We made a good living, owning shoe shops, where I worked with my brother. But life was always overshadowed by war; every six months or so we had a war with Israel. It made me see there was no place safe in Gaza. No life. No peace. No future. Nothing.

The reality became clear – I could do nothing in Gaza if I stayed. I started to think about leaving. Like many young people around the world, I have dreams and aspirations, not just for myself, but for my loved ones. I envision a future where we can live in peace, pursue our goals and thrive without fear. Unfortunately, the harsh reality of the Israeli occupation has severely hindered my ability to dream and achieve.

Many people told me to think about going to Europe, because you can find a good life and work there. Most people in Gaza, however, can never leave. Even so, I managed to eventually move to Turkey for a better life, with the hope for a

Baraa's family: Ahmed, Baraa, Mouen, Hasan, Bahaa and Mohammed

future that could not be found back home. But conditions were poor in Turkey and at the time, I couldn't get a visa to stay legally. I knew I needed to again relocate. However, it's so hard for Palestinians, Syrians or any people from the Middle East. People told me, "Getting to Europe is so difficult." My experience has shown this to be true; it's very, very difficult. I don't know why, but my Palestinian passport is not strong enough to get a visa.

I kept thinking about how I could find a way to leave for a better life. Desperation led me to search Google and YouTube, typing in phrases like, How can I go to Europe? I discovered countless stories of people making perilous journeys by sea and on foot. I started asking around, looking for people who could help me get to Europe. The reality was harsh; these smugglers demanded around €4,000. I didn't have that kind of money. Worse, they often lied. You could pay €4,000 or €5,000 and still not make it, or end up dead in the water.

At night, I often gazed at a cluster of five small lights flickering on a distant land. That spot called to me. It was the Greek island of Kos. Eventually, I decided to set out alone. I was in Turkey then and my destination was Greece. Arriving in Bodrum, I kept thinking, *I can't, I can't go.* The prospect of crossing the waters was daunting, especially in the morning, so I planned to go in the evening, because there was less chance of being seen. My only remaining choice was to swim.

At around 9 or 10 pm, I stood at the water's edge, staring into the darkness. The sight was terrifying. The water seemed endless and the danger overwhelming. I realised then that I couldn't do it alone. It was just too dangerous. Reluctantly, I turned back, the dream of crossing slipping away with each step.

With an increasing sense of urgency, I sought out someone brave enough to join me on the journey. Finally, I found a willing person from Gaza. With shared determination, we devised a plan and assembled the essentials for our swim to freedom. And so, on an October night, our hearts pounding with a mixture of fear and excitement, we set off. Under the cover of darkness, we started swimming. As we ventured deeper into the waters, there was a sense of hope in the air. The first two hours tested our resilience as we grappled with towering waves, each one more terrifying than the last. As we swam, there were four or five occasions, when we truly thought we would die. The journey we made is known as the "trip of death", a chilling reminder of the many people who had unsuccessfully gone before us.

Through some luck or fate, we found ourselves washed ashore at 3 am. As we stumbled onto the beach, relief flooded over us. We found comfort in the quiet of the night. It was only then that I called my family. I hadn't told anyone I was going. My hands shook as I grabbed my phone. "I'm in Greece," I said. That was it.

I eagerly awaited the arrival of my documents. I had told my family that, once I got my documents in Greece, I would come back to visit them. But they warned me that it might not be possible. They knew many people who had been waiting for documents for over five years. After two months of anticipation, they finally came, but it wasn't the coveted passport I wanted, just an ID allowing me to travel within Europe's borders. Although it granted me the freedom to travel, it barred me from returning to Gaza, where it was deemed unsafe. But Gaza is where my heart longed to be, with my family.

As I looked around Greece, I couldn't shake the feeling of displacement. The longer I stayed, the more I realised there was no life for me there. It's a poor country and, despite its beauty, a land of limited opportunity. There is no support to help you take care of yourself – nothing from the government or any other sources. After receiving my documents, I tried to find work and stayed in Greece for about five or six months. When I was younger, I had hoped I would someday speak English very well, but I couldn't achieve that where everyone spoke Greek. I decided I needed to travel to a country where English was spoken, where I could receive support and where I could build a future for myself.

In March, I decided I would travel back to Gaza to visit my family. Although my documents did not allow it, I decided to take the risk, especially since Ramadan was approaching and I wanted to be with my family during that time. Because there is no airport in Gaza, we have to go first to Egypt and then take a bus to Gaza. I booked a flight and prepared to leave. Before boarding, I called my brother and told him, "Tomorrow, I will be in Gaza." He was surprised and disbelieving, but I assured him that I would be there. I stayed in Gaza during Ramadan and Eid, helping my brother in the shops. After about three or four months, I went back to Greece.

In the meantime, however, the war that began on 7 October 2023 scared me a lot, because it was not like previous wars. I knew it would be terrible and long-lasting, as all the news reports indicated that this time it was different. Despite the warnings, nothing prepared me for the sheer magnitude of the devastation.

I was very scared for my family, both then and now. They live in the middle of Gaza, a very dangerous place to be during this war. My family even received a message telling them to leave our home. Near the start of the war, about a month in, my uncle, who worked as a photographer in Gaza, was killed by an Israeli bomb. Every day, I heard from family and friends about more people being killed – my uncle's friends, my cousins, all victims of this war. I am still frightened.

In the early days of the war, my family had fled to my brother's house. My brother is married and lives in a different area of Gaza. From Greece, I waited in fear for each call. I couldn't wrap my head around what was happening. Then, just four days after my uncle's death, my brother called me with the shocking news that our father had been killed.

I was in disbelief, unable to process the news. He explained that our father, who had a habit of going to the mosque every morning for prayer, had gone alone as

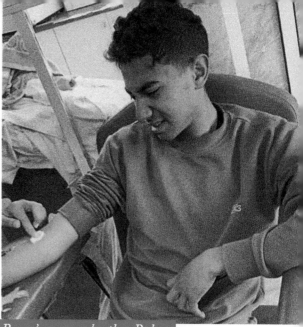

Baraa's younger brother, Bahaa

usual at 5 am, but that morning, tragedy struck. He was killed, possibly targeted, by an Israeli airstrike while walking towards the mosque.

My family were faced with the agonising decision of whether to inform our grandmother about the deaths of both her sons. As she was old and sick, we ultimately decided against it, knowing it would break her. For a month, we kept silent. Then, when we did eventually tell her, she too passed away soon after. We had shielded her from the truth, only for it to bring about further sorrow.

Every day, we hear news of more deaths. My cousin also lost his son. It's the same routine every day. Maybe one day, someone will call and tell me I no longer have any family left. For now, their grief and their suffering are reduced to a steady, painful decline. Deprived of the most basic necessities, they are facing a slow death, a life without food and water.

It's difficult to stay connected with my family in Gaza. Sometimes, I can only reach them once every three days, because there's no electricity or reliable communication. I have four brothers and three sisters. My mum is still alive. Two of my brothers and one sister are in Turkey, while my mum, two brothers and two sisters are still in Gaza. The war has had dire consequences for my family, forcing them to relocate seven times. Our homes have been demolished – the home I grew up in, my brother's home and those of my married sisters. On top of all that, my younger brother, Bahaa, not even 17, faces liver disease during this genocide.

Baraa's family being displaced

I was finally able to flee to Ireland for safety, via Italy. When I was questioned at the airport, I told them I was a refugee. They asked me, "How did you come here? Where are your documents?" I told them I didn't have any documents, but rather than sending me back, the guards told me that I could stay and request asylum. Initially, the government said, "We're sorry. We don't have any place for you to stay." But after roughly one month of being homeless, I was provided with accommodation.

The first month was difficult. There were no tents. I didn't know anyone. I had nothing and nobody, so I was sleeping on the ground outside the International Protection Office. I stayed in hostels on the nights when the rain was bad. I made friends from various places, including Palestine. Sometimes, I stayed with them, switching between different places each night.

The Ireland-Palestine Solidarity Campaign (IPSC) allowed me a chance to work with an Irish artist, Accidental Rapper, during a march that they held. We sang together for Palestine. The IPSC campaigns for justice for the Palestinian people, through raising public awareness about the human rights abuses. From there, some people shared my number to a WhatsApp group and I made contact with a lovely Irish family. They told me I was very welcome to come and stay with them. I moved in and I have been living there for about three months now. They heard my story and opened their home. They support Palestine and were very welcoming.

I hope to bring my family here or to Egypt or anywhere outside Gaza. My friends and what's left of my family are still there, and nowhere is safe. There is no electricity. You can't imagine what it's like. The news doesn't cover everything. If you were in Gaza, you would understand what I mean. Much of the news is filtered, especially in Western media.

My cousin Abed also wanted to go to Europe and I had told him we could go together. However, he left a month before me and we haven't heard anything from him since. After searching hospitals and other places, I contacted a lawyer to find out what could have happened to him. We learned that Abed swam with two other people. They made it, but he didn't. It's a terrible situation. I can't help but wonder if a shark might have been in the water.

Since arriving in Ireland, the people have been so lovely. I have found a new life here. You can work. You can really start your life. You can start anything, because in Ireland there is everything you need. Dublin represents safety to me. Yet, despite the comfort it has offered, I cling to the desire to reunite with my family, to take them away from the dangers of Gaza.

"MY HUMANITY IS BOUND UP
IN YOURS, FOR WE CAN ONLY
BE HUMAN TOGETHER."

DESMOND TUTU

Asad and Wafaa have been married for 26 years and have one son. Asad achieved a degree in English Literature and a Master of Linguistics, before receiving his PhD in Ireland. He is now a retired university professor.

Wafaa was a teacher in Palestine and has a degree in Science and Mathematics. She retrained in Ireland and now works for a mental health organisation.

Both Asad and Wafaa have dedicated many years of their lives to the Palestinian cause and support for Palestinian refugees.

IRELAND AND PALESTINE HAVE A LOT OF SHARED HISTORY.

ASAD

My name is Asad and I am a Palestinian refugee. My family was driven out of Palestine in 1948 and I was born in a miserable refugee camp in Rafah, which is now called Shabura refugee camp. We were dispossessed of all our property and belongings and we lived as destitute refugees in camps that were later built by the United Nations Relief and Work Agency (UNRWA). There were no jobs. People lived on UNWRA donations such as food, mainly flour, and oil. I went to an UNRWA school, where I worked hard to be a very good student and this led to a free scholarship from UNRWA to finish my BA in English Literature in Egypt.

On 9 June 1967, when I was 16, our home in the refugee camp was stormed by Israeli soldiers. I was at home with my father, my brother and two of my uncles. The Israelis shot their way into our camp. Five soldiers with guns confronted us, while other soldiers searched the house. They told us to face the wall with our hands up and to await our fate. Whether they were going to kill us or not, we did not know. On that day they killed many people. So we waited. All of a sudden, the soldiers told us to go outside and keep our hands up. They told us to run and as we ran, they were shooting after us. We made it to a house and knocked frantically, but the occupants were too afraid to let us in until we gave them our names. The next morning, we discovered that many of our neighbours, including a family of five, had been killed and many were thrown into the rubbish dump. Whenever I had to go for errands for the family, it was very risky, because there was a total curfew. The soldiers would rampage through the town shooting and killing indiscriminately. Nobody cared. No human rights organisation. No United Nations. Nobody.

Then I went to Egypt on the UNWRA scholarship to finish my BA in English Literature. I worked for some time, but I always dreamed of doing a postgraduate degree. In 1976, while working in Libya as a translator and journalist, I met two wonderful Irishmen, who changed the course of my life and made my future bright again. I was attending a religion conference, in which young Christians and Muslims were coming together to talk about peace between the religions.

I interviewed these two men for the conference. Professor Hayden was a Catholic priest, Professor of Education and Chair of the Department of Education in Galway University, and Sean Sherwin was a TD from Fianna Fáil. I told them that I dreamed of doing a postgraduate degree and had applied to the British embassy for a visa to study in the UK, but had been turned down. They told me, "Don't worry. Send us your paperwork and we'll fix you up in Ireland." I couldn't believe my luck! It was as if these people had come from heaven straight to me. I sent them the papers and soon I received word that I had been accepted to the University of Galway to study Linguistics.

But first, I had to overcome another difficulty. I had a travel document issued by the Egyptian authorities for Palestinian refugees. However, Palestine was not officially recognised as a state. As there was no Irish embassy in Libya, a friend told me to go to the Spanish embassy, where I could get a visa to Spain and then access the Irish embassy from there. However, the man at the Spanish embassy said that what I had was not a passport, so he could not give me a visa. At that moment, I was feeling defeated. Then I heard someone calling my name, a former classmate of mine. After I told him of my situation, he said, "Don't worry. I work here. You'll get your visa!" And I did.

I travelled to Spain, but the Irish embassy staff said my refugee passport needed to be renewed before they could accept it. This took about a month and a half with a lot of paperwork to fill out and a lot of back and forth between the Irish and Egyptian embassies. I then had to wait another few weeks. I was worried and anxious and my money was running out. After three months, the visa came through.

But there was more to come. The customs officer at the airport in Spain told me I had to report to the police in Madrid to tell them that I was leaving the country. Otherwise, I could not travel. Nobody had told me that. When I asked why, he said, "Because you have no state. You are stateless."

I said firmly to his face, "I am Palestinian! My country is Palestine!"

He explained that he was sorry but those were the regulations. As it turned out, I managed to board my flight to Ireland two days later. I was so happy. When I arrived in Dublin airport, I couldn't believe it. But I was hit with one last snag. As I produced my passport, the officer frowned and asked, "Where are you going to stay?" I explained I was a student and produced my papers. I was instructed to wait, while he phoned the Department of Justice. On his return, he said, "Listen, we will give you a visa for one month."

I left the airport and got a taxi to a hotel. I phoned Sean Sherwin immediately and explained what had happened. He assured me, "Don't worry. Don't ever worry. You are in safe hands!" He and his wife took me to the train station the next day to travel to Galway. But first, he took me to the Department of Justice to complain about my treatment at the airport. They apologised and gave me a renewable visa to study for one year, with Sean acting as my guarantor.

When I arrived in Galway, I met Professor Hayden and I stayed with an Irish family in Shankhill, who were extremely kind, lovely, amiable, human. You name it and they were it! I couldn't believe that I was in a nation of such great people. One day I went to buy a cup of tea at a park in Galway. The man who served me asked where I was from. When I told him I was Palestinian, he said, "You don't need to pay for your tea."

I was directed to go to Dublin to meet Professor Kader Asmal. He phoned Professor Conor O'Cleary, Chair of Linguistics in University College Dublin, a great man and intellectual, and they arranged an interview. I was accepted into UCD for the following academic year. However, as it was February, they told me I was most welcome to attend classes up until the course started. That way, I could study in the interim, which I did. Everything was going great!

I worked hard for two years. I had to study the linguistics course, for both undergraduate and postgraduate, and completed my thesis. I went on to study for my master's and passed with all honours. When I graduated in 1982, I was extremely happy to get my first degree from Ireland. However, when I went to the stage to receive my master's degree, the man said, "Don't leave yet. You have another to come." After ten minutes, they called my name again! This time, they gave me a BA! So I earned both a bachelor's and a master's degree in English Literature and Linguistics, covering both undergraduate and postgraduate studies simultaneously. I had attained two degrees in 24 months. I then went on to do a PhD with Professor O'Cleary. Finally, I went to Trinity to do another degree in Applied Linguistics.

Around this time, my Irish friends advised me to apply for an Irish passport, as my current travel documents were inadequate if I ever intended to travel. I was working for Sean Sherwin at the Abacus Institute and also as a journalist, which meant that I was eligible to apply. After three and a half years, my passport was approved. I was greatly helped by a lady in the Irish family I lived with. She was a solicitor, and she assisted me with the whole process and did not charge me for her services.

In 1983, I was living in South Circular Road. I was a member of the General Union of Palestinian Students, an activist for Palestine and also a member of the anti-Apartheid movement of South Africa. Ireland was so supportive of these causes, especially the trade unions. I was a member of the Friends of Palestine Society, along with Nessa Childers, daughter of the Irish president, Erskine Childers. I visited her family home in Donnybrook and met her mother and brother, Erskine Jr, who had written a book, *The Other Exodus* (1961), in response to the Leon Uris novel, *Exodus*, which was very popular at the time.

In 1985, I happened to be living in the area that was once Dublin's Jewish Quarter. The Israeli president, Chaim Herzog, came to Ireland on an official visit, during which he was to open the Jewish Museum. The day before the visit, the Gardaí came to my flat and requested that "All Palestinians in this area disappear from 7 o'clock tomorrow morning until 7 o'clock at night." I told them that we were harmless students, who only cared about our studies. They were apologetic and explained that the instruction came from Israeli security, not the Gardaí. They told me and my friends to stay in the library at UCD. I complied of course, as I didn't want to cause any trouble.

Chaim Herzog, originally from Ireland, was a general in the Israeli army and one of the ethnic cleansers of 1948. He was the chief of military intelligence, before becoming Israel's president. This man was a war criminal and is famous for tearing up the United Nations resolution that equates Zionism with racism. His son, also Isaac, the current President of Israel, is quoted as saying, "There are no innocent civilians in Gaza."

I eventually returned to Gaza in 1983 on a three-month visa to teach at the Islamic University. Israeli intelligence came to my house and took me several times for interrogation about my activities in Ireland. I was taken to the notorious Ashkelon prison, where they hooked me up to a lie detector. I was not afraid. I was actually very happy, because they had brought me back to my real "birthplace". I told them that my family is from Ashkelon and we had a big house and a large orange grove, which was probably still there and quite nearby. My grandad was the Mayor of Ashkelon and lived there until November 1948.

I was interrogated for hours by a colonel in the Israeli internal security service, Shin Bet. He was also a Professor of Psychology and played manipulative word games with me. He tried to persuade me to work for them, so that I could "stay in the country". I told him I would rather die. They cancelled my visa and kicked me out of Palestine.

I then lived in Kuwait for five years, teaching at the English Department of Kuwait University, where a former colleague from Ireland gave me a job. I returned to Palestine during a time of peace there, where I married Wafaa in 1998 and my son was born. I worked again at the Al-Azhar University of Gaza and I taught several courses, including some on Irish literature and history, including the 1916 Uprising. During that time, the Great March of Return happened, in which Palestinians would go to the border and look through the fence to where they used to live. I was one of its spokespersons and there were consequently many attempts on my life.

When my son was 15, he won a scholarship to study in America. For one reason or another, the US would not give him a visa. So I told him, "I will take you to the best country in the world, Ireland." And I did. He has been extremely happy here, having now finished his Degree in Computer Science and Business at Trinity and is about to start his Master's in Cyber Security at UCD. He also uses his musical talent to play for peace and justice in Palestine.

Since the genocide started in Gaza in October 2023, we have lost many family members. Our flat was destroyed, as well as my office at the University of Gaza. The refugee camp in Rafah, where I was born, is also destroyed. This war is not just a war; it is what I call a Palestinocide, ethnocide, urbicide, memoricide, politicide, historicide and an epistecide. They want to destroy everything Palestinian. Geography, history, place, politics, heritage, legacy, identity, memories and dreams. Unfortunately, they are being supported by the US and almost all Western countries.

Ireland and Palestine have a lot of shared history. Those who oppressed the Irish also oppressed the Palestinians. Churchill sent the Black and Tans to Ireland and later to Palestine, to terrorise and control both populations. The Israelis use the same techniques and administrative detention policy against the hunger strikers in Palestine, as was used in Ireland. In Palestine, we have Zionist settlers; in Ireland, you had the plantations. The Irish were kicked off their land and banished to the west, which also happened to the Palestinians.

This sense of support from Irish people is not new. They have been supporting the Palestinians for the last 70 years. The Irish streets are full of Irish people shouting for justice and a ceasefire, for our right to self-determination, for our right of return, for Palestinian freedom. The Irish people now are aware that Israel, which practises state terrorism, is not just a threat to the Palestinian people; it is a threat to all peace and security everywhere.

We have well over 1,000 resolutions by the United Nations calling for our right of return and compensation, our right to self-determination, our right to sovereignty and a state, and our right to independence. But the US Security Council veto keeps the Palestinian struggle in limbo. I believe that, if there is justice, dignity, equality and humanity, without the white supremacist mentality of Western superiority, we could free Palestine. I will end by saying injustice anywhere is injustice everywhere. Nelson Mandela once said, "The freedom of South Africa is incomplete without the freedom of Palestine."

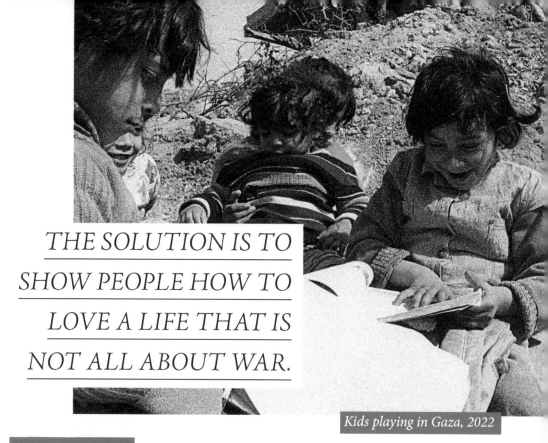

THE SOLUTION IS TO SHOW PEOPLE HOW TO LOVE A LIFE THAT IS NOT ALL ABOUT WAR.

Kids playing in Gaza, 2022

WAFAA

My name is Wafaa and I am a Palestinian refugee. In 1998, when I married my husband, Asad, I moved from the West Bank to Gaza. In the 20 years I lived in Gaza, they had three wars. My son was just seven years old during the war of 2008. My husband has an Irish passport and the Irish government was urging its citizens to leave Gaza during these times. However, my husband refused, because he did not want to leave his family or abandon the people of Gaza. Also, my mam had always told me to help and support people and never leave our land, especially during war.

When I first moved to Gaza, I had no family there. I had been a teacher in the West Bank and I began teaching in Gaza in order to meet new people and establish myself. I lived in the middle of Gaza's Tal al-Hawa district, beside the Jerusalem Hospital. We also had some friends in the north. During the wars, when the Israelis attacked, they always started in the north, and our friends would call us when they had to leave their homes. Throughout the three wars, we hosted many people in our home. During the wars, there was no food or electricity, but we learned how to manage. Opposite my house was an UNRWA school, where many people would shelter. I would visit and ask the women what they and their babies needed and I would go out and get it for them. We tried to help people in different ways.

My husband had family in Rafah in the south, but he didn't want to leave our home during the war. He said, "If we live, okay. If we die, okay. I can't live going from place to place running from war." It is so difficult moving from place to place. It is not normal, especially with a young child. So we stayed in our home during the three wars.

Our flat was on the third floor of a building that was otherwise empty, as the other occupants had fled. I remember when the first war finished, we had no windows left and most of the walls were damaged. People were returning and when I looked out of the window, I saw someone I knew. He asked how I was and asked if I had come back to see how my home was. I explained that we had never left. He was shocked. He told me to come outside and I did. When I looked back at the building, floors four to seven were completely destroyed. People asked how we could stay there with our son, but we replied that nowhere is safe, even if we had left. We always stayed positive. We had no windows but at least we had a place to sit. My people have been 76 years in this situation.

My son was born three years after I moved to Gaza. All I wanted was to be a good mother for him. Before the first war, he started attendance at a music school in October, but in December it was destroyed by the war. After that, they rented a new place and started the school again from the beginning. I tried to make sure my son had a good life growing up. I took him to sports clubs and music school. It is important to live a life that is not all about war. You get on with your life, you receive an education, you create memories. That is how you fight. Especially for the kids; they are the future.

My family saw my son for the first time when he was four years old. Israel would not allow me to visit my family in the West Bank. However, when my brother died, they gave me a pass for three days. It wasn't a happy visit; it was a very sad time in my life and I was also unwell. But at least my family got to meet my son. My brothers, one of whom has American citizenship, brought me to the border. He asked the Israelis if he could come with me into Gaza, because I was ill and had my child with me. They told him no.

There was a time when my mother was very ill. The family sent me the reports on her health and I would have to get help from a human rights organisation to go to the West Bank to see her. When my mam died, I was there with her, but the Israelis would not allow my son to come with me.

In 2018, we finally left our home. My husband, my son and I decided to travel to Ireland, because my son wanted to study there. My husband always spoke about Ireland to my son in glowing terms. He told him about the history of Palestine and the history of Ireland, because they are so similar. He and my son have Irish passports, but I have a Palestinian passport. I needed to get a visa to go to Ireland with them. I had applied for a visa three times, but each time it was granted, the border was closed.

One night, at 10 o'clock, my son came home with the news that the border was open and our names were on a list of people allowed to travel. However, we had to leave the following day if we were going to travel at all. It came as a surprise and we were unprepared. My Palestinian passport was still at the Irish embassy in the West Bank, waiting for a visa to Ireland. I told my son to travel with his dad and I would stay until I received my passport and visa in a few days. Then I would follow. However, I also have a Jordanian passport and my son persuaded me to travel with that, so that we would not be separated.

At half past twelve the next day, we arrived by bus at the Palestinian side of the border. However, the Egyptians would not allow us to cross until the following day. We spent the night sleeping on the bus. The next day we got through to the Egyptian side, where I saw about a thousand people sleeping on the ground. Some had been there up to three days. We spent another night there, hoping we would be allowed to cross. A lot of people who, like myself, had Jordanian passports were not allowed in. When he heard this, my son came to me and cried, as he had been the one to persuade me to travel on my Jordanian passport. I told him that God would look after us.

We waited through the night and they eventually called my name. I was brought into a small room, where they asked me a lot of questions. I explained that I wanted to travel with my husband and son to Ireland. Finally, I was allowed through. My son shouted and cried with happiness. We cried together.

While in Egypt, my sister posted my Palestinian passport to me with my Irish visa inside and we booked our tickets to Ireland. On 24 May 2018, at half past ten in the morning, we landed in Dublin airport and my Irish journey started. I was a teacher in Palestine and I have a degree in Science and Mathematics. I had worked as a supervisor in the Ministry of Authority in Palestine. I was also a volunteer in many organisations and worked among children with disabilities. When I got here, I needed to decide what I wanted to do. People spoke so fast here and sometimes I didn't understand a word, so my first step was to enrol in English classes, which I attended for two years. I got to Level 4 and I have a Certificate of Communication Skills.

I then started workshops to learn how to put my CV together. I attended many courses and I went to lots of different activities like painting, sewing and cooking, because I wanted to learn the culture. People would ask where I was from and would ask me questions about Palestine. It was good to be able to tell people about my home country.

I started attending sessions on mental health. I did a course to help the Arab and Muslim community here in Ireland, those with mental health problems. I now work as a volunteer for Cairde, an organisation that caters especially for people who have suffered through war. I also worked as a volunteer for a homelessness charity. I always want to help and support people, because I lived in such a bad situation in Gaza, so I know what it is like. When I think about what is happening to my people, I feel so sad for what they are going through. When you are finally safe, you want to help others. Sometimes I am overwhelmed with sadness, because the situation for my people is horrible.

We came here so my son could receive a good education and just this year, he graduated with a degree in Computer Science and Business. In September, he will start his master's in Cyber Security at UCD. I have been here for six years and I am so happy, because now Ireland is my second home. Every time I talk to my family and friends, I explain how the Irish people are so lovely. They support Palestinians and you can live a good life here, if you have a purpose. I try to do for the Irish people what they do for Palestine. I want to know the culture. I look and listen and learn.

My husband has lost 75 members of his family in Gaza. The survivors have had to leave Rafah and go to other places. We haven't had any contact with them for over two months. I am worried for my family in the West Bank, because they are being attacked by Zionist settlers. Our homes are gone and our apartment in Gaza has been destroyed. As well as family, I have lost many friends and neighbours in the genocide. When I go to demonstrations and marches for Gaza, I see so much support for my people. When I connect with people in Gaza, I always explain what the Irish people are doing for them. I use Facebook and Instagram to let the people in Gaza know that the Irish stand with them. I get invited to give talks and to speak at demonstrations. I speak about how we can help people, especially the children, when this war is finally over. Sometimes, we give donations and send money back to support families. These are the small things we can do for those who need help. When I walk through the streets in Ireland, I see people who walk and eat and play. I hope maybe one day that Palestinians can live like the Irish.

Everyone has a dream, especially children. They dream of the future. Even though everything is destroyed, I believe the people who live in the West Bank and Gaza will be free and the people who have left will come back again. I nurture the hope that Palestine will one day have peace, equality, security and liberation.

The Palestinian people are aware of everything the Irish people have done for them and they know that we stand with them in different ways. Maybe you can visit Palestine and meet the people sometime. Palestinians are so welcoming. They will do the best for you, because they love meeting people from different ethnicities and backgrounds. I love Irish people and I cannot thank them enough for everything they have done for us and for Palestine.

THE POWER OF
YOUTH VOICES

Adam's father is a Palestinian from occupied East Jerusalem and his family, originally from al-Lydd, was displaced during the 1948 Nakba.

Adam is about to start fourth class in Ireland and has a strong interest in geopolitics and the world around him. Like many children his age, he has been witnessing the ongoing conflict. On 29 June 2024, he felt the need to express his outrage and the emotions that many children are experiencing during these challenging times.

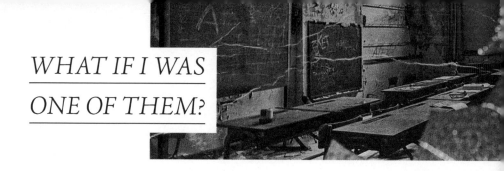

WHAT IF I WAS ONE OF THEM?

ADAM

My name is Adam and I am a proud Palestinian child.

Yesterday, as I closed the door of my classroom for the last time before summer break, I hugged my friends and said goodbye to my teacher. I wasn't sad, because I knew I'd see them again.

Imagine being in the middle of class and a bomb falls on the school? An American-made bomb paid by US tax dollars. My school in Ireland has about 100 children. If we were in Gaza, all of us would be dead or maimed or orphaned. The same scenes of chaos, distress and death would repeat for 265 days. That's 265 days!

This week, the United Nations revealed that there are over 21,000 missing children in Gaza. This is in addition to at least 15,000 dead. Can you imagine them, frightened, screaming under the rubble, waiting for someone to save them?

What if I was one of them? What if your kid was one of them? Your grandkid, your nephew, niece, neighbours? They didn't choose their place of birth. They didn't choose their parents, their skin colour or religion. If I was in Gaza today, I'd be starving to death. I wouldn't have a school. I wouldn't even know if I'll see dawn the next morning. Would my mum tuck me into bed at night? Most likely not.

I am just a nine-year-old boy, but I can see what is right and wrong in this world. What kind of world forces children to be witnesses to a genocide? What kind of adults allow this to happen?

Listen, world! Can you not see us? Can you not see them? The foetuses, the babies, the toddlers, the children and teenagers, who will never return to school. The world is a pretty dire place right now. The adults have a duty of care. You all have a duty to protect the innocent souls who are the future of this world.

I may be only 50% Palestinian, but I am 100% anti-genocide, like all of us here.

More about Palestine:

"REFUGEES DON'T LEAVE
THEIR HOMES BECAUSE
THEY WANT TO. THEY LEAVE
BECAUSE THEY HAVE TO,
AND THEY DREAM OF
A BETTER FUTURE FOR
THEIR CHILDREN."

MALALA YOUSAFZAI

A mother, a wife and a successful business owner, her strength in the face
of adversity has led to a life of opportunity for her two children. Despite
numerous years in direct provision, she never lost hope that one day her
family could live a life free from oppressive laws and start again.

> *WHEN YOU ARE SO DESPERATE, YOU WILL SEARCH FOR ANYTHING TO CALM YOU AND GIVE YOU HOPE, AND THAT WAS EXACTLY WHAT WE FOUND THOSE DAYS.*

ANONYMOUS

In 2008, my husband and I made the difficult decision to leave our home country, Iran, due to escalating tensions with the Iranian revolutionary police. It became increasingly clear that our family's safety could no longer be guaranteed. The revolution of 1979 brought to power an Islamist government, which drastically altered the lives of its citizens. The aftermath of the revolution was a period of turmoil, marked by the devastating Iran–Iraq War, which lasted for eight years. During this time, countless innocent lives were lost and many others were left physically and mentally scarred. I was just nine years old when the war began, yet the memories of those harrowing years remain etched in my mind.

After finishing high school with good scores, I completed a four-year nursing degree at university. Following a year of working as a nurse, I got married. My husband was also a nurse, working alongside me in the ICU. Together, we worked hard to provide a better life for our two children, a daughter and a son.

Life was not easy, particularly witnessing the suffering of individuals deprived of their basic needs. In the wake of the revolution, the country's condition

deteriorated rapidly. Day by day, the situation got worse; we were losing any sense of normal life. Women were stripped of even the most fundamental rights, including the freedom to choose what they wanted to wear. Every day, people were being arrested by revolutionary guards and imprisoned under false pretexts in a further violation of human rights.

I recall vividly an incident from my childhood, when at the age of 11, my 27-year-old cousin was arrested for producing homemade apple alcohol – a practice forbidden by Islamic law and which resulted in severe punishment. He suffered a horrible fate. They put him in prison, and while there, they poisoned him. Nobody could prove that his death was a result of the brutality of those in power, because they could do the same to anybody who challenged them. The absence of accountability meant that the same could be inflicted upon anyone deemed undesirable, casting a shadow of fear over people.

I remember clearly the day my husband and I got engaged. We were strolling hand in hand through a park when the revolutionary guards arrested us. In their eyes, the simple act of walking together was a violation of the rules under Sharia Law – men and women were not allowed to walk side by side. They were looking for proof that we were engaged. Despite our protests, they remained unconvinced, even when we showed them the only evidence we had: our engagement rings. It was a stark reminder of how deeply ingrained societal norms can be, even in the most personal moments of our lives.

I cannot forget that night. I didn't want to go with them and was reluctant to comply with their demands. Although we tried to explain that we were planning to marry in the coming months, they remained sceptical until they reached out to our families, who confirmed this was true. Under the law, if we were meeting each other without our family's permission, we could have faced either lashes or forced marriage.

After getting married, my husband and I left our hometown in the north of Iran for the capital city, Tehran. We rented a one-bedroom apartment and both began working in hospitals. My husband worked in the ICU of a public hospital, while I worked in the operating theatre in a private hospital.

Growing up in a family where religion was never imposed on us, I never practised it, especially after the revolution. Following the change in government, many Iranians found it difficult to adhere to Sharia Law, due to the suffering it caused. A colleague spoke to me about a friend of his who had recently embraced Christianity. He mentioned that this friend had been reading the Bible and had offered it to him, discreetly covering it with wrapping paper to hide its title. Reading the Bible is forbidden for Muslims in Iran and being caught with one can lead to severe punishment. If the authorities find out, the consequences can be life-threatening. My colleague, trusting me, recommended the Bible to me as well. I started to read it and found it incredibly interesting. Everything was discussed openly, even topics that would never be freely discussed in Iran. I was somewhat familiar with Jesus, but I had never had the chance to read the Bible before. In Islam, Jesus is considered one of the prophets, which is why it's confusing that the Islamic government doesn't want people to read a book about him. I shared the Bible with my husband and we began listening to Christian satellite radio. We also started going to meetings and an underground church. When you are so desperate, you will search for anything to calm you and give you hope, and that was exactly what we found in those days.

After a while, we learned that the revolutionary guards were searching for anyone participating in these meetings and that some participants had been arrested. As soon as we heard about the arrests, we decided to leave the country. We gathered a few belongings and moved to my uncle's house. We explained everything to him, knowing he had a contact who could help us escape. We left our house, jobs and everything we had worked for over many years, to save not only our lives but also the lives of our children.

After three days of hiding at my uncle's house, someone came to collect us and take us to another city near the border of Iran and Turkey. He was a smuggler. We couldn't even call our parents to tell them, as we feared the phone would be monitored. At night, we went with someone else in another vehicle, to cross the border. I cannot explain the emotions we felt and the stress we were under. We were quiet, unable to talk due to the tension. Thank God, we were lucky enough to cross the Turkish border without being arrested. We arrived early in the morning to a city called Van. We were exhausted and anxious, not knowing where we would go next.

The smuggler kept us in a house that was far from the city. He would bring us food and water. We stayed there for nearly 10 days, constantly asking him when and to where we would be moved. His only answer was, "Whenever the time is right", adding that our destination was unclear, but it would be somewhere in Europe. My poor children, just 12 and 10 years old, were agitated and uncomfortable. As I remember, we were in Turkey for almost three weeks, before flying to Ireland. At that time, we had no idea where Ireland was, only knowing it was in Europe and close to Britain. Once we arrived in Ireland, our stress began to ease.

During the flight, we were all quiet and tired, but we couldn't rest because we kept thinking about what we needed to do when we arrived. We worried about what would happen and what we would have to say. The smuggler had given us instructions, but when you're stressed, it's easy to forget. We arrived around midday and I'm not sure how we made it through, but we did. At the airport, we tried to find a bus to the International Protection Office (IPO). Our English wasn't perfect, but it was decent enough. Eventually, we found the bus and had enough money to buy tickets to get to the city centre.

It took us hours to find the IPO. We approached a porter in front of a building. My husband spoke to him, as I was shy about speaking to unfamiliar males. He was very friendly and I believe he felt sorry for us when he saw the children. He wrote down the address and told us where to go. We arrived at the IPO with only a backpack each. When we introduced ourselves, we handed over our bags. They were very good to us, which made us feel relaxed. My husband and I were asked a few questions, but since our children were underage, they didn't question them. After completing several documents, which took many hours, it was evening. We, along with other refugees from different countries, were sent by bus to the Kilmacud Refugee Centre in south Dublin.

We were all so hungry. The centre provided us with warm food and gave us a room with two double bunk beds. Our bathroom, located outside the room, was shared with others. That was where we stayed for two weeks. During our time there, we met a mother and son from Iran and a lady from Afghanistan, with whom we could communicate. It was a challenging situation, but we felt a sense of safety, which was a great comfort.

After two weeks, we received a letter telling us we were to be transferred to another centre. Sadly, we had to bid farewell to our new friends, as they were being sent to different accommodation. It wasn't within our control to choose where to go, which seemed fair enough. The lady from Afghanistan tried persuading the centre to allow her to come with us, but they didn't grant her request. Instead, they sent her to Mayo, while we went to Monaghan.

Our stay in Monaghan lasted four months. During the first month, the four of us lived in a single room; this was standard in that centre. Some of the rooms had their own bathroom, but we shared communal bathrooms and showers with others, which was challenging. At times, it was uncomfortable, witnessing men using the women's shower and bathroom. We asked the manager of the centre if he could give us another room with a private bathroom and shower. He told us that we would have to wait until another family moved out, before they could accommodate our request. After two months, we were finally allocated a room with its own bathroom and shower. We were overjoyed!

The manager explained that we would have to wait, because they needed to clean and prepare the room and he promised to arrange it by the following week. However, we couldn't wait any longer, so we offered to do it ourselves. We asked him to give us the necessary paint and cleaning supplies, eager to make the room liveable as soon as possible. He did, and my husband and I took on the task. We were also given some furniture from a second-hand shop, which we cleaned and organised in the room. My husband also had to clean up the area out the back of the room, which was littered with rubbish and nappies.

Life was incredibly tough there, especially as my children had to start school.

There was no bus service for them that we were aware of at the time, and we were in the countryside with narrow roads and no footpaths. I had to use taxis for the first month, for which no assistance was provided. Adults received €19 per week and a few euros were allocated to each child. We received €57 per week for all of us and, although it wasn't easy, we did our best to save it for the children's taxi fares, so they could get to school.

I should mention that the centre provided us with food and washing powder, which alleviated some of the expense, but it still wasn't enough, especially when you wanted to buy something extra for your children. Fortunately, the school helped us with the children's uniforms. After a month, my children could take the school bus, which was a great relief.

After four months there, they decided to transfer us to another centre in a different location, because an inspector had visited and felt that we shouldn't all be staying together in one room, especially since my children were 12 and 10 years old. We couldn't understand why they didn't recognise this issue when they first sent us to Monaghan. The Monaghan centre was more suitable for single refugees, not families. We were upset, because it meant the children had to change schools again, but we were also hopeful about moving to a better place.

They relocated us to Athlone, where we were given a mobile home consisting of three small bedrooms. We had our own shower, bath and kitchen, as well as a small living room. We started painting the interior of the mobile home and cleaning it; again, doing our best to make it feel like a home for our family. Once more, our children had to attend a new school and wear new uniforms.

It was an incredibly difficult time for all of us and if I were to go into detail, it would take many pages to explain. My husband's mental health was affected and at one point, he confided that he wanted to end his life, because our situation was so uncertain. As a father, he was overwhelmed with anxiety about our children's future. I also want to mention that in both Monaghan and Athlone, we found solace in attending church, where the people were incredibly helpful. Without their support, who knows where we might be by now?

After 19 months in the centre, we finally received our refugee status and had to move out. We were granted Irish status on 31 March 2010, which coincidentally was our wedding anniversary. It was a momentous day for us all. In June, after much searching, we found a house in Dublin and moved in. Both my children were immensely happy and relieved. We rented that house for 11 years.

My beautiful daughter achieved her dream of becoming a fully qualified dentist after studying for five years at Trinity College Dublin. My son earned his bachelor's degree in Science and then completed his master's in Data Analysis. Currently, he is working on a research project on lung cancer with two friends and he is doing exceptionally well. Their project was recognised by a scientific magazine and they were interviewed by science journalists.

I am incredibly proud of both of my children. They had hard times, but despite facing many challenges, they never let their situation define who they are. Instead, they have always been resilient. I also pursued higher education and went to college, studying beauty therapy. After working for a few years, I opened my own business in 2018 with one of my college classmates. I am still working as a beautician and running my business. My husband has been working as a taxi driver since 2014. My daughter bought her own house and we all moved in with her. We have been living there for two years now.

Thankfully, those difficult days have passed, although life always has its ups and downs. I hope that by sharing our story, we will provide people with some insight into the refugee experience in Ireland.

More about Iran:

Direct provision was established in Ireland in 2000 to meet the needs of people around the world who, for reasons such as war, abuse of human rights or conflict displacement, seek refuge. Countries that become places where people seek safety and protection have their own policies and procedures governing who can stay and how their needs are provided for once they arrive in the country.

Through the system of direct provision, Ireland provides state-funded accommodation, which is outsourced and run for a profit by companies that operate within the private sector. Upon entering the direct provision system, an asylum seeker is assigned to an accommodation centre. These are normally hostels or hotels, where they are provided with three meals a day. During their stay, they have the freedom to live and travel within the State. However, their freedom and autonomy have conditions, and the management need to be notified about any stays outside of the centres.

Asylum seekers are given a means-tested Daily Expenses Allowance. According to Citizen's Information, as of 2024, this allowance is €38.80 per week for each adult and €29.80 for each child. Those who availed of direct provision from 2000 to 2017 were denied the right to work. The Supreme Court ruled in May 2017 that this was in breach of the Constitution. While waiting for a decision on their application, asylum seekers are now only required to wait for six months before they are allowed to work, but they can start applying for work after five months.

Direct provision has come under huge scrutiny from human rights organisations such as Amnesty International. Calling for an end to direct provision, they note that "Ireland's direct provision system has been a human rights scandal. Direct provision has failed utterly to fulfil Ireland's human rights obligations to people seeking protection here. Instead, it has been 21 years of people being hurt and marginalised, and 21 years of lives put on hold." (End Direct Provision, Amnesty International Ireland)

Amnesty highlights that many applicants have been left waiting more than the stated six months and sometimes end up spending years in direct provision, often in remote areas, their lives in limbo. Further to this, they noted that the living conditions, such as sharing with strangers, did not meet the State's duty to protect the dignity of people who have come from situations of trauma. They remarked that direct provision ran like an "institutionalised regime", which can harm and hinder people.

In 2017, the Ombudsman was given official remit to examine the numerous complaints made about people's experience in direct provision. From this, the Ombudsman published *The Ombudsman and Direct Provision: The story so far* (2018). In this report, they outline their findings about direct provision complaints concerning food, cooking facilities, attitudes of staff towards residents and fear of the complaints procedure due to feeling like it would hamper their cases. It also notes that some complaints fell under cultural misunderstandings and genuine disparities in care between centres.

In February 2021, the Irish Government published a White Paper in which they announced their plans to end direct provision, to be replaced by a service called the International Support Service. Under this plan, direct provision centres will be closed by the end of 2024. Further to this, applicants will be placed in a "reception and integration centre" with a decision on their application due to be made within a four-month period.

More
about:

> "TO BE A REFUGEE IS TO LIVE IN LIMBO, ALWAYS WAITING, ALWAYS UNCERTAIN ABOUT WHAT TOMORROW WILL BRING."

KHALED HOSSEINI

Brian is a father and a carer. His story begins when he defected from the army to fight for a better life, free from corruptive powers.

BRIAN

My name is Brian and I'm from Zimbabwe. I've been in Ireland for nearly six years. I came here seeking asylum because my life was under threat. I was a soldier before I arrived here. I defected and I was on my own. The army was looking for me and if they caught me, I would not have survived. By the time I left, there was an opposition party forming against the government. Some of those who had defected were joining the opposition. Some were unlucky, like two of my friends, who were caught and one died. I managed to flee and came to Ireland.

At 23 I joined the army, because I admired it as an occupation. However, after three years, it wasn't working for me anymore. Financially, I could not look after my family. I had signed a seven-year contract and I was in my fourth year, but I just couldn't manage. A soldier at the time earned a salary of 170,000 Zimbabwean dollars, the equivalent of roughly €170. Inflation was high and with that money, you had to live, send your children to school and look after the family.

I knew I had to leave. However, my contract had not yet ended and in Zimbabwe, this is a crime. Defection from the army can lead to legal consequences such as imprisonment, court martial or in extreme cases, capital punishment if the defection is considered treasonous or if it occurs during conflict or political unrest. If you are caught, they will take you to a barracks, where you will spend at least five years being physically punished. There is a fifty-fifty chance that by the end, your body will no longer be fit and able, as it will have suffered too much.

I met with my friend after he had left the barracks. Even before he told me what had happened, I could see just by looking at him how badly the abuse had affected his physical state. There is no proper medication in Zimbabwe.

Hospital care, the whole system, is broken. He couldn't manage to get proper help and passed away soon after.

With the life that was facing me, I knew I had to take a risk, because either way, things were not going well. When I left the army, I went to another town rather than go home. If you defect, they will come looking for you. My friends were caught, because they had gone home. The army went to my old address, but were told that I wasn't there. I fled to South Africa and I sought the help of people who could help me secure safe passage to Europe. I stayed in South Africa for about five months. It was tough being away from my family, not talking to them. I was afraid they might also be at risk. I had to send my children to the country, afraid that the army would come for them.

The political situation is bad in Zimbabwe. Those in power want to stay in power, because they know the crimes that they've committed. They feel that if an opposition government came in, they would be in danger of being arrested and even their lives would be under threat. So they will try everything possible to remain in power.

Daily life in Zimbabwe is hard. It's tough for an ordinary person to get a normal meal. Very few families can afford three meals a day. The food they eat is nothing fancy, just a meal to keep them moving. If you're poor, you're poor. If you're rich, you're rich. There's nowhere in the middle. Usually, if you are poor and you are struggling, there is a 99% chance that you will never rise out of it. You will always struggle.

To survive, it's all about corruption and bribes. Although I don't agree with it, I had to adapt during my time in the army. When the situation was getting tough, especially when the opposition was active, if I saw a civilian that I felt was "in the wrong place", I would demand that they pay me to look away. People are afraid of the army, so they will give you what you ask for. In Zimbabwe, this is normal; it is a way to survive. Everyone wants to survive. The leadership is so corrupt, and once it's corrupt, everyone becomes corrupt.

———————

When I arrived in Ireland, I was in a panic. As you start to make that journey, all you think is, What's going to happen? Will I be accepted or will I be sent back? So far, I had been lucky not to be sent back from South Africa, so I hoped for the same in Ireland. I was directed to the Department of Justice on the day I arrived. From there, they sent me to a direct provision centre in Finglas, close to Charlestown. I stayed there for three months. As I didn't know what to expect, I thought at first that everything was top-class. But the longer you stay, the more like a prison it is, because you don't have your own rights, you don't make your own decisions. You are told what to do and you can't say no. Everyone is sharing a room. If you are single, you are one of four in a room, with people from different countries, different backgrounds and different cultures. When you ask people not to do something, they'll say, "This is my place, just mind your own place. I've got every right to do whatever I want here." It was tough. After a few months, I got transferred to Clondalkin. Here, it was the same thing again. You couldn't make decisions for yourself. You were given rules, told what not to do and you were sharing again, four people in a room.

People who are in direct provision have experienced trauma. Some are supported, some are not. It depends on your solicitor. If your solicitor is supportive, you might get access to a social worker. If not, then you're on your own. I was in direct provision for nine months. They gave me a temporary work permit, while they reviewed my case. I worked as a care assistant, which was very different from my life in the army. I was a frontline worker during Covid. Your work permit is not a given. You renew it after the first six months, then for one year. One day while at work, I got a call from HR to say my permit had been denied and that I was no longer eligible to work. However, they were kind to me and gave me an extra month's work, because I had been with them a long time. After that, I decided to stop, because I did not want to put the company at risk. To this day, they regularly check on me and ask if I have my papers so that I can come back to work.

Unfortunately, the Department of Justice gave me a deportation order. They told me to leave the direct provision centre and that I had to look for my own accommodation. I still had opportunities to appeal, but for now, I was denied refugee status. I've been out of direct provision for nearly two years now. Once you've been denied, they will cancel your work permit and you won't be allowed to work. It's a shame, considering I was working as a health care assistant. I thought maybe the minister would give me the benefit of the doubt.

Every month, I have to go to the Garda National Immigration Bureau and sign on. Here, they give me another month or two to stay further. I have no passport and there's no Zimbabwean embassy here. My country is considered an unsafe country and has no embassy. I am stuck in limbo. I can't apply for a passport to leave and they can't send me back without one, even though I was issued with a deportation order.

I have been paying rent for almost two years now, living off the money I saved working as a care assistant. I've written to the minister several times asking them to allow me to work, because my savings are nearly gone, but they haven't replied. Only yesterday, I got a response to a letter I had sent six months ago, and that was only to say they had received it. I'm almost dry. I even wrote to social services to ask if they could give me any kind of allowance – we used to get a weekly allowance of €38 but it was stopped. They said, "No, you're not entitled to anything." Then I wrote to see if they could give me temporary accommodation and again, they said no.

I have a baby boy here, he's four and he was born in Ireland. He has his difficulties. He's nonverbal, which means he can't speak, but he can hear. So, he has his own way of doing things. He stays with his mum. Legally, I can apply to stay in Ireland on the grounds of guardianship. The Department of Justice said I had to get a DNA test, which costs €1,500. I wrote to a barrister and said that I wouldn't be able to raise that money right away. They told me there was nothing they could do; the barrister must be paid. So, without a permit to work and earn money and no passport to leave, this is an incredibly tough situation I find myself in.

For many years, I believed my baby had my name, but one day I saw the birth certificate and my name was not on it. I asked the mother of my child why this was the case. She said that she feared they would deport her if they knew I was the father. When she went for her interview, she told them that she didn't know who the father of the child was. So now it has made everything crooked. She had obviously panicked and wanted to stay and protect both herself and my child.

My other children are back home and they need my support. If I tell them I'm not allowed to work, people don't understand. They think that maybe I am getting money and enjoying my life here, that everything is okay and I am forgetting my family.

Sometimes, I don't feel like calling home. My daughter is 19 and studying to be an accountant. She's renting a place. I am trying to provide for her and do my best by her, but I owe two months' rent for her accommodation. My little boy is 14. He was in a boarding school, but now he can't attend because I can't afford to send him.

During my time in direction provision, I was the Community Chairman. I worked to give a voice and support to the residents. At times, management made bad decisions that impacted the residents and I spoke up for them. It felt like a war sometimes. Funding was given to the centre, but the residents rarely got to see it or benefit from it. In many ways, they try to silence you in any way they can. I learned quickly that if you spoke out or if you said no, then you're no longer on their side.

I hope that one day I might get an email from the minister saying I can stay in Ireland, and then I can start living a normal life. For now, it's not a normal life. I don't want my landlord to think I'm not working and start asking questions about how I am surviving and where I get money. Because if you don't go to work, people think maybe you're living a dirty life. Sometimes I wake up in the morning and think, okay, let me just go to the city centre, spend time there, come back around five, and maybe they'll think that I'm doing something. I just hope that maybe one day, I'll get my papers and start living more. I get stressed sometimes, but even if it pains, I'll just say, "Okay, I'll soldier on."

It's hard to be here. I've got parents back home and I'm the only child who's here. They know that their son is in Europe, that Europe is wealthy, and if you work, you earn money. So when they see other families with children in Europe bringing things back home, they will start asking, "What's happened?" I grew up in a Christian family and sometimes when I talk to them, I feel they think that maybe I've changed my way of life. All I want is to bring my children here and try to make sure that they finish their education and live a normal life again. I would like to go to college. Right now, I can't even do this. I'm in limbo. If you look for government colleges or universities, they will ask you, "Are you in the asylum system?" If you say yes, they will ask you for the blue card, the refugee card. If you don't have these things, you can't go to college. I was offered a place to do nursing in UCD, but because I had no permit, I couldn't accept. The only place that I can get into is a private college, but to go to a private college you need money.

I want the people out there to know the real situation that's happening for some people. They think when people are in direct provision, they are in heaven, and everything is good, but this is not the way it is.

More about
Zimbabwe:

> ## "HOW WONDERFUL IT IS THAT NOBODY NEED WAIT A SINGLE MOMENT BEFORE STARTING TO IMPROVE THE WORLD."

ANNE FRANK

Donnah is a mother and advocacy professional dedicated to human rights and social justice. As Project Coordinator for the Doras Migrant Victim of Crime support project, Donnah addresses critical service gaps for victims of domestic and gender violence, human trafficking, racism and hate crime. She also co-founded the Movement of Asylum Seekers Ireland (MASI) and established the Limerick-based community group, Every Child Is Your Child.

DON'T WORRY. WE'LL BE VOTING FOR YOU. WE TAKE CARE OF OUR OWN.

DONNAH

My name is Donnah and I have been living in Ireland for ten years. I moved to Ireland in 2014 with my three children. Now I have four. The eldest girl is 20, followed by her sister, who is 16, and their brothers, 14 and 4.

I originally come from Bulawayo, Zimbabwe. Bulawayo is a beautiful city with a significant Western influence. Walking through its streets, you might feel like you're in Limerick or somewhere in England, due to the strong British influence. During my secondary years, I attended an all-girls school with a very British curriculum. I studied Cambridge O-Level and A-Level subjects. People often comment on how good my English is. They ask how long have I been speaking it. Well, my whole life, really.

I come from a politically active family, which has greatly influenced my experiences and shaped who I am today. My father, who passed away earlier this year, was a veteran of Zimbabwe's fight for independence, after which the country gained its independence. Many of his family took up positions within the political structure and some remain active in politics today.

I left Zimbabwe at around age 16 and moved to South Africa. The political landscape in Zimbabwe evolved over the years, with the ruling party breaking up into factions, due to ideological disagreements and policy execution. My mother was one of those who distanced herself from the main party. She played a key role in establishing a significant women's league movement at the time. However, the ideas my mother and her colleagues were advocating clashed with the dominant ideologies of the ruling party, of which my father's family, including my father himself, were strong members. She came to distance herself from the main party and this led to her fleeing the country.

It was around this time that my own political activism, and in a way my radicalisation, began. I understood why my mother left. She sat me down and explained the situation, emphasising that it was for both her safety and ours that she had to go. It made sense to me at the time, although I didn't fully grasp that I might one day find myself in a similar situation. For me, it was simply a matter of accepting that she was leaving, with the promise that we would join her at some point.

During those years, I spoke out against military conscription being introduced in Zimbabwe. This policy was set to start with my own cohort of high school graduates, and it included requirements like shaving our heads and undergoing compulsory military training. For many of us, this was shocking.

Back in 2002, we didn't have social media or even mobile phones. It was all very grassroots, with group meetings at the park and city hall, where we would gather with other students who were facing the possibility of conscription. Most of us were students, and women were included in this too. We were given the nickname "green bombers", because of the green uniforms we were supposed to wear as conscripts. Part of the group was set to be trained in the Congo, which felt outrageous, given Zimbabwe's strongly Westernised culture. The schools we attended were similar to those in Ireland, so the idea of being forced into a military uniform and shipped off to training camps was unacceptable.

On the last day of our exams, buses were set to take us to the military camps. We tried to warn people to avoid the last exams if possible, advising them to go to their rural homes, hide or even lie about their age to avoid conscription. Our goal was to build enough confidence among people to protest and refuse to participate. Some did end up going to the training camps, while others managed to avoid it. It's unclear whether those who went were conscripted involuntarily, but there was certainly a significant number who did participate.

We were adamant that we were not going to comply with these new policies and spoke out against them. At the time, this was considered quite radical and we faced numerous threats to our safety. There were several incidents involving me and my friends that made us realise we might no longer be safe in Zimbabwe. So, at the age of 16, a group of us left for South Africa. We were young and inexperienced, meeting new people and making friends. I entered a relationship with a man, who would later become the father of my three children. In hindsight, it was probably a relationship of convenience for me. At that age, what I craved most was security, someone who could provide stability and safety, especially as I was only 17 and unsure of what I was doing.

This person expressed being deeply in love with me and wanted to be my provider. Initially, the relationship was wonderful, especially in the first few years. However, as I grew and developed my own ideas and ambitions, it became clear that our visions for the future did not align. I was becoming less compliant with his expectations, particularly as I sought education and new experiences. This disconnect eventually led to the breakdown of our relationship, especially after the birth of our son, who is now 14. Due to the fallout, my life became unsafe. There were threats to reveal my identity and location to people back home. Coupled with the abusive treatment I was receiving from him, I became really fearful. At that point, I began considering my options, including whether I should leave the country.

I relocated to a different part of the country, desperately hoping to escape him, but he still tracked me down. There was a heart-wrenching period when he took our eldest child and I was unable to see her for three years. It felt like an eternity, filled with worry and pain. At that time, the youngest was still breastfeeding and my other child was a toddler. His reasoning for taking our daughter was that if I wanted her, I had to return to him. Essentially, I could not have one without the other. He claimed my return would fix the family unit and the relationship.

I kept insisting that I would not go back to that situation. It felt like his behaviour was either a form of punishment or a method of exerting control, although it was hard to understand his exact motives. It felt like a deliberate attempt to control the situation. The emotional toll was overwhelming. We turned to the police for help, but they could do nothing without current addresses or phone numbers. However, his last known phone numbers were disconnected and the addresses were outdated. As we reached out to friends and acquaintances, the responses were disheartening. They were all in the dark. It felt like my child and her father had vanished from the face of the earth.

It felt like being in limbo, existing without direction. At the same time, I had to be present for our two other children, who constantly asked about their sister. "Where is she? When are we going to see her?" I tried to reassure them by saying that she was with Granny or that she was just visiting friends.

It was horrific to deal with these questions and the constant reminders from others asking where the other child was. Meanwhile, people around us seemed to move on, forgetting the situation, which only added to the difficulty of navigating through this painful time. However, I had become self-sufficient, having worked hard to get an education and build a stable life.

In the third year, when I finally found her, it was a moment of overwhelming relief mixed with anger. That week, it happened that my ex-partner had been arrested. With this, his partner at the time reached out to me on Facebook, asking for my daughter's birth certificate to change her school. I responded, filled with disbelief and concern, "Wait a minute, where are you?"

I managed to get his partner to agree to meet up. Then I rushed to the police station, telling them through tears of anxiety, that I knew where my daughter was and begged them to assist me in bringing her home. This they did and I finally reunited with her that same week. The relief was overwhelming, but short-lived. Almost immediately, I started receiving chilling threats from his family, demanding that I return her. The threats felt dangerously real. In South Africa, where anything can happen, I was starkly aware of the terrifying potential of the people I was up against and what they might do.

During that period, I had enrolled in a Business Management Diploma programme and graduated. I was working at a fantastic job in an office automation company, specialising in printers and similar products. Despite this, the fear and uncertainty drove me to make the difficult decision to leave everything behind and start anew.

I explained my situation to the owner of the company and his support was incredible. He assured me there were options and suggested I seek refuge in countries where I wouldn't need a visa. He even offered me an advance on my salary. "Donnah, do what you need to do," he said. "If it doesn't work out, you come back home. We'll have you back." The company had been instrumental in helping me, from accompanying me with the police to retrieve my daughter, to ensuring I reached a place of safety.

I vividly remember the day I walked into the travel agency. "What's the next flight out that doesn't require a visa?"

The agent replied, "To Ireland."

I was taken aback, but didn't hesitate. "Okay, Ireland it is. Which flight?"

We boarded a plane to Dubai, but while waiting for our connecting flight, things took an unexpected turn. The immigration officers pulled us aside, scrutinising our passports and asking about money. They wanted to see my bank cards and work documents. I was relieved to have everything in order, but when I tried to make a purchase at the duty-free shop, my card was declined. It had been flagged for suspicious activity.

Amid this stress, my younger daughter, about six at the time, asked, "Mommy, why are we the only black people here?" I was taken aback, but amused by her innocent observation. A woman approached us and asked if she could touch my daughter's hair. I was stunned and amused. This was really happening. It wasn't negative, just an unexpected part of the experience.

Eventually, an immigration officer came to us and said, "Look, you can board the flight." Then he added, "I wish you the best of luck in whatever you're going to do." I thought, Oh my God, does he know? I'm like, okay, that's weird, but we've made it this far. We boarded the flight and arrived in Dublin, but the experience was far from pleasant. I was already feeling nervous, unsure and a bit sad. I didn't know what I was doing or where we were going. I tried every delay tactic I could think of, hoping to be the last ones in the queue. I wanted to avoid others from the plane knowing our business. While people chatted with me about their plans – weddings, seeing family again – I was evasive.

"What are you going to do here?" someone asked.

"Oh, just … you know," I replied vaguely. "We're on holiday, touring around. That sort of thing."

This was in September and we were dressed in our summer tops. When we got off the plane, it was freezing and foggy. None of us had coats or even sweaters.

We approached the immigration officer. "How long are you guys going to be staying, and where?" he asked.

"I have no idea. I was hoping you could actually help me with that."

He took our passports, placed them on the desk and muttered, "Not you people again. You just come over here and confuse the system."

I was mortified. I stood there, my teeth chattering from the cold, and my children were right next to me, equally unsettled.

Then he asked, "Where are you from?"

"Well, I'm actually from Zimbabwe, but I'm coming from South Africa."

He started cursing under his breath, saying something like, "Here we go again. I'm done with this." It seemed like he was wrapping up his shift. He told us to wait. Soon, another officer appeared and asked what we were doing here.

"I'm not really sure," I responded. "I'm here seeking help, but I don't know what kind of help exactly. I think I might be in danger where I'm coming from."

"Are you seeking asylum?"

I hesitated. "I suppose. I'm not familiar with the terminology. But yeah, I suppose that's what I'm doing."

He then took us to the back, where I sat with the kids. They were hungry and cold and we waited there for about six hours, while our fingerprints were processed, among other things. The officer asked if we had accommodation and, of course, we didn't. They arranged a taxi for us, which took us to the Balseskin Reception Centre.

When we arrived, we were told to report to the International Protection Office (IPO) on the following Monday. We were then placed in a shared room with another family from Zimbabwe. Seeing that we desperately needed warm clothes, a woman from the family directed us to a room with donated clothing. She then asked, "So, what's your story?"

I was confused. "What do you mean, what's my story?"

She explained, "Well, have you been processed?"

I said, "Oh, yeah, we're done with all of that."

She started laughing. "Oh my God. My dear, it's not over. You'll need to explain to the IPO why you're here. After that, you might be transferred to another centre."

She then gave me a crash course on the asylum process. She said I needed to start thinking about my reasons for seeking asylum, based on grounds like political persecution, religion, race or membership of a particular social group. I was overwhelmed; it all felt so intense.

I will never forget that following Monday. The security guard knocked on our door around 7.30 am, reminding us to get ready for the bus that would leave at 8.30. I tried to get the kids ready in time, but we missed breakfast. So, when we made our way to the IPO, the kids were already hungry and cold. The processing took about six hours, finishing around 3 pm. During that whole time, the kids had nothing to eat or drink. They'd gone the entire day without a meal.

When we finally finished, they told us we could head back to the centre. I was bewildered though, as the bus had dropped us off outside the IPO and I had no idea how we were supposed to get back. The officer handed me a printed map and pointed out where we were and where we needed to go to catch the bus.

To put it in perspective, the IPO was on Mount Street, near St Stephen's Green, and we needed to get to Mountjoy Square. Imagine walking that distance with a four-year-old, a six-year-old and a ten-year-old who hadn't eaten all day! It was raining, we had no umbrellas and we were wearing light jumpers. I tried to use the GPS on my phone, but I had no SIM card. I attempted to withdraw money but my card was blocked. I literally had nothing in my pocket. We kept getting lost, constantly stopping people to ask for directions. No one knew where we needed to go.

At that point, I was feeling utterly defeated. The kids were tired, hungry and cold, and I was running out of options. Just when I thought things couldn't get worse, a man approached us. He asked, "Are you lost?"

I told him, "Yes, terribly lost. I need to get to Balseskin Reception Centre in Finglas."

He seemed puzzled and admitted he didn't know what that was, so I explained it was an asylum seeker centre. He didn't understand what seeking asylum meant. I was shocked. How could someone not know about asylum seekers?

He said his name was Ken and he was Irish. Despite not knowing where we needed to go, he said he was picking up his kids from school. He offered to come back after dropping them off at home and help us find the bus stop. I was sceptical, but decided to trust him. We waited and, true to his word, he came back. He drove us around, asking people for directions, but no one knew. Eventually, he dropped us off at Jury's Inn, telling us that there was a bus stop just around the corner. Maybe a bus driver would know where we needed to go. He gave me 20 euros, saying, "If you find the bus, at least you'll have some money." I was overwhelmed with gratitude and deeply moved by his generosity.

Ken's kindness was a lifeline during a difficult time and I remain grateful to him. To this day, I still wish I could reconnect with him and thank him for his incredible support. He had given me his business card, but I've since lost it. I took the kids to a small shop nearby, an Arabic store. We walked into the shop and I told the kids, "Let's just get some sandwiches." Despite how hungry they were, they kept insisting, "No, it's fine. We just want water." I was adamant, urging them to pick something, anything. Eventually, they settled on some crisps.

I then turned to the shopkeeper and asked, "I need a SIM card. How much is it?"

"Five euros and comes with five euros of credit."

I thought, perfect, and bought it, along with the crisps. After paying, I had about seven euros left. With the SIM card in hand, I finally had internet access and could use the GPS on my phone. I entered the address from the map into the GPS, and it said we were just two minutes away from the bus stop. I was so relieved. However, I feared that the last bus had already left. Apparently the final one was at 5.30 pm. Thankfully, when we got there, all the buses were gone, except one. I showed the map to the bus driver, who said, "This bus goes to Finglas, but only as far as the Finglas Shopping Centre. From there, you'll need to take another bus or walk."

At this point, I was willing to do whatever it took, so we got on the bus. When we reached the Finglas Shopping Centre, the driver informed us that the connecting bus had already departed. He looked at us sympathetically and said, "So what I'm going to do is this: I'll take a risk and drive you there and drop you off. It's only a three-minute drive, but a 25-minute walk in the rain for you." He drove us directly to our destination and didn't charge us for the ride. I was immensely grateful.

By the time we arrived at the centre, it was after 7 pm and the canteen was closed. There was no more food. Exhausted and disheartened, we went to our room, knowing we'd have to wait until the next morning to eat again. The next day, with a working phone, I was finally able to call my bank and start to get things sorted.

This was the beginning of our new life in Ireland. I could buy things for the kids, such as cookies and squash. We were also getting some basic necessities that we could keep in the room. It's a bit embarrassing to say that, after four days in the country, we were only now getting things like washcloths, soap and toothbrushes!

The two younger kids were too little to grasp the situation and my relationship with my eldest was still fragile. We were just beginning to reconnect and make sense of everything that had happened, after spending three years apart. So, there was a lot going on for all of us in different ways. For me, it was especially confusing and filled with fear of the unknown and uncertainty about what would happen next. My biggest fear was that if this didn't work out, we might have to go back. We were warned that this might be the outcome, given where we were from.

In my asylum process, the burden of proof was on me. I had to provide every possible piece of evidence to explain why I feared being sent back to my country. Despite having pictures, articles and other proof about my family's political affiliations, I was afraid to fully disclose this information. My concern was that if I revealed too much and was later denied protection, it could lead to severe repercussions if I were to return home.

I began receiving threats on my Facebook account from senior officials in Zimbabwe. These threats were even visible on my public profile. I was targeted primarily because of my family's political connections and the fact that my mother had already fled the country. I was seen as bringing shame to the family and deviating from the expected political path. There was an expectation that I would align with their political stance. It wasn't just my father; the whole family was involved in the party. It took immense bravery to navigate this situation and I had to be courageous to protect myself and pursue asylum.

We were coming from South Africa and were told our case would be prioritised, meaning it would be dealt with within two weeks. It was indeed processed in that time frame, but we received our first refusal. That alone was incredibly stressful, because I kept thinking we might be sent back. There was so much misinformation and conflicting information coming from different sources. People at the centre who had been there longer were often misinforming and misleading us. At the same time, reliable sources were telling us things like, "You don't have the right to work. You don't have the right to education," and other similar restrictions.

As someone with a professional background, who was used to working and providing for my children, we were accustomed to a certain lifestyle. Suddenly, I was in a situation where I could neither provide for them nor work. We had moved from a stable environment, where the kids had their own rooms, friends and went to school, to a place where we were living in a shared space with strangers.

We were sharing space with families from Zimbabwe and Nigeria. The setup was like adjoining rooms in a hotel: two rooms connected by a bathroom. So, there were three families in total – two families in one room and our family in another, with a shared bathroom between us. We lived with that arrangement for about two months. Then we were transferred to the Knockalisheen Centre in Limerick. Direct provision back then was very different from what it is now. On the negative side, the reception conditions were poor and the quality of food and living conditions was extremely inadequate. The centres were often isolated and segregated. We couldn't work, attend school or even know if we might be transferred at any moment, which was frightening.

However, there were positives. People who were aware of the conditions were strongly advocating for reform, spreading the message that such living conditions were unacceptable. At that time, there was also heightened awareness and discussion about the Magdalene Laundries scandal, which kept issues of institutional mistreatment in the public conversation. There was a great deal of empathy, sympathy, understanding and a sense of welcome in the communities. This warmth and friendliness were also evident in the reception I received from the two strangers I had met when I first arrived.

However, it was also disheartening to meet people at the centre who had been there for years, some as long as ten, which underscored the challenges within the system. Some people I met would tell me, "My children were born here," and I remember seeing other kids, some around 12 or in their teens, and immediately thinking, Oh my God, this cannot be my story! This will never be me!

That's what sparked my activism in Ireland. When I had only been in Knockalisheen for two months, I met Sue Conlon, who was the CEO of the Irish Refugee Council at that time. Sue, along with then DOJ Junior Minister, Aodhán O'Riordain, visited the centre to inspect the rooms. The centre manager had painted and spruced up certain blocks. I remember lingering around, observing the visit, and eventually pulling Sue aside to tell her, "What you're seeing here is not the reality."

Sue responded with interest, asking if I had more to share. I told her I had a lot to say and invited her to see my room and block to show her the real living conditions. The manager looked furious, but I persisted. I showed them my room and space, where my kids and I lived. I also called on other residents to show their rooms, the kitchen and other facilities.

By the time Sue and Aoidhan left, they had a clear understanding of the living conditions. Sue exchanged contact details with me and I explained that my asylum case was being decided again in two weeks, without legal representation. I had attended the interview without any support. Sue gave me her business card and encouraged me to contact the Irish Refugee Council for assistance.

A couple of weeks after meeting Sue, she also connected me with Doras, an independent organisation that promotes and protects the rights of migrant people in Ireland. Here, I met incredibly welcoming people, like Aideen Roche, Karen McHugh and John Lannon. They were some of the most amazing and hospitable individuals I've ever encountered. Their kindness made me feel that maybe everything would turn out okay.

During the time between meeting Sue and getting involved with Doras, I started documenting all the issues in the centre. This included the poor quality food, the lack of consideration for people with special dietary needs and the limited food availability outside specific canteen hours. There were also invasive room searches with no respect for privacy. For example, staff would just enter the rooms unannounced, even when people were undressed or coming out of the shower.

Seeing these injustices, I began talking to other residents, encouraging them to join me in taking action. By the time I connected with Doras and learned about their campaign against the direct provision system, I knew that was where I needed to be. It was a small group then, but I felt it was the right place to channel our efforts for change. I felt strongly that I needed to be with the people at Doras. It was clear that we didn't just need reforms; the entire direct provision system had to be abolished. I didn't want to see myself or anyone else stuck in this situation ten years down the line. So, I joined the group and coincidentally, similar movements were happening across the country, including in Cork, with activists like Lucky Khambule. They were protesting the terrible conditions in their centres as well.

We decided to protest in our centre too, effectively shutting it down. About a month later, along with two other residents, Kyle Phiri and Felix Dzamara, I got in touch with Lucky. We realised how much our causes aligned and it became clear that this was a widespread issue that needed a united front.

One day, we decided to bring together activists from Cork and Limerick. Our first meeting focused on sharing our experiences and highlighting the flaws in the system. In our second meeting, we discussed what we should call ourselves, what our identity would be and what we were advocating for. We agreed on key demands: the end of deportations, the abolition of direct provision centres, the right to work and an increase in the minimal allowance of €19.10 that we were receiving. Many of us were skilled professionals eager to contribute, but because we were refused the right to work, we were losing our skills and facing depression. We were determined not only to avoid ending up in that situation ourselves, but to ensure no one else would.

That is how MASI (Movement of Asylum Seekers in Ireland) was formed. We began organising protests, inspired by their success in Cork and Limerick, believing it was the only way to get the State's attention. These efforts led to significant changes in the operation of direct provision centres and the international protection system. Although it's not perfect, the introduction of the International Protection Act in 2016 and the right to work were major steps forward. Our movement played a crucial role in these reforms. Initially, we were given very little support, but we fought hard for our rights and now almost every migrant has the right to work, with access to nearly all sectors. We're still going strong.

I want to highlight a key issue we addressed in 2018. By then, my daughter was starting secondary school and it became clear that we were missing a crucial aspect: the rights of children in direct provision centres. No one was discussing the challenges faced by children or the financial burden on parents trying to raise children on €19 a week.

I remember a particular day when I was feeling the weight of these issues. The routine in the centre was incredibly monotonous. If you weren't working or volunteering, you spent most of your time in bed. I remember a particular instance when my younger daughter had a book fair at school. The fair was on a Tuesday, but our weekly cheque only came on Thursdays. She wanted €5 to buy books and pencils, but I didn't have it. I had to tell her no, that we wouldn't get the money until Thursday. She responded, "Of course you don't have the money. How could you, when you're always lying in bed?" Even at her young age, she could see how the situation was affecting our lives. It was a harsh reminder of our reality. I thought, oh my God, this is having a direct impact on the kids.

I realised my six-year-old was right: How could I possibly have the money, when I was always lying in bed? That same year, when my daughter was starting secondary school, I was struck by how outrageous the costs were. At that time, no charities were willing to help us. They would tell us we were outside their jurisdiction. There was a lack of understanding and a reluctance to be associated with the direct provision system, even when people were aware of it.

I started talking to some of the other women in the center and said, "We need to do something for ourselves if we're going to manage this."

My background is in marketing and sales, so I thought the best way to tackle this issue was to start a community support group. Along with other women in the centre, we set up "Every Child is Your Child," focusing on raising funds and highlighting the challenges faced by children and parents in direct provision. The group aimed to address the struggles parents face in providing essentials like uniforms, books and extracurricular activities. We also sought to address the exclusion children experienced, such as missing out on sleepovers and other typical childhood activities.

The group was a massive success. By 2019, we were supporting direct provision centres nationwide with school uniforms, stationery, textbooks and more. In 2020, we took a break during the pandemic, but our impact had already been significant.

If more people understood the challenges and the daily struggle of being in direct provision, they would see the immense pressure to maintain composure and appear like you have everything under control for the sake of your children. Crumbling simply isn't an option. I remember taking long showers in the bathroom just to give myself a chance to cry, because there was no other time or place where I could let my guard down. You must always present a happy face and seem like you have it all together. This is the harsh reality for every single mother in direct provision. I don't believe you'd find anyone who would tell you otherwise.

One of the key issues I highlighted throughout that initiative was how the role and responsibilities of being a mother were stripped away from us. I remember a day when my child, who was in third class at the time, came home and asked me, "Mom, what's Mac and Cheese? Everyone at school keeps talking about it." Imagine trying to explain what Mac and Cheese is, when all he knew in direct provision was rice and gravy with a sausage or rice and gravy with a piece of chicken.

At that time, there were no cooking facilities in any of the centres. One absurd rule is that you cannot have food in your room, which is particularly problematic for people with health conditions like diabetes, who need to eat at specific times. Neither are there fridges or microwaves allowed in the rooms.

This was something MASI had to fight hard to change. Even today, only a handful of centres have cooking facilities. Sometimes, restrictions are used as tools for punishment or control. A few years ago, we had to step in and prepare a protest over a case involving a pregnant mother, who was denied an extra burger that was about to be discarded. She had already received her daily share, but requested the extra burger to keep in her room for later.

Despite my initial hope that I would not be in direct provision for ten years, I ended up there for seven. The only way I was able to leave was because I finally gained the right to work. During our campaign for the right to education, the University of Sanctuary group from the UK came to Ireland and established its programme here. I was invited to join the steering committee for this initiative. One of the first universities to offer Sanctuary Scholarships was the University of Limerick (UL). At that time, I was already pursuing QQI Level 5 and Level 6 courses at the Limerick College of Further Education, but my ambition was to attend university. I became one of the first recipients of the Sanctuary Scholarship.

Completing my degree and gaining the right to work were game-changers for me. Coincidentally, Doras was hiring a maternity cover policy officer and I got the job. With my first month's salary, I began looking for a house. I was determined to leave direct provision and start a new chapter, even if the situation was temporary. Fortunately, at that time, rental prices were not as high as they are now and I found a wonderful home.

Within three months of starting work, I managed to move out of the centre after seven years. My case was still unresolved at that point, but after eight years in Ireland, I was granted refugee status. When Covid arrived, I had completed college, found my house and received my refugee status. It all came together.

I worked at Doras during 2019–2020. After that, I took a break due to the pandemic and had my son in 2020. In 2021, I returned to UL to complete a master's in Peace and Development Studies. As the world began to reopen, Doras was recruiting for a Project Coordinator for their Victims of Crime Support Project. I applied and got the job. I've been working on this project since 2022.

I always say that someone has to take action and if you have the courage to step up, just do it. People will follow, support you and stand in solidarity with you. That's been what has kept me going over the years – the incredible solidarity, encouragement and love from the Irish people and from those who have become like family to me. There were people who were crucial in advancing my case, such as Donal O'Kelly and Lynn Ruan. Lynn, in particular, was instrumental in ensuring that my case received the attention it needed. I am deeply grateful for her support.

Looking back, when you're younger, you often think you're untouchable. You just dive into things with a rebellious attitude, thinking we're going to say no and do our own thing. In Zimbabwe, it was fun and seemed like a game at the time. We didn't fully grasp the seriousness of our actions or the gravity of the situation. All we knew was that we didn't want to shave our heads or conform.

There was a certain naivety and foolishness to it, but we were also aware of the broader issues. We saw human rights atrocities, people being tortured for joining opposition parties and how certain lifestyles such as LGBTQ could lead to death. The public discourse was tense and you could feel the change in the air. Despite this, we didn't take it seriously enough or understand the potential consequences of our actions.

There are many things I wouldn't change, but one thing I wish I'd done differently is how I handled my relationship with my ex-partner. I should have been braver and fought more for myself. I stayed in that situation longer than I should have, even though I had the power to leave. I chose to stay and I regret not standing up for myself more.

When I think about my eldest daughter now, I marvel at how precious she is. It makes me reflect on my own past and wonder if I was that much of a naive child myself. It's a strange realisation, but one that's part of growing and understanding how far we've come.

The worst part was losing contact with my siblings and my mum during that time. I had no way to reach them or for them to reach me. When I left home at 16, I didn't have a phone and mobiles were uncommon then. My mum didn't know where I was and I didn't know where she was. It was a heart-wrenching, isolating experience. We only reconnected in 2015, when I was in Ireland and joined Facebook. One of my old school friends, who was in Canada, happened to be the sister of someone who was friends with my younger sister, who was also living in Canada. That's how we managed to get back in touch. It was a miracle.

When my sister saw pictures of me with friends in Ireland, she recognised me and exclaimed, "That's her! That's my sister!"

None of my family knew where I was. Nobody knew about my children or my life. I was completely alone and the loneliness was overwhelming. Reflecting on our reunion years later, it's hard to put into words how profound it was. It was December 2015 and we hadn't seen each other since July 2002. My mum had fled to the US with a group that later moved to Canada. By the time she could reunite with my siblings, I was already lost to them and no one knew where I was. My mum first came to Ireland for Christmas in 2015 and met her grandkids for the first time. It was surreal and deeply moving – she had left me as a child and returned to see me as an adult with my own children. It was one of the best Christmases of my life!

Living in Ireland has been a refuge for me. The sense of safety, security and love I've found here is beyond anything I could have imagined. Ireland has provided me with a profound sense of belonging and acceptance. Almost every person I've encountered here has shown me kindness and warmth.

When I stood for the local elections, something extraordinary happened. Not once did I face negativity or racism. For every door I knocked on, I was met with warmth and support. Even online interactions were overwhelmingly positive. The only negative experience I've had was with the direct provision system, but aside from that, I've felt embraced and loved throughout my journey.

The other day, just before the election, I was driving home, when my neighbour, who is also my landlord, stopped me. He said, "How's the canvassing going? Are you ready for election day?" I admitted that I was feeling a bit anxious. "Don't worry," he reassured me. "We'll be voting for you. We take care of our own." His words were incredibly comforting and moving, and made me feel deeply supported. I was nearly in tears. Although I was not elected, the support from my local community was incredible and the irony of receiving my citizenship a week later made me feel at last that I truly belonged.

As for a lasting message, I want to address the current climate. It's easy to dismiss the hateful rhetoric of a loud minority by labelling them as just a small extremist group. However, it's crucial to recognise that their words and sentiments impact every individual they target. For anyone from a migrant background, those voices carry a heavy, crushing weight. Now, more than ever, it's essential for the majority to raise their voices even more loudly to drown out the negativity with positivity and support.

We must focus on valuing people as individuals rather than generalising, based on their backgrounds. I think there's a tendency to make broad statements like, "People from South Africa are good," or "People from Nigeria are bad." Every place has its share of challenges and difficult individuals. Even though I've met so many amazing people in Ireland, it's important to remember that others might have different experiences and could come here with a perspective that reflects their own struggles. Ultimately, it's about recognising each person's unique story and fostering a culture of appreciation and respect. Let's keep amplifying the positive voices and making sure they resonate far and wide.

More about Zimbabwe:

"NEVER DOUBT THAT
A SMALL GROUP OF
THOUGHTFUL, COMMITTED
CITIZENS CAN CHANGE
THE WORLD."

MARGARET MEAD

Joe is the CEO of WALK, an organisation that supports people with
disabilities in Dublin and Louth. Joe, like others around the world,
watched as the war in Ukraine was projected in real time onto our
screens and was compelled to take action.

THANKS FOR SAVING OUR LIVES.

JOE

When I was 13, my parents fostered Patrick, a 10-year-old boy who had an intellectual disability. My sister worked for St Michael's House and Patrick used to go to school there. One day, she turned to my mam and said, "Mam, there's this little boy in the class. I don't think he's ever been to a St Patrick's Day parade. Can I bring him to the parade with Joe?" My mam first said no, but eventually gave in and said yes. Patrick lived in one of the largest institutions in the State, a tiny young boy living in a locked ward with adults. It was heart-breaking. He began to stay with us some weekends, and then for the summer. Finally, my parents could not bear to take him back to the grey, soulless building. Patrick hated it there.

I remember just before he came into our lives, the Irish Press did an article on fostering and adoption and on their front page was a picture of my now-brother Patrick at 10 years old. The caption over his head was "The Blue-Eyed Boy Nobody Wants". Well, I am proud to say my family wanted him and he became a major part of all our lives.

Joe and the Ukrainian families he rescued

WALK is a community and voluntary organisation. The services and supports it provides are rights-based and rooted in the belief that all people have the right to live self-determined lives within an equal and inclusive society.

When the war broke out in Ukraine, I read reports of the distressing plight of institutionalised people with disabilities dying in their beds, because they had no way of escaping. Others were starving because staff had to leave and they had no one to support them. It broke my heart. Knowing where Pat had come from and working with WALK to develop models of support that are inclusive of people with disabilities, I was appalled. I remember thinking, these people are just like Pat; they need care, love, help and support.

I was in touch with a charity in Kyiv called "With Warmth in Your Heart", who were desperately trying to help Ukrainian people with disabilities, particularly intellectual disabilities. They highlighted the frightening lack of information or media coverage about these individuals and that, in reality, people with disabilities were being abandoned because most did not have the capability to reach the borders. For them, there was no escape. In Ukraine, children and adults with disabilities are often housed in large institutions, many of them already cut off from their communities. As each day of the war goes by, the risk of them being abandoned and forgotten dramatically increases. I spoke to my colleagues in WALK about how we could support charities in Ukraine. I watched videos online and asked myself, "Why do human beings act in this way – inflicting terror on each other like it's some sort of game?" I looked at photographs of a facility that had been bombed. I forced myself to look, so that the images could be imprinted on my brain. I knew that I needed to do my bit.

My dad died in 2021 and he had loved Pat with all his heart. So, in Dad's honour, I decided that I would go to Ukraine and see if I could help. I told my wife Catherine I was going, saying to her, "If one person comes home with me, that could be one more person that didn't die."

I didn't have the right to ask anyone to go with me, to put themselves at risk. However, a colleague of mine, Kevin, offered to come. The staff at WALK volunteered to collect aid. Kevin had made contact with Alex, who runs a charity in Ukraine that supports older people and people with disabilities, who are either living in the community with families or in institutions. They needed adult nappies, food, mobility aids, personal hygiene products, and more. Alex said he needed to get a couple of families out if possible. Kevin and I agreed to take annual leave and go to Ukraine. At the beginning of the war, it was impossible to get across the Ukraine border. Catherine promised to stand by me whatever I chose to do, but she really didn't want me to cross the border. I said, "Okay, I'll do the next best thing. I'll see if I can meet people at the border." I've always been empowered by Catherine's love and support.

However, about a week later, we completely lost contact with Alex. Kevin rang me while I was driving to a Shamrock Rovers match with my 11-year-old son, Sean.

"Have you heard anything from Ukraine?"

"No, I can't make contact."

"Neither can I. So, what are we going to do?" We decided we'd take the weekend to think it over and keep trying to re-establish communication. We were hoping it was just a cell tower that was down. If there was still no contact on the Monday morning, we were going to knock it on the head, give the money raised to Inclusion International and send over the items we had collected through a company bringing aid to Ukraine. Then Catherine received an email from a lady in Ukraine called Olena, married to Oleg. Their daughter, Daria, 12 at the time, has severe intellectual disability, autism and epilepsy. She has a service dog named Jess. They had been stuck in their apartment in Kyiv since the start of the war. Daria's epilepsy had been well controlled up until that point. But, of course, with everything that was going on – stresses, strains, noise and lack of medication – it became unmanageable. The basement wasn't safe for Daria, so they chose to stay in their apartment day and night. Olena said she heard that we were planning a trip to the border and asked if there was any possibility that we could accommodate them. Catherine said to me, "But you've changed your mind. You're not going now." I read the email and I looked at the photos of Olena and Oleg. There was a picture of the three of them taken a few weeks earlier – in the park in the snow, taking selfies, living their best life, or at least a good life. I handed the phone back to Catherine and said, "Tell her we'll get there as fast as we can. Ask them if they can hold on."

I then rang Kevin. I told him about Olena, Oleg and Daria, and of Catherine's and my decision. "I don't want you to decide now and I don't want to put you at risk. If you want to stay, we're perfectly fine with that. Think it over and ring me in the morning." About an hour later, I was at the match and I got a text from Kevin. "Is it morning yet? I'm in."

We met on Monday morning in Dublin. We piled the minibus high with aid; we were bringing it to a humanitarian aid centre in Poland. Catherine would stay in contact with us the whole way and keep us updated on emails and phone calls we were receiving.

We knew we wanted to get to the town closest to the border, so we went to a place called Lublin. Another family had found out that we were on our way. It was initially Natasha and her two children – a daughter, 5, and a son, 14. The son (now my new best pal) has cerebral palsy. A gorgeous kid. After they contacted us, things went a little bit astray for them because Viktor, the father, was away fighting and Natasha doesn't drive. They were trapped in Kyiv.

Kyiv is about 650 kilometres from the Polish border. But then Natasha sent an email to Catherine, saying, "We can't get out. Thank you for your kind offer and we wish you well in the future." They were about 30 kilometres from the border, but they couldn't get any further. So, I told my wife, "Tell them not to move. I will come and collect her." We figured we would get in on our Irish passports, but we might not get out again!

A lot of work was done here in Ireland by Catherine; Adam Harris from the autism charity AsIAm; the Minister for Disabilities, Anne Rabbit; and Senator Mary Seery Carney. I became good pals with a man I never met, called Dominic.

He works in the Irish embassy in Poland and gave us letters of support to get in and out. We also had letters from our own organisation, WALK, to prove legitimacy for what we were doing.

It then so happened that, on 19 March at about 5 pm, as we were still driving through Poland, an emotional phone call came through from Catherine. "We've got some fantastic news! We're after getting a letter from the Ministry of Defence in Ukraine. Viktor, the dad, can pass through the border to bring his family across." So there were celebrations and lots of tears in our minibus.

Olena and Oleg left Kyiv on St Patrick's Day. They reckoned it would take them three days to get to the border, but they did it in one day and emailed us to say, "Happy St Patrick's Day! He is a wonderful saint – we made it to the border." The following day, their apartment complex was blown up. A mother and her child, who was in school with Daria, were killed in the bombing. When people tell me that I had no business going or ask me why I did it, their story is the one I tell.

We had just left Ireland and were driving through England, when Catherine rang.

"How many seats have you got in that bus?"

"Jesus, I don't know. It's packed to the roof with boxes. Why?"

"I've just been talking to Adam Harris. He has a young lady and her son, who have made it across the Polish border and they're looking for safe passage to Ireland."

"Okay. They're welcome to come back with us. I know there's room. So far, we've only got seven people and a dog." (The dog was Daria's support dog, a golden labrador. Ironically, we had a harder time getting it back to Ireland than we did the people!)

We took the most direct route to the border. We had some very funny moments, as you do in these situations. When tensions are high, we're typical Irish lads; we crack a joke or do something stupid to break the tension.

As we drove through Holland, we got another phone call from Catherine, asking if we had counted the seats yet, because we have another mother and her son, Olha and Bohdan (7), who has autism. We also had Max and Jullia,

Aid being delivered to displaced Ukrainian refugees

Aid being brought to Ukraine by Joe and his crew

Joe and his son holding a banner containing the Irish flag, Ukrainian flag and Shamrock Rovers crest

who had made contact through Adam Harris from AsIAm. I just said, "Yeah, we've got room." I told Kevin he might be flying home.

As we drove through Germany, we passed a convoy of tanks and armoured personnel carriers on the backs of 40-foot flatbed trucks; they were all heading for Ukraine. A silence descended in the van. I looked at Kevin and said, "Shit, it's getting real now." We were quiet for a minute and then he said, "Is there a fucking reverse in this?" We just laughed and drove on.

We then met some of the families we were bringing back. We got there quicker than we anticipated and went looking for the humanitarian aid centre. We found that and a refugee camp together. That was a very surreal and humbling experience. You look at these people and realise that four or five weeks earlier, they were living a normal life. Then you look at them now and they're in this centre. The people who are supporting them are great people, but the centres were overrun.

We were offloading the stuff, which included baby products, dry baby food, creams and nappies. As soon as they heard there were nappies in the yard, you could see the mammies and daddies coming out. These people were now reliant on us to bring them much-needed aid. The staff were so grateful. They thanked us so much, we had to say, "Stop, stop, stop. Stop thanking us!"

Some people in my sector said we shouldn't have gone until we had all the answers. Well, if we had waited until we had all the answers, there might be seven people dead today who aren't because we went when we did. I always say, "Excellence is the enemy of the good." Sometimes having a good

A group of volunteers getting ready to rescue families from Ukraine

plan is far better than having an excellent plan because in the time it takes to have an excellent plan, the good one is gone. So, we waited for the rest of the families to arrive, and we got ready to come back to Ireland.

Many months later, Viktor showed me a video clip. It was bodycam video footage of soldiers going through a blown-apart house, roof gone, walls down, windows gone, doors down. I asked him where the video was taken and he said, "That's my home." The sudden realisation was that if Viktor hadn't been given leave to bring his family across the border, they would have gone home. They might have been in the house when that happened.

We then waited for the rest of the families to arrive and we got ready to come back to Ireland. We were driving back from Lublin and the children were amazing. We discovered that Daria likes trad music and loves "Wheels on the Bus" and "Old McDonald". There's a clip of us where you can see me nodding and singing along. We stopped at a playground and we watched the two kids on the seesaw, laughing their socks off. Jullia was standing beside me.

"Jullia," I said. "We had a great leader in Ireland, a fella called Bobby Sands, and he said that our revenge will be in the laughter of our children, and those children are already laughing. We're already getting revenge now."

"Thanks for saving our lives," she said.

"I didn't, you saved your own life. All I'm doing is giving you a lift."

I couldn't imagine what it would be like to be in a position where you are forced to put your trust and faith in people you have never met.

People asked after I returned if I would go again and the answer was one hundred per cent yes. I would go in the morning. When we came back in with the families, there was a lot we had to figure out such as accommodation, registering the children in school and sorting out social welfare. We brought the four families to Dublin airport to complete all the necessary paperwork and avail of accommodation. However, when we arrived, we spoke with numerous interpreters, who explained that the families could only be accommodated in a hotel for a night, possibly a week. Then they may have to move hotels regularly and there were no facilities at that time designated as disability-friendly. At this stage, we had two children with disabilities who were ill, one with autism who needed medical treatment for epilepsy, and the other experiencing physical deterioration, due to their cerebral palsy. As Yuvenni had no physical mobility aids, he required constant assistance; he even had to be physically held by his mother to sit up straight.

We could not in all conscience abandon these families, who had already suffered so much, and traumatise them further by putting them into a system that was not suitable to meet their needs. However, the Irish Refugee Centre, Department of Education, Cheeverstown House and the HSE were extremely helpful and supportive.

My new best pal, Yuvenni, is only 14 and has cerebral palsy. I got him a laptop so he could communicate with his friends again. I brought him to Dublin to get fitted for special shoes; the GoFundMe helped with the likes of that. His family had to leave Ukraine without his wheelchair, but Cheeverstown House donated one and he's able to walk with sticks that help him if he has the correct shoes.

Joe bringing rescued Ukrainian families to visit his favourite football team, Shamrock Rovers

Yuvenni meeting Shamrock Rovers player, Aaron Greene

On 7 May 2024, Olena, Catherine and I were asked to address the Oireachtas Disability Committee in Leinster House to outline how Ireland could support people with disabilities from Ukraine. Olena made history as the first Ukrainian woman to address an Oireachtas committee. I was honoured to be part of it.

Three of the families remain living in Ireland. Jullia and Max discovered that they had family in the US and have moved there to live. I embarked on my next journey in June 2022, with Viktor, Mason and Dan. We borrowed two vans and filled them with aid. A friend, Brian Mason (no relative), a fellow Shamrock Rovers fan who lives in Warsaw, gathered up another vanload of aid for us to bring. So we hired a third van in Warsaw and headed off for the border. We were to meet our Ukrainian friends from Kyiv at a hotel on the Polish side to give them the aid.

Unfortunately, however, they were not permitted to leave Ukraine and meet us. So I decided to bring the aid across the border myself. With one aid van, I drove on my own to the Poland/Ukraine border. In my naivety, I thought the process of getting aid into Ukraine would be simple. However, I soon learned the hard way that this was not the case. Most of the Polish guards I encountered were anything but helpful, although most of that was due to the language barrier. However, using Google Translate, I was able to explain to one guard that I had driven all the way from Ireland with essential aid. That did the trick. The guard then took the time to explain the system and show me where to go and what to do. On that occasion, it took me five hours to get across the border. Later that evening, I went over with the second load, and the next morning with a third. Each time, it got easier as I learned the system.

I went again in October 2022 with another group of volunteers: Alan, Dave Pat, Mason, Eoin, Viktor and Fran (RIP). On this run, we were bringing five vans of aid over. We partnered with the charity, With Warmth in Their Heart. Incredible people doing incredible work. We were asked if we could help a mother, her three children and their cat and dog to evacuate, which we did. A beautiful family, beautiful children, a baby born under bombing and shelling. When we met this family, the dad had to stay behind. It was heartbreaking to watch a family being torn apart. The journey home wasn't without its difficulties, as the English border police would not give the family permission to travel through the UK on a temporary visa. So, we drove back from Calais to Brussels and arranged to have them flown to Ireland. Thankfully, they are now living safe and well in Mullingar and the children attend local schools.

In May 2023, I returned to Ukraine, this time with volunteers: Pat, Jimmy, Patrick, James, Viktor and Eoin. We brought aid and had four vehicles to donate, three four-wheel drives and a van. Having learned the lessons from the previous trips, passing through the border was easier, as I knew the best border crossing to use and the times to cross. What's more, I had all the necessary paperwork.

We met some local people. One was an elderly man who hugged and kissed us and thanked us for coming all the way from Ireland to support his people. One thing that stayed with me was that he said it was the first time, since his wife had passed away six years earlier, that he was grateful she wasn't around. His house had been destroyed in the first days of the war, and he was grateful she didn't have to see it. That night, we stayed in a hotel on Maidan Square, and the same night, 139 missiles and rockets were fired at Kyiv from Belarus. Thankfully, the air defence systems were fully operational. On this trip, we also went to visit the aunt and grandmother of one of the families who had come back with us to Ireland. That was an exceptionally emotional time for everybody, as we handed over gifts and letters from their loved ones in Ireland, and they did the same to us. The grandmother was so grateful that we had got her grandchildren to safety at the war's start. I promised to continue to look after them and support them until they could return to their homeland. She also made me promise to come and visit again, which I hope to do sometime in 2024.

So far, we have brought over €750,000 worth of aid and €200,000 worth of vehicles. I've been to Kiev, Lviv and Oman and other places in Ukraine on about six occasions now. I have met the most amazing people and laughed and cried with them. Our last trip for now was in November 2023, where a team of volunteers brought to Uman six ambulances full of humanitarian aid that had been donated to us. We handed them over to the organisations, Save UA and Eleventh Border Guard. I am now planning my next trip to Ukraine and look forward to adding to this story.

> ## "YOU MAY CHOOSE TO LOOK THE OTHER WAY, BUT YOU CAN NEVER SAY AGAIN THAT YOU DID NOT KNOW."

WILLIAM WILBERFORCE

Olena is a devoted mother to her beautiful daughter Daria and their playful golden retriever Jess. A full-time carer, Olena embraces the opportunity to learn new skills, with a particular passion for embroidery.

MY SOUL IS STILL UNEASY ABOUT UKRAINE. EVERY MORNING BEGINS WITH CHECKING THE NEWS TO SEE WHICH UKRAINIAN CITY HAS BEEN BOMBED AND WHETHER THERE WERE CASUALTIES.

OLENA

I'll tell you our story of meeting Ireland, which we have come to love with all our hearts. Our family of three – me, my husband and our daughter – lived in an apartment in a high-rise building in Kyiv. We led an ordinary life filled with everyday chores, joys, experiences, work, study, walks and trips. Our lives were also shaped by our daughter's epilepsy, a condition we've been managing since 2010. This challenge taught us to live in the moment, appreciate the small things and always be prepared for an attack.

After the war broke out in February 2022, we were faced with serious problems. My daughter could have a seizure at any moment and I also have health issues that limit my mobility in the advent of bombing attacks. There was also the lack of access to life-saving medicine for our daughter, which she must take every day. Because this medicine is unavailable in Ukraine, we had previously purchased it in Europe, but the commencement of the war meant that this was no longer possible.

My husband and I faced a dilemma. On the one hand, it is scary to go into the unknown with just one suitcase. It wasn't clear how this could even be possible

Olena and Jess on the beach

for our family, where two people have serious health problems. We also have a large dog, a golden retriever. In the first month of the war, evacuation trains from Kyiv were overcrowded and our car would not cover the long distance to the border. On the other hand, if we were to come under direct attack, we wouldn't have been able to flee.

Then, on 13 March 2022, I saw a post on Facebook by a woman named Catherine Kelly. An Irish organisation was offering to help Ukrainian families, who had children with disabilities, to travel from Poland to Ireland. I quickly wrote to Catherine and received a prompt response. She allowed us to bring our dog, which was very important to us. We made the decision immediately, despite knowing almost nothing about Ireland.

The journey was filled with anxiety. My greatest fear was whether we could make it from Kyiv to the Ukrainian-Polish border. My husband and I frantically searched for different options to ensure we reached Lublin in time. In our darkest moments, various strangers appeared and helped us without asking for anything in return. A Ukrainian volunteer took our entire family, along with our large dog, in his small car to the Polish border. A Ukrainian border guard noticed we were struggling and arranged for us to travel in a Red Cross car driven by an Austrian volunteer, who helped us cross the border. Polish volunteers then provided us with shelter in a refugee camp, where we had a roof over our head, food, attention and care for three days. A Polish family of volunteers drove us to another city to ensure we arrived on time at our appointed meeting point. And that was just the beginning.

By 17 March, we had crossed the Ukrainian border. Three days later, we met two wonderful Irishmen, Joe Mason and Kevin Power, who brought a group of four families to Ireland.

In Ireland, Joe Mason, Catherine Kelly and the staff from the charity organisation, WALK, and the voluntary organisation, Cheeverstown House, surrounded us with care and attention. They helped us to find housing and solve numerous organisational issues, becoming true friends who were ready to help at any moment.

We have been living in Ireland for almost two years now. We are learning English, my husband works and volunteers and I care for our daughter. In the autumn of 2023, she started attending a special school and is very happy there.

I use the half-days when my daughter is at school, as well as the evenings, to learn new skills like hand embroidery and sewing bags. This is truly relaxing for me and an opportunity to create interesting gifts for our new Irish friends.

Hand-embroidered bags made by Olena

Olena, Daria, Oleg and Daria's service dog, Jess

Daria at school

We are very grateful to the Irish Government for enacting laws that help people, even those not mentally prepared for a move, to survive in a foreign country. These laws have been crucial for our family, providing my daughter and me with access to highly qualified medical care, modern treatments and necessary medications. This support is vital for us.

In Ireland, we have seen the potential for a full life for people with disabilities, including mental disabilities, through the work of organisations like WALK and Cheeverstown House. I am amazed at how well the support system for these individuals is structured, with years of proven success. In Ukraine, only recently have efforts been made to socialise adults with intellectual disabilities. While we have many development centres for children on the autism spectrum, there are very few places that work with teenagers and adults.

I appreciate that it's possible here for adults of any age to find a job or place of study. In Ukraine, after the age of 40, getting a paid job is problematic. I am grateful for how attentive and friendly people are here. To be honest, I had the impression at first that the Irish never swore. However, after working as a parking manager, my husband dispelled this myth! We still have cards from our first Christmas here, sent by unknown schoolchildren. They somehow found out our names and the name of our dog and left very warm wishes. It was such a lovely surprise.

Ireland is an incredibly beautiful country. In our free time, we love travelling around the island, admiring nature, walking along the cosy streets of small towns and large cities and sitting by the shores of the Irish Sea.

My soul is still uneasy about Ukraine. Every morning begins with checking the news to see which Ukrainian city has been bombed and whether there were casualties. Our relatives and close friends remain in Ukraine, and we worry about them deeply.

I yearn for the day we can drive the Russian forces out of our country and ensure they never threaten us again. I am endlessly thankful to the tireless and courageous Irish who have not only given shelter to my compatriots here, but also continue to help those who remain in Ukraine. I want to acknowledge Joe Mason and his team for their significant and much-needed humanitarian assistance for people with disabilities and to thank them for their unwavering support. I am grateful to fate that we ended up on this emerald island and met incredible people who will forever remain in our hearts. I want to end with the words of my husband, spoken during our early days in Ireland: "Apparently, I did something good in my life, since we found ourselves in this wonderful country."

"LOVE AND COMPASSION ARE NECESSITIES, NOT LUXURIES. WITHOUT THEM, HUMANITY CANNOT SURVIVE."

DALAI LAMA

Olha works in IT and is a dedicated mother to her son Bohdan, who has ASD. She is currently furthering her studies in English.

ONCE AGAIN, MY SON BROKE DOWN IN TEARS, BEGGING ME TO RETURN TO THE SAFETY OF THE BASEMENT.

Bohdan sheltering in a basement

OLHA

My story begins on 15 December 2018, when my son's father, a paramedic, returned for a vacation from his military service in eastern Ukraine. The day before he was due to leave and return to work, the house caught fire and he died. The house was no longer suitable for living and life took a dark turn. However, over time, I began to rebuild.

On 23 February 2022, the day before the war began, I received congratulations from my colleagues on the anniversary of my work at an IT company, along with wishes for many more anniversaries ahead. My contract was extended and I felt happy. Life was getting better.

The following day, my daughter, who is 27, woke me up with a text: "We have been bombed." She lives in Hostomel. Over the course of the day, she texted:

12.30 pm: "A Russian helicopter was shot down, a Russian prisoner was captured, the military ran in front of my house. I'm not leaving the house."

2.30 pm: "Russian troops captured Hostomel, but they have not yet reached my house. I'm still planning on staying here, but the people around the village are packing up to leave."

4.10 pm: "My boss warned me that I am in danger, because of my work at [name of IT company] and I must leave my house. It was practically an order. [Husband] and I are getting out of Hostomel, we're taking the dogs and cats. We're staying with [husband's] relatives near Kyiv in the Boryspil district."

I lived in the Borshchagivka area of Kyiv, about 25 kilometres from Hostomel. We constantly heard explosions. After my daughter had moved to a relatively safer place, I calmed down a bit. I began making rounds of the neighbourhood, looking for basements where I could hide my seven-year-old son, Bohdan.

On the morning of 25 February, the Armed Forces of Ukraine blew up two bridges that connected Hostomel, Bucha and Irpin with Kyiv. After the explosions, evacuation by car was almost impossible. My daughter's house was located along the road near the Hostomel-Bucha-Irpin-Kyiv intersection, where a convoy of military Russian equipment was later stopped and destroyed. There was heavy fighting. If my daughter hadn't left, she may not have survived.

From that date, Hostomel endured relentless shelling from aircraft and heavy weapons. The situation fluctuated constantly, with Hostomel alternating between the control of the Armed Forces of Ukraine and that of the Russian Federation. Basic necessities such as water supply, electricity and gas ceased to function. With temperatures dropping below zero, civilians sought refuge in basements. There was a severe scarcity of water, food and communication. Hostomel was in hell.

On 2 March, my son and I took refuge in basements, only returning home occasionally to cook and eat. Small stores still had long-term storage products, but supermarkets were completely empty. I was contemplating leaving Kyiv, but the train stations and trains were overcrowded, posing a challenge to any escape plans.

The company I worked for set up a general chat for employee communication. One of my colleagues shared that her relatives had managed to leave Kyiv on an additional evacuation train to Khmelnytskyi. Instantly, I made up my mind. At the time I was living in my mother's apartment. I told her about my decision and asked her to pack my son's belongings. I told my daughter about my decision and she supported me.

Just then, I received the devastating news that my ex-husband's wife had been killed in Hostomel. Within 40 minutes, we had left the apartment and headed towards the railway station. Our destination was the Lviv region, to stay with my son's godmother, a close friend who had invited us to stay with her at the onset of the war. I remember that day minute by minute; it's etched in my memory forever. The weather was freezing, with heavy, wet snow falling. My son was in tears, feeling threatened and scared, begging to return to the basement. My mother tried to reassure him, saying we were going to a resort, but he sensed the truth. I hugged him tightly, speaking to him like he was an adult. "We must try to leave; it is dangerous to stay here. Help me, please. I need your support. Today is our chance to get out of this horror."

We went to the nearest bus stop, but public transport had been suspended for quite some time, leaving us with only the hope of catching a passing car. With three of us waiting and cars already packed, our chances seemed slim. I urged my mother to return home, hoping it would increase our odds of being picked up. As we hugged, tears streaming down our faces, my mother took a few steps away. Suddenly, a car pulled up with only one empty seat; it was going to the train station. Grabbing my son, I jumped in. Inside, people began talking with my son, helping to ease his fears.

As it turned out, there was no evacuation train scheduled for that day. However, the timetable said there was an electric train to Khmelnytskyi due in three hours. Although we had no idea whether the train would indeed arrive, we decided to wait. That train became our ticket out of Kyiv. Few knew of its existence, so there were vacant seats in the cars. To avoid drawing attention, the train ran with its lights off. Occasionally, we heard air raid sirens blaring and distant explosions, increasing the tension of our journey.

We arrived in Khmelnytskyi at midnight. But now the problem was how to reach Lviv. With no buses or cars available, the station was overrun with huge crowds of people. Trains pulled in, but the doors stayed shut on the platforms due to overcrowding. We missed out on four or five trains, running across the snowy platforms hoping to find an open door. Once again, my son broke down in tears, begging me to return to the safety of the basement.

I approached a strong-looking man and asked him to help me force open the doors of the next train. Kindly, he agreed. He hammered on the doors until the conductor, fearing damage, gave in and opened them. Although the train was packed, we managed to squeeze in. Standing in the cramped space throughout the night, we finally arrived in Lviv.

There, my son's godmother welcomed us with open arms. At last, we were safe. The memory of peaceful sleep in a warm bed, without the sound of sirens, had become a distant one. However, the constant stream of news meant we were always in a state of nervous tension.

———

By 16 March, it had been two weeks since we found refuge in warmth and comfort. However, we were staying in a remote village, where essential services like schools, kindergartens and playgrounds were non-existent. My son had no other children to socialise with and I couldn't find work. How would we move forward? Desperate for a solution, I turned to the internet in search of ways to leave the country. On the website of a group called Autism Europe, I discovered numerous contacts for organisations across different countries that assist individuals with autism in fleeing Ukraine. I reached out to more than 20 organisations, pleading for help with the following message:

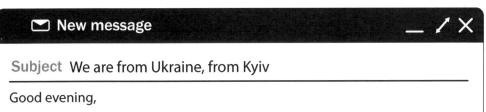

📩 **New message**　　　　　　　　　　　　— ✏ ✕

Subject We are from Ukraine, from Kyiv

Good evening,

My name is Olha, my son Bohdan (6.0) has ASD. We are from Ukraine, from Kyiv. Now we near Lviv.

I would like to come with my son for some time to Ireland. Is is important for us to resume communication with people, children, specialists. Bohdan speaks Russian, understands Ukrainian.

We have international passports.

I could work remotely if my child could attend kindergarten and be more financially independent.

I know a little English, but I had no communication practice.

I would be grateful for any help, information.

Olha

SEND　✎ ▣ ↓ ☺ 🗑　　　　　　　　　⋮

Adam Harris from AsIAm, Ireland's autism charity, was among the first to reach out to me. He sent both an email and an SMS, telling me that they had two available seats on a bus from Lublin to Dublin scheduled for Sunday. This bus was specifically for people with disabilities and these were the last two seats available. He offered to arrange this for us if we were interested. With only four days to Sunday, I knew I had to decide quickly and arrange our journey to Lublin.

We had several meetings on Zoom with Adam and his team to arrange our journey. My son again felt fear and uncertainty. He cried and asked to stay. It was incredibly difficult to stay calm and confident, to reassure him and negotiate with him.

The next stages are a blur. We were able to leave the village and cross the border on foot. Then, we relied on hitchhiking and the kindness of volunteers to reach various points in Poland. On the day of departure, we were at the shopping centre in Lublin. I was filled with such excitement that I hadn't been able to eat for days. It was surreal to believe we had a chance to leave, to completely change our lives. The thought of losing this hope was unbearable. When we finally met Joe and the other Ukrainian families, tears streamed down my face. All the worries seemed to vanish. We were safe. The four days on the road weren't difficult because we were not just escaping, we were heading towards a new life. Joe and a dedicated team of people looked after us, providing food, entertainment and even gifts for the children. When we got to Ireland, we were accommodated in hotels.

Finally, we found ourselves in a house in Cheeverstown, where everything, from groceries to beds and towels, was provided. Despite not being paid, the team generously fulfilled all our requests. Paula, Denis and Kasia, who worked in Cheeverstown, warmly welcomed us into their homes, introducing us to their families and the local customs. They even gave us gift cards to clothing stores. I finally had the chance to take off my tracksuit, which I had been wearing since the beginning of the war.

I was keen to start working as soon as possible, but I couldn't find a specialised school for my son. As he had experienced bullying in Ukrainian kindergartens, I couldn't bear to send him to a regular school. Three months of unsuccessful calls and emails only led to long waiting lists. Paula came to our rescue by helping us secure a spot at a suitable school. We are so grateful to her for this. Without a school, returning to Ukraine would have been our only option.

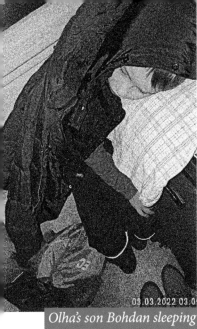

03.03.2022 03.0

Olha's son Bohdan sleeping
during the train journey

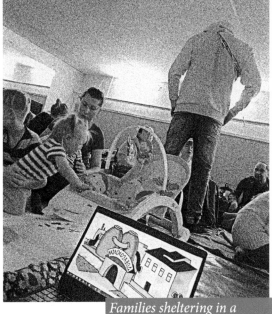

Families sheltering in a
basement with their children

The Irish are very friendly, polite, open people who support and accept us Ukrainians unconditionally. One aspect that particularly struck me was the Irish attitude towards individuals with special needs. During our first week here, we visited the playground in Tymon Park one evening after the rain. A group of children aged about 9 to 12 were playing there. They invited my son to join them, offering help, extending a hand, catching him from high heights and providing support. My son couldn't believe he was playing alongside these older kids, who not only accepted him but also treated him with understanding and patience. It brought tears of happiness to both of us. We were both crying.

It hurts me to write about it, but in Ukraine, he had no friends. It's difficult to discuss, but our society back home is not yet ready to accept the special needs of others. A special school, a programme of adaptation and socialisation and the care of patient and loving adults have changed my son beyond recognition. He has blossomed, opening like a flower. He is developing successfully and has begun to speak English. His development (and even growth) is rapid.

For more than half a year, I studied English in three online courses and did homework seven days a week. But I still don't understand English well and I can hardly speak it. Therefore, it is almost impossible to find a job in my speciality. Ireland provides us with many opportunities to realise our potential. That's how I got into the programme of the Ibec Academy, which helped me to get a job, despite my level of English. I have been working for an Irish state-owned company for a month now. My colleagues are supportive, friendly and patient with my style of work and my English.

My mother and my daughter are staying in Kyiv. Mum is too old to change where she lives. My daughter, a lawyer who defends people's rights in the European court, does not want to leave Ukraine, although she has the opportunity. She sees her future as being there. I tell my friends from Ukraine that my fairy tale in Ireland continues. I appreciate what I have. I am blessed with Ireland and the Irish, and I accept each new day as a bonus, as a gift and not as a given. I would dearly like to stay here for my son's future.

"WE HAVE A MORAL OBLIGATION TO HELP THOSE WHO HAVE BEEN FORCED TO FLEE THEIR HOMES."

ANGELINA JOLIE

Natalia is a mother and wife living and working in Ireland while continuing to support those bravely fighting for her homeland.

I AM A PERSON WHO IS AFRAID OF CHANGE, BUT IRELAND AND ITS INHABITANTS GAVE ME THE OPPORTUNITY TO FEEL NEEDED AND NOT ALONE.

NATALIA

We are an ordinary Ukrainian family of four: Natalia, Viktor and Valeria Firsovski, and our son Yevhenii (Yuvenni), who has cerebral palsy. Fleeing from the war was incredibly difficult. The fighting in our village took place just 25 kilometres from where we were hiding. It was a terrifying experience that is hard to describe in words. Our home in Irpin was destroyed.

On the Internet, we read about Catherine Kelly and Joe Mason, who help people with disabilities. They offered to help us get to Ireland. Crossing the Ukrainian-Polish border was challenging and the journey there took us two days. However, the four days on the road to Ireland were a real test, both physically and emotionally, for the children and me. Thanks to Joe Mason, director of the crossing, who supported us and sang songs to help during the trip, we felt a little better.

Arriving in Ireland at night, we were placed in a beach house on the seashore. It seemed like a deserted place at the end of the world. We didn't know what to do the next day, but we knew very well that there was silence and peace outside the window.

I am a person who is afraid of change, but Ireland and its inhabitants gave me the opportunity to feel needed and not alone. Currently, my children go to school and have made friends, while my husband and I work, despite the language barrier. We have wonderful friends – Joe and his family, the Sisters of the Holy Faith – and good neighbours. My daughter is very worried about her relatives and our country's military. At every opportunity, we collect and deliver parcels to those defending Ukraine.

Thanks to Joe, Catherine, Kevin, Sandra, the tireless volunteers and the staff at the school where my daughter was welcomed, we felt that we could continue to live, while getting used to Ireland's customs and rules. Finally, I want to thank all residents of Ireland for the much-needed support for Ukraine. You are all wonderful and very caring people.

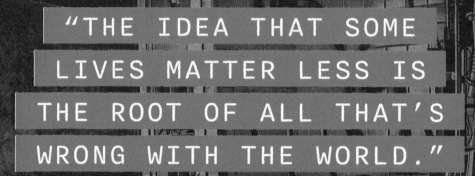

> "THE IDEA THAT SOME LIVES MATTER LESS IS THE ROOT OF ALL THAT'S WRONG WITH THE WORLD."

PAUL FARMER

Uliana is a proud mother to her three daughters. She studied medicine and earned her Master's and PhD in that field. Along with her mother, her husband and family, she fled Ukraine in 2022 and has established a new life in Ireland. Uliana strives to always develop and better herself for her children and family.

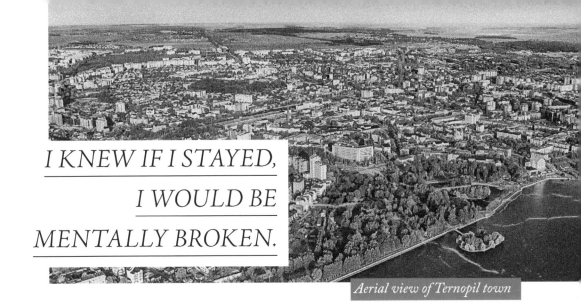

I KNEW IF I STAYED, I WOULD BE MENTALLY BROKEN.

ULIANA

I was born in the city of Ternopil in Ukraine. Until 2022, I spent my whole life there. Normally, I am a person who really struggles with change. I will always do my shopping in the same place. I will go to the same hairdresser and doctor every time. I have set habits and routines.

I enjoyed learning languages in school and was even thinking of studying English or French afterwards, with a view to maybe moving to another country and working as a translator. I then realised that it would be too much of a change and wasn't for me.

So, when I finished school, I decided to study medicine. When I was 18, I got married and started a family. We had three children. I was so busy during those years, planning what I wanted to do with my life, where I wanted to work, how I could develop professionally. By the time we had our third child, I had gained my Master's and PhD.

I was working in two hospitals at the same time. One was a hospital for people with alcohol disorders and the other was a private hospital as a GP, specialising in gastrointestinal conditions. Government jobs are not paid well, not enough to survive on, whereas private companies pay more. However, this only applies to private hospitals in big cities, where the pay is better. In Ukraine, my city is not considered big, so I had to work at two jobs.

Just before the war started, my youngest daughter was 11 months old. My middle child was 10 and my oldest was 13. I was on maternity leave at the time, which in Ukraine is three years. For my first two maternity leaves, I only took about two weeks off before I went straight back to studying. So I never had a lot of time to spend with them at that young age. With my youngest, I decided that I would spend more time with her and with my other two daughters. At that stage, I was also very tired from working two jobs. I felt burnt out.

When you are a doctor, you are dealing with people's problems, some serious, some minor. I needed a break and to spend more time with my kids. I got my girls into music, swimming and volleyball and we even tried horse riding. However, swimming was their favourite pastime. I would go with them to all their activities. We'd go for walks and spend time at home together. I was generally helping them to learn about life. Nobody was expecting a war.

People were talking about the possibility of a war, but my family never believed it would happen. My grandmother was from Russia and we had lots of Russian family. Alerts were being broadcast on television, notifying us that the war had started. We were shocked; we didn't know what to do. We went to buy food, but the shops were empty. It was February and it was cold – we have "proper" winters there! There were huge queues early in the morning for the banks and shops, but the queues for fuel were unbelievable. You needed to be there for at least three hours before you got fuel and there was a limit on the amount you could purchase. Chemists ran out of supplies of Paracetamol and Ibuprofen, because everyone was buying them, not knowing what to expect. Sirens were frequently going off, especially during the night.

We lived in a two-bedroom apartment, a small one. They were built in the 1970s, so it was an old apartment block. My bed is located beside the window and I was sleeping there with my youngest child. I kept her with me, because I had a fear that something would happen, especially when the sirens went off. Most nights, my children slept in their clothes in case we heard a siren and we needed to go to the basement.

The government was trying to find places for people to hide. In my town, we hid under very old buildings, so it was not safe. Schools had the best places to shelter, because they were built during the Soviet era and they had good basements you could stay in during the sirens. However, the basements in really old apartment blocks did not have that safety. People were trying to clean them up and make them better for sleeping in, but they were dirty and cold.

The war started in February and the first of March is my eldest daughter's birthday. I remember it so clearly. We'd just had a big party in January for one of her sisters and I wanted to give my eldest a birthday party too. I was trying to arrange something for the family, but those plans were interrupted by the war. I kept looking for a birthday cake, but I couldn't find one. We wanted to invite her friends over, but it was not safe. One of her friends was living just across the road and I convinced her mam to allow me to collect her and bring her over for a little celebration. We made some tea and served it with a cake, which I finally managed to buy after a lot of searching. These are small things, but I remember them so clearly.

We were living in the west of Ukraine and people were saying that it was safe. However, while the first attacks happened in the east, there were also bombings in the west. My eldest child developed a sleeping disorder after the war began. She was walking around in her sleep, talking, gathering her clothes and trying to leave the apartment during the night. I was sleeping only about one hour a day. Life as we knew it had stopped.

To be honest, I didn't know what to do. It was at that point that I started to think about leaving the country. I never wanted to leave and my husband wanted to stay. However, I managed to convince him, because I knew if I stayed, I would be mentally broken.

We packed everything that could fit into the car. We were not sure where to go, so we headed towards the Polish border. However, we had to pass through military checkpoints. The soldiers stopped us with their guns and asked questions about where we were going. The kids were so scared; they had never experienced anything like this before. The soldiers were checking all our documentation to make sure it was in order. Usually, it takes about four hours to get to the border from our city, but it was going to be very different this time. Some people were left in queues for up to 24 hours. Fortunately, we were allowed to go into a special queue for people with families. Ukraine is divided up into what Ireland would call "counties", we had to travel through different counties to reach the border. It took about five hours just to enter a different county.

On reaching the border, we were all so tired and we did not know how many hours we were going to have to wait again before being allowed to cross. Then some border control personnel approached us. They explained that there was a woman with a newborn baby, who could not cross the border, because nobody had a place for her in their car. We had my youngest, my two other kids, myself, my mam and my husband. We had no space at all. However, after pulling over and checking how the woman was getting on, I said to my family, "We need to take her."

The baby had been born just two days before in Kyiv, in a basement. The mother had come to the border on her own and she had just one bag with her, mainly things for the baby. She explained that her mam was just across the Polish border waiting for her. She sat in the front seat with her baby and I sat in the back with one of the kids on my lap. My mam had another on her lap and our youngest was in her baby seat.

Crossing the border took a long time. Because of the volume of people leaving the country, to cover one kilometre took five hours and it is illegal to leave the car when you are crossing the border. The lady with the baby was starting to panic. She wanted to get out of the car, because it was taking so long and the baby was crying. Then all the kids started crying. I begged her to stay calm until we crossed the border and she could meet her mam. When we finally arrived on the other side, the patrol officer was shocked. I don't think he had ever seen so many people packed into one car! I was worried that he would stop us, because it was against the rules, but he let us through. The lady also met up with her mam, who was able to greet her two-day old grandchild.

We went to Warsaw and there we found somewhere to stay. A relative of ours had a small place, so we stayed with her. It was a one-bedroom flat but we all managed to fit. Of course, we had no other choice. My oldest kids slept for a whole 24 hours. I even had to check that they were still breathing! I think they were just relieved to be in a safe country and I felt that too. Finally, I was feeling calmer. After two days there, we started to think about what we should do, because Poland at the time was overcrowded with Ukrainians. People could not find places to live and work was hard to find. We had to consider all our options.

Initially, we thought about Spain, because my husband had a friend there, but he told us we would need Spanish to find a job. Then we heard Ireland had started to take people in. I only knew a few bits of information about Ireland and mainly from an Irish woman I had chatted with once on public transport. I also knew that it rained a lot! However, to be honest, I think what made us choose Ireland was the language, as I knew some English. Some people asked us why not the UK, but at that point, they had not yet opened their borders to Ukraine's refugees.

We stayed in Poland for a week to settle in, before we made our next big trip. A lot of Polish people were so good to us, bringing us food for the kids and even a stroller for my youngest child. From Poland to France it takes about a day or two in the car, so we stayed in Germany for a night with a family who took us in. We had never met this family before, but we had been calling everyone we knew. Someone found that family for us and they offered to take us for a night. I can't even remember their name. Since the war broke out, I think the trauma had affected my memory of what was happening to us at the time.

Then we came to Cherbourg in France and I remember I had to ask my friend over the phone to buy me tickets for the boat, because I did not have a euro account. It's those small things that show how hard it was for people. As I had a little bit of English, as well as some Polish and French, I was able to ask people where to go, but many Ukrainians don't even have that. We had made contact with some Ukrainians in Ireland, who said they could help us find accommodation. However, I could not tell them exactly when we would arrive.

We were not planning on staying in France, as we wanted to go straight to Ireland. However, the crossing was cancelled because of a storm. It was a Sunday and everything was closed. Nobody was answering the phone. We needed to find a hotel to stay overnight. I don't know why I was not using the internet but I definitely remember walking from hotel to hotel to find a place to stay. When you are in a normal situation you would think normally and google hotels, but I was running on adrenaline and just acting on instinct.

We finally found a hotel with a vacancy and the following morning, we managed to contact the ferry company. They told us they would have a place for us on a boat in one week's time. We didn't have the money to stay in a hotel for a week. So we then went to the city administration to see if they could help us. When we got there it was difficult, as I needed them to speak French very slowly to me, so I could understand. They got us some refugee accommodation and we went there straightaway. We met Ukrainians there who told us that people were going to the port and waiting for any kind of ferry or boat coming in, asking if they had places left. Fair play to those companies, because they were helping people for free.

The next day, we went to the port and learned there was a boat leaving that day. The company staff said that, although we had tickets, they could not provide us with a cabin. So we had to stay in the seating area. They promised they would try to provide us with a room, but it went in order of how many kids you had or elderly people and people with disabilities, but in the end, we did get a cabin.

We arrived at Rosslare. I had been contacting people in Ireland from the boat and they had found us accommodation close to Tramore on the south coast. We had the car, but my husband had never driven on the left-hand side before, so that was a challenge for him! He was going very slowly, but I appreciated that as well. We went straight to Waterford to meet people, who would show us the way to our accommodation. When we arrived in Tramore, a family took us in. They had a very nice house with a holiday home right beside it and they allowed us to stay there. They were a lovely family. Everything started to feel better for us, because we felt their support. A Lithuanian family helped us too, locating a woman who showed us how to complete all the documentation needed for our kids to go to school and to fill out the forms needed for us to stay in the country.

I tried to get my children into school straightaway. Not everyone in the family agreed, but I felt certain they would settle better that way. I loved the school in Tramore from the first day, as the people were so helpful. I was shocked, as they didn't know me or my family. In fact, they didn't know any Ukrainians at all. I think that's what helped us the most – how much people did for us.

My eldest daughter found it hard to settle in and she struggled to make friends, even though her level of English was quite good. My middle girl, who didn't enjoy learning English before, now has a bit of a Dublin accent, especially words like "bus" and "one". Yet I still can't pronounce those words correctly. It's good that I can laugh about it now.

It was also time to start looking for a job. My English now is at a level where I can work. I can understand people and I can speak with some fluency. However, when we arrived, I was only just able to manage. I was still unable to talk for a long time or express myself easily.

I knew I would not be able to practise medicine in Ireland straightaway. To become a doctor here, you need to complete a lot of steps. You need to pass your English test, basic medicine test, chemistry, biology and physics. A lot of this I had completed in my first year of college, which was so long ago. Then you need to pass your practical skills test. It's a different education system, different medical system, a different society altogether. So far, I have not heard of any Ukrainian refugees who are now working as doctors here.

For this reason, I started to look at jobs that were related to medicine. A lot of people were telling me to just find any kind of work such as cleaning, because I needed most of all to be settled. I understood what they meant, but I had studied too hard and too long to abandon medicine. I decided that if I could not find something in the medicine field, then I would think about looking for a job elsewhere. At the same time, I kept thinking, I have a small child. How can I manage to work?

Even if you were qualified as a doctor in Ukraine, you cannot work as a nurse here. I did find work as a dental nurse in Waterford, but I realised that there was a lot I needed to learn. It was also a long commute, which Ukrainians are not used to at all. A 30-minute commute in Ukraine is considered crazy! I was there for two weeks and the owner of the dental clinic really wanted me to work there. He said, "Stay here and we will figure out the hours. I can give you fewer hours if you need." They did everything to help me, but it is hard to train someone with poor English. I wanted the work, but I finally had to tell them that it was not for me.

I then began looking at the pharmaceutical industry, as it is closely related to medicine. I had read that in Ireland, it is of a very high standard. Every time I went for a job, I think my English was the main challenge. I was so confused, because in Ukraine we do not have formal interviews, more like just a chat. It's mainly your CV that matters.

I read a lot and did extensive research on how to get a job, using whatever online resources were available, such as LinkedIn and Jobs.ie. I think that is why I succeeded. I had great support from my husband too; he really tried to help me. Through networking, I found a Polish family from Dublin and they told me about a pharmaceutical company that was hiring. They were just finishing trials and were getting ready for production on a new cancer drug. I applied and received a call-back. I was required to do a logical-technical test and if I passed that, I would proceed to an interview. I worked hard to prepare myself, reading what I could about the company. I knew of it, but had never heard of the drug they were working on. It was new, very effective and much in demand around the world, and also expensive. I passed the test, got the interview and the job! What's more, when they called to tell me the job was mine, they said that they had not expected me to have such good English!

The big problem was that the job was in Swords, but I was living in Tramore. For the first month, I was living with the Polish family who first told me about the job. The family had also gone through a lot. I think they knew how difficult life in a new country could be and that is why they showed me such kindness and opened their house to a stranger. I was living there four days a week, doing 12-hour shifts. It was a huge adjustment for myself and my family. I would go home to Tramore when I was not working. It was the first time my children were without me for long periods of time, which was stressful for them. Their dad was minding them, which was probably very stressful for him too. I knew I had to change something, because I could not stay with that family forever. They were so good to me and the kids would call me auntie, but I knew I could not keep doing the long commutes.

I started writing to a lot of Facebook groups, looking for accommodation. That's when I got a message from a woman named Mary. She said she had a house between Ashbourne and Swords and she invited me to come and see for myself, with a view to moving in with her family. I could tell from her messages that she was an honest and trustworthy person, so I called straight back and agreed to meet. I previously described myself as someone who did not like change, who would never move abroad, and here I was in Ireland learning to survive. My husband was with me for the whole journey and fair play to him too for that.

Once the decision was made to move in with her, Mary helped me to get the kids into schools in the area. I had always said education is the most important thing for them and Mary agreed. She gave us all kinds of tips and tricks on how we could make things work, always reassuring me that everything would be fine and not to worry. I felt from the start as if we were connected. We moved in with Mary in August 2022 and stayed until April 2024. Mary and Cathal, her husband, drove me to and from work every day for almost two years! They also dropped off and collected my kids from school. Not everyone can do that, support a stranger for two years.

Sadly, my husband made the decision to move out. Since coming to Ireland, he had become depressed. In Ukraine, he did not have to join the army, because we have three kids. He wanted to stay and defend Ukraine, but he is not the type of person who could kill someone or hold a gun. He was so attached to Ukraine, it was very hard for him to adjust to Ireland. He helped our host family with the garden and did jobs around the house. However, he had no English at all, which was very isolating for him. He was a lawyer in Ukraine and the main provider, but here his main job was to mind the kids when I was at work.

I remember when he moved out, I was desperate and didn't know what to do. Mary said, "Look, we'll deal with that. It'll be okay." As I had no car and couldn't drive, she and her husband gave me a gift of driving lessons. She and I are now jointly renting an apartment in Ashbourne and it is working well for us. I think when two strong women come together, great things happen!

I always considered myself a soft person, but coming here has made me more determined to provide for my kids and give them everything they need. A marriage breakup is difficult. There is no rule book for these things. Nobody tells you how to handle a war, displacement, a marriage and three children, trying to redefine yourself in a country that does not recognise your years of studying for a Master's and a PhD. Retrospect is a lovely thing, but when you're in the moment you can only do your best. I just wanted to provide everything I could for my kids. Their father also had no rulebook on how to manage either. It just shows the impact of war and its ripple effect. He always supported me with getting the kids to safety and providing for them as best we could. He did as much as he was able to do. My oldest daughter now lives with him.

I think that it is important to talk as well. If you hide all of your problems and stress, it builds up. If you are able to talk about your problems, not only will it help you, but it can also help others. They might take inspiration and know that they are not struggling alone. You take strength from other people and that's what makes us human, not to hide our problems. You see so many people coming into the country, fleeing from war, struggling, and by talking with them and sharing, I realise that my situation is not all that uncommon.

Much of my childhood in Ukraine in the nineties was difficult. There was no money and a lack of food. The first time I went to the cinema, I was probably 17 or 18. People are always surprised when I tell them that we never had holidays. My mam never had money for them, despite being a doctor. We didn't even have coloured photos as children. My mam always remembers when I was three years old, I asked her to buy me a chocolate and she started crying, because she had just bought bread for us. However, I had one big advantage – very strong women in my family. My mam raised me without my dad. My grandmother also had very little money, but she was a great influence on me, giving me inner strength and a desire to succeed.

Mam is now a lecturer in a university in Ukraine and she is head of her department. She came all the way to Ireland with us and, when we were settled in, she returned to Ukraine. She comes to visit every now and then. I don't think feeling safe really bothers her. For her, the main thing was for me to be safe. My whole life, she was dedicated to me. Now she is dedicated to her grandchildren.

My mam's cousin is now living with me. When the war started she was living just outside Kyiv. She was living in the basement for weeks, going upstairs just once a day to have a shower. They were living in fear that Russian soldiers would arrive and kill everyone. Even now after a year, when she speaks about it, her body starts to shake. When people see us, they think that we Ukrainians are okay, because we are safe from the war. But the fear remains and we just have to deal with it.

Now, I am in Ireland. I'm renting a house, I have my job and I have my kids, but I still don't know what to expect in the future. I think I am settling in well and I really like Ireland. The main thing I like about it is the people. They are friendly, but they also respect your boundaries. I like how children are treated in school. This could be why my daughters settled into school so amazingly well. Nobody was commenting on what they wore or where they were living. After some initial shyness, they made friends easily. I like that my daughters can practise swimming in the National Aquatic Centre.

I got so much support here that I did not expect to receive. I like the people I work with. I love the nature in Ireland. Yes, it's raining and windy, but I really like it here.

"AN INDIVIDUAL HAS NOT
STARTED LIVING UNTIL
HE CAN RISE ABOVE THE
NARROW CONFINES OF HIS
INDIVIDUALISTIC CONCERNS
TO THE BROADER CONCERNS
OF ALL HUMANITY."

MARTIN LUTHER KING JR

Mary is a mother of seven children, who works as a head of sales and customer service. She is also an entrepreneur. She has opened her home to numerous families who have come to Ireland to seek refuge. She selflessly provides a springboard to empower people in taking the next steps of their new lives.

WHILE WE MAY FEEL POWERLESS ON A NATIONAL OR GLOBAL SCALE, WE POSSESS IMMENSE POWER TO OFFER KINDNESS AND SUPPORT WITHIN OUR OWN BUBBLES.

Mary, Uliana and her daughters

MARY

Human behaviour is a complex interplay of many factors, driving some individuals to acts of kindness and others to less altruistic actions. While the reasons behind these behaviours can be deeply intricate and varied, reflecting on personal experiences can offer insights into what motivates us to choose one path over another.

At a high level, understanding why people behave the way they do is challenging. Yet, on a personal note, I can pinpoint why I love to help others succeed, a trait deeply influenced by my parents.

My father was the ultimate giver, always helping those in need. He donated much of his money to charity and was known in the area as a charismatic and supportive man. My mother often invited people in need to dinners and parties. These qualities rubbed off on me and my happiest moments are when I see the smiles on others and know that my support has helped them on their journey through life.

After finishing school, I spent three years studying in France and Denmark. At 18, I lived with a French farming family, a lovely couple with four children, who cared for me and encouraged me as if I were their own. This experience taught me the importance of support, especially when living abroad.

Upon returning to Ireland at age 21, I soon married and started a family that eventually grew to seven children. When numbers six and seven were born, I realised I needed help and sought an au pair. Through a Brazilian agency, I met Leonora and Fatima, two women from São Paulo in search of a better life, with very little English but a lot of heart. Instead of choosing one, I welcomed both into our home. They became integral parts of our family, with Fatima even holding her wedding celebration on our farm.

Fatima's marriage led to another opportunity to help. Her Mauritian husband mentioned he had a relative, who was struggling. She had come to Ireland to earn money to support her family, having left her husband and children behind in Mauritius. I invited her to live with us for six months until she found her footing. This act of support was deeply fulfilling, as I watched her grow and then move on.

At the beginning of Covid, I welcomed two young girls from Brazil, who had been ostracised by their community for being a lesbian couple. We provided a safe and supportive environment for them, helping them gain confidence to return to Brazil two years later.

When the Ukraine war started in February 2022, families began arriving in Ireland in March. I immediately contacted the Red Cross, offering a three-bedroom house. However, the process was slow, involving numerous forms and Garda vetting requests and interviews, but no family was assigned.

By July, I decided to take matters into my own hands and find a family in need through Facebook. I joined Ukrainian Facebook pages and monitored them daily. Soon, I saw a message from Uliana, a desperate mother working in Swords, while her three daughters, husband and mother were still in Tramore. She felt incredibly lonely without her family, especially her 15-month-old baby.

Within a few days, the family came to view the house and by August 22, they had settled in. One of Uliana's primary goals was ensuring her children received the best education. Over the past two years, they have not only attended Irish schools, but also continued attending Ukrainian school online. Upon their arrival in my home, I immediately contacted local primary and secondary schools and, thankfully, they started school that September.

For a few months, they lived independently, using their car to travel to and from the farm. However, the trauma of the war and their flight from Ternopil took a toll on Uliana's relationship with her husband. One day, she watched as her husband and eldest daughter left, leaving her devastated and wondering how she would manage living in such a remote location.

We held a family meeting and agreed to support Uliana, her two younger daughters, Kseniia (11) and Dariia (17 months), and her mother (Granny) in the best way possible. My husband Cathal took on school duty, driving Kseniia to and from school five kilometres away. Kseniia, an aspiring Olympic swimmer, trains four times a week at the National Aquatic Centre. Cathal and I shared these journeys and I even enjoyed my 6.30 am Saturday drives, feeling that there is no better gift than kindness. Uliana worked four-day shifts in Swords, so evening drop-offs and early morning pickups became routine. Cathal also handled Granny's weekly shopping trips.

Each week, Uliana and I would sit down and plan the schedule, which we have done for nearly two years. Reflecting on this busy time, I fondly remember our daily chats during car journeys, which helped us understand each other's cultures and beliefs. This experience has been incredibly rewarding for my family, watching Uliana's family grow and flourish in their new Irish society with great determination. It makes me happy and proud of all they have achieved.

The world is undoubtedly a challenging place right now, with terrible atrocities occurring daily. It is easy for us, as good humans, to feel small and inadequate when we witness such suffering and injustice. However, while we may feel powerless on a national or global scale, we possess immense power to offer kindness and support within our own bubbles.

I have always believed that, although I may have little influence over the grand scheme of things, I can make a significant difference in my immediate environment. This approach not only brings comfort and joy to those around me but also creates a ripple effect of positivity. My interactions with international families, though fleeting, leave behind a treasure trove of wonderful memories. These moments of connection and kindness, though temporary, are the true legacy we leave behind.

In the end, it's the small acts of kindness and the warm memories we create that make a lasting impact. By focusing on what we can do within our reach, we contribute to a better world, one person at a time.

More about Ukraine

"TO STAND IN SOLIDARITY WITH REFUGEES IS TO STAND FOR HUMAN RIGHTS, FOR JUSTICE, AND FOR THE BETTERMENT OF OUR WORLD."

KOFI ANNAN

Abdulai is a committed activist, advocating for the rights of refugees, asylum seekers and migrants in Ireland. Abdulai was awarded the National Activist of the Year Award at the 2023 Black and Irish Awards Gala.

I FIND HAPPINESS
AND FULFILMENT IN
SEEING SOMEONE SMILE
BECAUSE OF SMALL
ACTS OF KINDNESS.

ABDULAI

I was born in Baw Baw Village, which is situated along the coast about 25 kilometres south of Freetown, the capital of Sierra Leone. I lived there with my mother, my late father, and three of my siblings. My background is very humble, and when I was a child, we struggled a lot.

I am the second-born in my family, with an older sister and two younger siblings. Although times were often tough, I learned something important: even when we had little or nothing and struggled daily, my parents, especially my late father, went out of their way to help others. Despite our hardships, my dad always advised us to be kind to others, which is an outlook that has stayed with me. He also had a strong desire for us to have a quality education. Sadly, my father passed away in 2011, but his influence remains with me.

We lived in a rural village. While we had a primary education locally, after primary, I had to walk about seven kilometres to the secondary school. After doing this for a year, my dad sent me to live with one of my uncles. My uncle was living in Agoofarm, which was about two kilometres from the school.

Abdulai during the 2023 Black and Irish Awards Gala

I did well in school, but living with my uncle wasn't without its challenges. He was a good man, and I still appreciate him for showing me love and support; however, my aunt treated me differently to how she treated her own children. This caused me a lot of anxiety. There were times when I would return home, weary from the day, only to be greeted by a mountain of domestic chores. It wasn't that I minded doing them – far from it – but the way she spoke to me hurt. However, I persevered, as I was determined to continue my education and not disappoint my parents.

In my family, no one had ever completed secondary education, let alone dreamed of going to university. I was driven by a fierce resolve to change that. In my junior secondary education, I was top of my class from JSS1 through to JSS3 (equivalent to Junior Cycle). In Sierra Leone, after completing their JSS3, students sit the Junior SAT and can choose to stay in their current school or apply elsewhere. I yearned for a different environment, a school where I could grow alongside ambitious peers.

I moved to St. Edward's in Freetown, an all-boys school famous for its high academic standards and historical ties to the Catholic mission. My biological grandma's friend (who I also called Grandma) agreed that I could stay with her. Grandma had a four-roomed house. In the house, there was Grandma, her three daughters, their four children, myself and another cousin. My cousin and I slept on mats on the floor.

I worked hard in school, striving to excel. My time in Freetown was a period of personal growth and discovery, although life there was often difficult for me. My aunts (my grandma's daughters) weren't particularly kind. I remember vividly the daily grind my cousin and I endured. We were the ones who had to do all the dirty jobs at home: all the household chores, cleaning, shopping at the market and preparing meals. There were plenty of other children in the house to do these jobs, but my aunts' children were exempt and everything fell to us. One of my aunts worked in a market that was over two kilometres away, and we made the trek there regularly to buy essentials, then rushed back to cook before my afternoon classes at St. Edward's. One of the most hurtful comments from that time was when one of my aunts referred to us as "slaves" for the family. It still hurts to this day.

My cousin and I were only given one meal a day, so hunger was part of our life. Lunch was a luxury I couldn't afford. My grandma was an amazing human being, but she was afraid of her daughters. Despite her fear, she found ways to secretly help me. She would sneak me food and sometimes slip me some money, always careful not to let her children see her kindness towards me. She is someone that I owe a lot to.

I chose to use these hardships as motivation, as a reason to stay focused on the bigger picture: gaining an education. It was incredibly tough, but those experiences helped make me the person I am today. Freetown lay the foundations for my resilience and determination. It was a period of profound growth and learning, not just academically, but giving me an understanding of the value of perseverance and family support during adversity. Despite the physical distance from my family, our bond remained steadfast.

———————

The only way to have a better quality of life in Sierra Leone is through education. However, secondary education is generally only available in the cities. Many young people who come from rural areas like me are lured to the city under the guise of receiving a better education. However, it is common that many are exploited by their host families, with many using students as servants in their houses. And because the students don't have any other options, they must accept it. The younger people in the villages are unaware of this because people don't want them to fear pursuing the education they need. When students return to the villages, they are celebrated for striving to create a better future for themselves and their families. They never talk about the exploitation.

As I was finishing secondary school, my father passed away suddenly. I think his death was one of the worst moments in my life. He was my role model; he taught me kindness. Even when we had little, he went the extra mile to help others. He holds a special place in my heart. At this point, my dream of attending university and earning a degree seemed unreachable. With no one to support me financially after my father's death, I was heartbroken. Being the eldest male in the family, I had to return to my village to take his place to help my mother and siblings.

Driven by my painful experiences in the city, I realised that I needed to take action to prevent other young people from being exposed to similar situations. So, when I returned to the village, I started working at our beautiful community beach, River Number Two. I worked as a waiter and used my earnings to support my family.

I set up a charity with two of my friends with the aim of creating a network to protect the younger generations. The charity supports less privileged children in our rural area, advocating on their behalf and encouraging them to pursue education and other opportunities without having to go to the cities, where they might face exploitation and abuse. However, I faced a significant dilemma. On the one hand, I view education as a crucial tool for empowering children. On the other hand, I was discouraging parents from sending their children to urban areas and I questioned whether I was right to do this. I was torn between protecting them and empowering them. Although this weighed heavily on me, my primary goal was to provide meaningful support to these children.

Founding this charity elevated my standing in the community. People began to see me as a role model. However, the local politicians saw me as a threat and thought I was becoming too popular. Some even accused me of being sponsored by other political parties due to my growing influence.

When you look at Sierra Leone in general, it's a country blessed with an abundance of resources, both human capital and natural wealth. We have gold, diamonds, bauxite, and other valuable minerals, despite being a nation of just seven million people. Yet, our people continue to struggle. This boils down to leadership, or rather, the lack thereof. Our leaders often prioritise personal gain over serving the people.

During this time, I connected with and organised young people and rallied communities to take action, organising clean-ups, fundraisers, and other events. This activism sometimes led to clashes with authorities. It was like a war between me and them. My mother was constantly in tears, because I was arrested on a number of occasions – not because I disobeyed the law but because of what I stood for. I was torn between continuing the fight for justice and sparing my mother's pain.

There are numerous cultural practices in Sierra Leone that I dislike, particularly those concerning the treatment of women. These practices prevail not only in Sierra Leone but also in other African countries. It's disheartening to see women confined to their homes and not treated with the respect they deserve.

In Sierra Leone, we have two predominant cultural practices, one for the women, the Bondo society, and one for men, the Poro society. The Bondo society is a secretive tradition steeped in mythology. Even talking about the society, women believe, puts them at risk of "curses" and "demons". Female genital mutilation (FGM), which is rampant in Sierra Leone, is a central pillar. Girls as young as five or six are forced to endure immense pain and trauma. This inhumane practice is often carried out by the Sowei (elders) in the society. Most politicians, even the women in power, are part of this Sowei council. Currently, we have laws in Sierra Leone that prohibit FGM, but they are not implemented. The Government will do nothing because they are part of this system. Even the First Lady boldly said that she's part of the Bondo society and went through FGM herself, so she has nothing to say against it.

I went through the Poro society – the society that is responsible for organising the initiation that prepares boys and young men for adult life. In Sierra Leonean culture, being part of the Poro society is a significant aspect of one's identity. Undergoing their rituals is seen as a mark of respect and manhood. Similarly, for women, going through the Bondo society is viewed as essential to being considered a real woman.

If you haven't gone through these societies, people may treat you as less than a man or woman. But how can any society that captures, humiliates, and beats young boys and girls be considered a culture? These horrific rituals have been in place for generations, passed down from our great-great-grandfathers and maintained by our leaders. Around 80 to 90% of people are forced into these practices. If you've experienced them, you'll understand how harmful they are.

However, some volunteer willingly. For instance, when I went through that society, I was around 17 or 18, not a child. I was eager to go through it, wanting to fit in and not fully understanding what it entailed. Societal pressure leads young men and women to feel they have no option but to endure these practices. They want to interact with their peers without being seen as "less than human". Unfortunately, our people, especially our leaders, seem to accept it. Anyone who challenges this is seen as an enemy and will face suppression.

We have numerous political prisoners in Sierra Leone who have committed no crime. They have been detained for years simply because they stood for justice and human rights. Sadly, there are no human rights in my country, no accountability. It's a tragic situation.

When the charity I established began to grow, it incorporated the entire community, with social clubs coming together. The foundation not only impacted the children, but also supported their parents with financial assistance, creating a ripple effect throughout the community and surrounding areas. The local people wanted me to run for a councillor position in 2018, but I refused, despite their attempts to start an electoral campaign. A political position was not my goal. All I wanted to do was support people. Unfortunately, this also made me a target.

Life became increasingly difficult and I was forced to leave Sierra Leone. There was no other option. Going through the legal route was nearly impossible, especially given my situation at the time. I sought out an agent who ran a paid human trafficking operation. These agents can secure visas, often using fake information. He charged me 3,000 dollars.

I left Freetown at midnight and I travelled to Dublin via Amsterdam. When I arrived at Dublin airport, I had to go through immigration. The documents I carried indicated I was an official attending a conference in Ireland. The trafficker took my documents and, presenting as the supposed leader of the delegation, he approached immigration, while I stayed back.

Presentation of a prize to a pupil in the primary school in his village

A poster about Abdulai, shown around Longford and in the direct provision centre

After we cleared immigration, we took a bus into town. There, he gave me information about the International Protection Office (IPO) and handed me the address and 20 euros before leaving me on my own. I was completely lost. Back home, we mostly heard about larger countries like the US or Australia, but I knew nothing about Ireland. I had many questions about where I would stay and how I would manage, as I knew no one here. It was a challenging journey, to say the least.

The night I left Sierra Leone, I had a heavy sense of guilt, but I had no other option. I knew that if I wanted to continue to make a meaningful difference, I had to leave my country.

I came to Ireland in November 2018. When I arrived, I had no idea about the climate. The lowest temperature I had ever experienced back home was like a nice summer's day here. I arrived in just trousers and a t-shirt and I still remember when they opened the plane door and the freezing wind hit my skin for the first time! I was in shock, shaking, thinking I couldn't survive. I summoned up the courage to face the cold, encouraged by a kind flight attendant who said to me, "Man, you'll be fine, you won't die."

I distinctly recall the moment when I saw the Spire. All I had was the address of the IPO; I had to make it there to formally declare myself an asylum seeker. It took hours of asking people for directions.

I was hoping for a better start here, but I entered the asylum process and was sent to a direct provision centre in Longford, where I ended up spending over three years. I hadn't anticipated how tough it would be. I was placed in a tiny room with three adult men from different countries and cultures in a hostel housing over 80 males. I found it very restrictive.

To cope, I had to find ways to disconnect, as staying in the hostel all day made my mind race. I signed up to work with the volunteer centre in Longford. This allowed me to meet and help others. In 2019, I was elected as a volunteer ambassador, promoting volunteering within Longford. I also volunteered with other organisations, such as the Movement of Asylum Seekers in Ireland (MASI).

While in direct provision, I was determined to seize any opportunity to educate myself. During Covid, I was studying Applied Addiction and Community Development in the Institute of Technology in Carlow, through An Cosán. I tried to study for exams, but living with two other men in one room made it hard to concentrate.

Throughout my time at the hostel, I often respectfully questioned management about their treatment of residents. I proposed creating a resident support group to collaborate with the management and improve conditions and to connect people to services like social welfare, education, and mental health, because they didn't have those in place. Eventually, the management agreed to the formation of the group. This ended up being so successful that it enabled many people to leave direct provision, find jobs, and integrate into society.

I asked for a quiet environment where I could study but they refused. As a result of my questioning and actions, management disliked me. One morning, I returned to the hostel after spending a night in a quiet space where I had been studying. I was ordered to leave the hostel because I had spent the night out. I was shocked. Although the rule supposedly prohibit this, I knew many residents who had been out for three or four days at a time without any issue. I had only gone out to study, which was something they couldn't provide for me. It was clear that this was just an excuse to get rid of me.

They called the Gardaí to escort me out. When the guards arrived, they recognised me from my community work. "We know this guy," they said. "He's a good person and a volunteer ambassador." My photos had been displayed all over Longford, even in the hostel. The guards asked, "Where do you expect him to go? He has no family here in Ireland."

Unfortunately, they didn't have the authority to compel the management to take me back. However, they were very kind. They offered me a place to stay at the Garda station for the night so I could make a plan. I had already built a large network with various services and organisations through my volunteer work, such as MASI, Comhlámh, the Irish Refugee Council, and many others. So, I decided to email the Department of Justice about my situation and copied in all of these organisations. Feeling frustrated, I explained what I'd been through and how I'd been treated.

To my surprise, in less than five minutes, I received a call from a woman named Niamh, who was one of the volunteer board members of Comhlámh, an organisation that supports people in their journey towards social justice. She said, "Listen, Abdulai, here's what I want you to do. Take the train to Dublin, and I will pick you up from there. Just get yourself to Heuston Station, and I'll be waiting for you." I was nervous, to say the least. I had been expecting an email response from the Department of Justice, but instead, I received a call from a total stranger asking me to travel to meet her in Dublin. Her voice was reassuring, and she seemed genuinely excited to help me.

When I arrived at the station, an elegant woman stood next to her car, waving at me. She welcomed me with a warm hug. It was so surreal. She drove me to her home, a beautiful house with a large back garden. When we stepped in, she handed me a key and said, "This is your key. Here is your room. This is the fridge. Make yourself at home, and if you need anything, don't hesitate to let me know."

I was in shock. I could find no words, feeling like I was in a dream. When I got to my room, I fell to my knees and cried. It was one of the most beautiful moments in my life.

If I were to talk about Niamh, it would take all year. Later, I learned that I wasn't the first person she had helped; she had assisted refugees and asylum seekers before.

Every day was a great day. We went for walks and had coffee together. She showed me around Dublin and helped me with everything I needed. I lived with her for five months and she helped me secure accommodation in Dublin.

Kingdom Heritage Foundation SL (Sierra Leone), Christmas Celebration in Milton Margain School for the Blind, Freetown

Even when I was leaving, she told me to keep the key and that I was free to come to the house at any time.

And now, here I am. Fast forward to being a final year law student at Technological University Dublin and a community link worker, with big plans for the future, especially for my charity, the Kingdom Heritage Foundation SL (Sierra Leone).

The charity, which I started along with two friends, has had no external funding. We have been doing everything out of our own pockets. Despite the financial struggles, I had a strong urge to create an impact and I used whatever money was available to try.

From Ireland, I continue to do some advocacy work back home in Sierra Leone. This is challenging, especially with the documentation and logistics. However, we've managed to support visually impaired children at the School for the Blind.

During the festive season in Sierra Leone, one of the happiest times of the year, everyone is out on the streets, enjoying themselves. However, visually impaired kids often miss out on these experiences. Our organisation tries to fill that gap. We got together a team of volunteers and we organise events with music, food, and drinks at their centre, spending the whole day with them. This has been one of our biggest accomplishments, bringing joy to these kids during Christmas.

Recently, one of my friends who helps run the charity reached out to me about a young girl who had lost her parents and was struggling to

Abdulai with his friend, Niamh

Immigrant Council of Ireland 'Leadership Academy' 2022

pay her university fees. She was on the brink of quitting, and her situation reminded me of my own when I lost my father. I was able to send her about €150, which was all she needed for her fees, but it was one of the most fulfilling things I've done. Helping her gave me a sense of purpose and hope that I can continue to support other ambitious young people who lack opportunities.

This charity work is very close to my heart. I dream of helping people for the rest of my life. The charity continues to struggle financially, but our aim continues to be to help as many young people as we can. I find happiness and fulfilment in seeing someone smile because of small acts of kindness.

Our charity has a big vision. Currently, it operates within a small community in Sierra Leone, but the goal is to expand across the country, reaching deprived villages and providing children with opportunities to realise their potential and improve their lives. My dream also extends beyond Sierra Leone to other countries facing similar challenges.

Globally, many children are struggling, and our broader aim is to reach as many of them as possible. I am a firm believer in humanity and know that with collaboration from like-minded individuals, we can give children worldwide the chance to pursue their dreams and become valuable members of society.

"HUMAN RIGHTS ARE
INSCRIBED IN THE
HEARTS OF PEOPLE."

MARY ROBINSON

Niamh lives in Dublin and has been actively
involved in finding homes for refugees in Ireland.

I BELIEVE WE SHOULD WELCOME PEOPLE LIKE ABDULAI WITH OPEN ARMS.

NIAMH

My name is Niamh and I am from Kildare town. In 1997, at the age of 17, I moved to Dublin to study science at UCD and went on to work in technology.

A pivotal moment in my life occurred in September 2015. I had been working in London and as I was on my way home, walking through Gatwick Airport, I saw the heartbreaking image of Alan Kurdi, the young Syrian boy whose lifeless body washed ashore near Bodrum in Turkey. The image was broadcast across multiple big screens and it moved me profoundly. It was a period marked by the war in Syria, triggering a wave of people fleeing for their lives. Forced to take perilous, overloaded boat journeys, the grim reality is that thousands of people died while attempting to cross the Mediterranean.

This moment ignited a determination in me to use my skills meaningfully. I did some initial research on the experiences of people arriving in Ireland seeking asylum. Housing and isolation immediately jumped out as major pain points. First impressions matter greatly. For many, arriving at a direct provision centre and experiencing the harsh realities of the system can be disheartening and difficult to endure and bounce back from. The appalling situation we see now of people seeking asylum being left homeless on the streets of Ireland, without access to services, is not going to be easy for people to recover from. Those who do get off the streets are now "housed" in military tents, often with protestors outside, claiming Ireland is full, which is deeply inhumane.

Drawing on my experience with two-sided marketplaces, facilitating point-to-point contact without a middleman, I envisioned a solution that would support capturing the public goodwill towards refugees and putting the necessary operations, safeguards, technology and staff in place. This would facilitate the smooth and safe operation of a programme, matching these offers of accommodation with people in need. I recognised that, although there was a housing shortage, there was also some underuse of housing resources in the form of empty spare bedrooms. I was encouraged when a charity called Uplift had significant engagement from the public offering to welcome refugees into their homes.

Initially, we had no formal support but, with sound advice from well-meaning individuals, our project caught the attention of the Irish Red Cross. Shortly afterwards, I attended the Web Summit in Dublin and organised a fringe event calling on developers, user experience professionals and product and data experts to join forces. We aimed to build something impactful. This journey has been a testament to the power of compassion and community and the impact we can have when we unite to address humanitarian crises.

So, we created a website for the Irish Red Cross, called the "Register of Pledges", where people could offer their spare bedrooms to refugees. Offers began to come in. At the request of the Red Cross, we expanded the platform to allow people to pledge goods and services, designed to address the needs of people on arrival in a new community. The Red Cross expanded their migration team to include two caseworkers, who conducted outreach in direct provision centres, such as Mosney, where asylum seekers often faced prolonged processing times without much opportunity to integrate into Irish society. These caseworkers reached out to young men from Syria and Iraq, offering them an avenue to leave Mosney to live with Irish families. They also met hosts and matched them with guests, to allow maximum benefit for guests, hosts and host communities.

When I launched the Red Cross website, I felt compelled to lead by example. A young Syrian man, who spoke little English, came to live in my home. The Red Cross provided invaluable support, handling the extensive paperwork and logistical challenges. Language barriers can significantly delay integration, but we managed remarkably well. Many hosts, including myself, bonded with their guests and with other hosts as we celebrated our guests' milestones and witnessed their growth. It was a privilege to be part of this community.

Nine years have passed since the Register of Pledges began. The programme saw slow but steady progress from the time the first guests moved in with hosts in 2017. Then, in February 2022, Russia launched its military operation in Ukraine, which brought a surge of activity, with 20,000 pledges in a few weeks. During this period, I took three weeks off work and enlisted volunteers from corporate Ireland, who generously donated their skilled technologists and call centre staff to help manage the influx of pledges of spare rooms. While there were operational challenges during that busy time, the initiative scaled rapidly and housed many in need.

With scale, however, came sacrifices. Early on, the focus was on providing comprehensive wraparound supports, with caseworkers knowing their service users and taking the time to understand and address their needs and aspirations. However, the international protection process lacks the appetite to provide people with personalised care. There are rarely any formal vulnerability assessments. No effort is made by the State to help those arriving to integrate with their communities and, because they do not take the time to understand an individual's vulnerabilities, needs and skills, they don't understand the barriers they face.

This brings me to the email I received from Abdulai, who I had met once before. I volunteer with Ireland Says Welcome, a member group of the charity, Comhlámh. One of our members, who runs multicultural arts events, had met Abdulai. She recognised his interest in global justice and thought our group would be a good fit for him. At our meetings, he didn't speak much, but his contributions were always valuable.

Abdulai faced significant challenges, especially in the direct provision centre. These places are tough for anyone who struggles with injustice, because injustice is so stark in direct provision. The lack of respect for the autonomy of residents is disheartening. He had organised a residents group to liaise between residents and staff at his direct provision centre and he was studying for a qualification in, I believe, addiction and community development – a Level 6 qualification.

Abdulai channelled his frustrations positively, navigating difficulties with diplomacy and striving for good outcomes for everyone.

However, his leadership led to strained relations with the staff and eventually, he was asked to leave the centre. I've heard many stories of people being told by staff in direct provision centres to stay in line or risk affecting their asylum case. Facing homelessness, he emailed the Department of Children, Equality, Disability, Integration and Youth. He cc'd a number of charities and included my personal address, having met me through Ireland Says Welcome. I felt for him as, although he had made an eloquent appeal, the department rarely responds to, or acts on, any appeals or complaints, and the emails most often go unanswered. I decided to reach out to him directly. I offered him a place to stay, telling him to get to Heuston Station and I would look after him from there.

Seeing Abdulai's relief on his arrival was profound. He had endured a long journey from Sierra Leone, a country with many difficulties, and had spent years in Longford's direct provision system. The distance from Freetown, Sierra Leone, to Longford, Ireland, both physically and metaphorically, was immense. Given all his efforts in studying, volunteering and activism, I believe we should welcome people like Abdulai with open arms. There's a misconception that people seeking asylum here want to stay on social welfare. In reality, most people I know want to work, send money home, look after their families and be good citizens. They want to avoid further trouble in their lives and strive to contribute positively to society. This has been my consistent experience.

During Abdulai's stay, we became friends. We were very close to the city, so there was always a lot of life around – walks in Phoenix Park and on the beach in Sandymount. Abdulai, originally from Freetown and surrounded by the sea at home, had been in Ireland for over two years without seeing the sea. I will always remember how his eyes lit up when we went to Sandymount beach.

In June 2024, I attended Sierra Leone Day at a church in Harold's Cross. There must have been a couple of hundred people from Sierra Leone there and the food was amazing. Experiences like these have enriched my life immensely.

I really hope the Government takes action on the housing situation. Irish people who fall into homelessness and people trying to leave direct provision shouldn't have to face a housing market where demand outstrips available supply. This situation becomes very competitive and adversarial, which has proven to be disastrous for social cohesion. Furthermore, when securing a rental property using the Housing Assistance Payment, approval from Local Authorities can take up to 12 weeks. Then people need to pay the deposit and multiple months' rent in advance, amounting to thousands of euros.

It's all too easy to fall into homelessness, whether you're Irish or a refugee. The safety nets aren't there, and the Government isn't addressing the issue adequately. I've seen the numbers grow from 1,000 to 10,000 on the Dublin City Council's homeless list, with 14,000 homeless across the country. Meanwhile, there are tourists staying in Airbnbs that should be homes, while homeless Irish people and international protection applicants live in hotels that should be used for tourists. The Government is now resorting to military tents for emergency accommodation, but the homeless on arrival numbers are so great that the Government cannot even manage to offer all of them a tent.

I have a particular perspective from spending so much time understanding the needs of humanitarian organisations and reading reports from the UN and various white papers and research. The housing crisis is at the root of the social cohesion breakdown we're witnessing. Of late, the housing problem is being framed as an immigration issue. The sight of tents along the canal gives the impression that we as a nation can't cope. Why are people being left homeless told to get a tent from a charity, only to have those tents taken away before eventually being moved to a military tent? It's completely mismanaged and unnecessary. A better system should be put in place tomorrow.

I enjoy meeting people I wouldn't otherwise encounter. My life is broader and richer. For instance, I love an Iftar during Ramadan, even though I'm not Muslim. I enjoy Eid dinners and Sierra Leonean gatherings. Life is more enjoyable with these diverse experiences. At the micro level, helping Abdulai and others has been a pleasure. While filling out forms can be tedious, the overall experience of helping people to integrate is an honour. At the macro level, I continue to look for opportunities to apply technology effectively and ethically, while respecting people's human rights. This is challenging but worthwhile.

More about
Sierra Leone:

"YOU MAY NOT CONTROL ALL THE EVENTS THAT HAPPEN TO YOU, BUT YOU CAN DECIDE NOT TO BE REDUCED BY THEM."

MAYA ANGELOU

Lariche was born in the Congo and is a mum, a wife and a regular on our television screens, in the series *Gogglebox Ireland*. She is a woman of strength and kindness. Lariche and her Irish husband continue to use their platforms to challenge and to create awareness and compassion.

BE BRAVE

LARICHE

One night in 2022, my husband Gary and I treated ourselves to a date night. My mam took the kids for a sleepover and we went to our local. After a while, Gary suggested going into town. After some initial reluctance, I agreed, as we had not been into the city since before Covid. We danced the night away, finally letting our hair down. Normally, we would have left earlier to avoid the taxi queues, but the club staff recognised us from television and we chatted with them for a bit, before heading home.

As we were walking down the street, one of a group of seven men, aged between about 18 and 22, hurled a racist comment at us. On reflex, Gary turned and said, "What did you say?" Immediately the group became aggressive. I appealed to everyone for calm and we tried to walk away. Next thing I knew, I was slapped in the face, followed by a punch to the jaw. My attacker kept delivering blow after blow, punching me in the ribs, arms and face, eventually knocking me to the ground. I grabbed his jacket and pulled him closer to make it harder for him to punch me.

I thought I was going to die. Thoughts ran through my head. Should I have kissed my children more? Told them I loved them more? I hope they think I was a great mam. Will I see them go to college or get married? I held on so hard to my attacker that my nails were ripped off. I turned to see my husband being dragged into a laneway by four of the men. When he tried to stand up, the men kicked him in the chest and back to the ground. I was sure they were going to kill him. I released my grip on my attacker and he got off me.

As I stumbled over to my husband, I felt the blood streaming down my face. The sound of the kicking was getting louder and stronger. I threw myself over him and covered his head, while screaming, "Someone help us! Please help us!" Nobody came. All the while, I was also being beaten. My final plea was "Please, please stop! He's down, there's nothing left. Just stop, please! We have a family, please stop! I need him, he's all I have." The next thing I remember was one of the men shouting at the top of the laneway and they all ran off.

My dad had always said to me as we were leaving Africa, "I need you to be a soldier; you're my first born. Be brave." I have been through a lot in my life, but this incident hit me like no other. The aftermath left me wondering how I would have got through it, if not for my family and friends around me. I was physically and mentally scarred; my husband was lucky to be alive.

The psychological effect of this racist attack was immense and stays with me to this day. This is why I want to share my story – of my early childhood in the Congo and my family's move to Ireland, to encourage others to pause and think.

My name is Lariche. I'm 37 and I've lived in Ireland since I was six. My family came from the Congo. War had been raging there and my dad always said that he didn't want to raise his kids in that country. So he and my mam decided to work, save as much money as they could and get out. That was their plan for us.

I don't remember much about my nanny, but I still remember being brought from one house to another, either my nanny's or my auntie's house, because they kind of reared us when my mam and dad were trying to work. And then, obviously, the war got bad. Civil war. My dad knew we needed to leave. "Nobody is safe," he said. "The kids won't be safe." My mam agreed to do whatever was needed. They didn't tell anybody we were leaving, in case someone let it slip.

I was six at the time and my two brothers were a year-and-a-half and nine months old. I remember we waited until the middle of the night. They got a vehicle, put us in it, and drove all the way to Angola. When we got to Angola, there was a civil war going on there too. There were all sorts of terrible things happening, people killing each other, people everywhere carrying guns. My parents had to find somewhere to stay and what we ended up in wasn't even a house. More like a garden shed.

For protection, my dad got thin sheets of metal and put them along the sides of the shed. When we slept, he would put me and my brothers in the middle between him and my mam. There would be loads of pillows between us all too. The idea was that if they did shoot bullets, they would hit my mam and dad and the kids would be okay. Dad would say to my mam, "If it hits me, at least you'll hear it. You'll have time to escape." Dad had made a little manhole at the back of the shed, so we could escape if anything happened. It was covered with tin and led to a jungle of sorts. "When you hear the gunshots, take the tin cover off, grab the kids and go."

I remember the night it happened, Dad saying he could hear firing, people screaming. He got the manhole ready. Mam grabbed us and Dad said he would follow. He needed to stay behind to cover the manhole, so they wouldn't catch us. My mam put my baby brother on her back and tied him with a rag around her. She dragged me and my other brother by the hand as we ran away. My brother and I had little backpacks but my mam had nothing. There was no time to grab anything.

Mam was trying to count her steps because, once we left, we were in the dark. Dad had walked the route with her, giving her instructions: "Count 100 steps to here, stop, turn left, 50 steps to here …" She was running from people with guns, through a jungle, with three kids and counting her steps. We had to go through a small swamp. The water was only up to my knees, but it was probably 30 feet wide. We had to go through that, not knowing what was underneath. There could have been alligators, but you're in the dark, so you don't know. And all the time hearing gunshots in the background. That was the risk we were taking. It goes to show how dangerous it was to stay.

Mam got us to the coast. Dad said he would meet her there, so she stood waiting for him. The people running the boats eventually told her that we would have to go. What do you do? Dad had said that we would have to go without him, if he wasn't there in time. So we had to get on the boat without him.

He had always said, "When you're going, remember, you're going to Ireland. When you get off, tell them that's where you're going."

Mam was confused at first. "Ireland? Why are we going to Ireland? Isn't there a war there too?"

My dad was well educated and he was able to reassure her. "No, no. You're going to the south of Ireland. You're not going to the north. Make sure when you get out, you go to the south of Ireland."

We didn't know where we were going; we were just little kids. Mam was keeping us wrapped up and sitting there with us on a boat. She said later it was the scariest thing ever, because she was on her own. Not able to swim, with three young children and not a word of English. She didn't even know if we were going to make it in the boat. All she could say was "South of Ireland, south of Ireland."

We got to England and stayed there for three days. Mam didn't know if someone would take her children away from her, so she had to be on high alert, not knowing where my dad was, who she could talk to, who she could call.

Then we arrived in Ireland. As refugees, we were put in a hotel. We stayed there for months. With three kids, Mam was given £19 per week. She would go out every day to the pay phone and leave us in the hotel, saying, "Don't answer the door to anybody else." She would ring back home to see if anyone had heard from my dad or knew where he was. It was heartbreaking to see, because she'd come back and we'd be asking where he was. We were kids; we were lost. We waited for Dad, wondering if he was ever going to turn up.

And then, somehow, she made contact with him! He told her not to worry, to stay where she was. He said he would find a way to get to Ireland. Every day from six to seven, Mam would go to the pay phone and wait for the phone call from my dad … and wait and wait. Four or five weeks had passed since we'd heard from him. At that point, she had convinced herself that he was dead.

She considered going back to the Congo, because we didn't know Ireland at all. We came to Ireland on humanitarian grounds, so Mam was waiting for the paperwork to be processed. If that didn't come through, we would be deported. We were at the embassy every day. With little English, my mam fought hard for

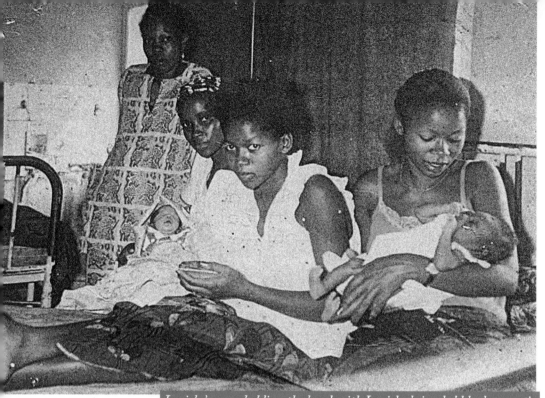

Lariche's mom holding the bowl with Lariche being held by her auntie

us. They explained that if we were deported, we would be sent back to Angola, not the Congo, because we came through Angola. Mam begged them not to send us back to Angola. She explained that her husband couldn't get out of there and was probably dead. "If you send me home, these small kids, they'll be dead."

I remember in the hotel, Mam would go into the other room to pray (she's Catholic) and it would break my heart, because I would hear her crying. I was only about six or seven, but I could feel her pain. My brother would keep asking, "Can we go home, Mam? I don't want to be here. Can we go home?" To stop him from crying, I would tell him, "It'll be okay. It'll be okay." My brother would ask my mam what was wrong when she cried and she didn't know what to say, because we were just kids. Mam was trying to protect us.

One day, there was a knock on the door and she put me and my brothers in the bathroom. She thought it was immigration coming to get us. We laugh now, thinking of her putting us in the bath with the shower curtain over us. She went out to the door. I heard her scream and then she started crying. I didn't know what was happening, so I tried to keep my brothers distracted. I remember waving my baby brother's toy in front of him, trying to stop him from crying.

Then the bathroom door opened and there was my dad! He actually found us. I started crying, but I didn't really understand, whereas my mam understood and she was sobbing. Absolutely sobbing. I still remember it.

Dad never really told us what had happened to him in Angola. I would eavesdrop over the years to pick up a few pieces. I know that when he tried to escape, the army in Angola got him. They had blocked the manhole and caught him. They put him in a cell with other prisoners and he said it was the most horrific and inhumane experience of his life. They weren't fed. If there was a bit of water, everybody was trying to take it, like animals, just to drink and survive. There was no toilet roll; everybody had to go in the same place. They eventually gave him a gun and forced him to join the war. To survive, that was his only option.

One day, during war duty, my dad put the gun down and ran towards the border. Because he had escaped, they were hunting him down. When he got to a boat, only women and those with children were allowed on. There was a woman there with two children and he begged her to allow him to hold a child to get onto the boat, or he was going to be shot. Eventually, she felt so sorry for him that she agreed. If it hadn't been for that woman and child, he would be dead.

It was hard for us growing up in Killinarden, Tallaght. They gave us a bed-share house and we were sharing with four or five different families, which was mental. My dad was fighting for us to stay in Ireland. The day I started school, I remember walking in and all the students and teachers staring, because I was the only black person there. I would often come home crying. Mam found it hard too. I'd hear her talking to Dad. "I don't want to be here. Is there anything else we can do?"

I still remember the first time someone called me the N-word. I didn't even know what it was. I was with Mam when it happened. I said say hello to a kid I knew and their parent said, "Don't talk to that n*****." My mam was heartbroken. I laughed it away, because I didn't understand. She came home to my dad and said, "We're not welcome here."

For me, I can genuinely ask, "Do you think people want to leave their country?" My mam didn't want to leave, but there was a civil war on and she had no choice; she had small kids. She had to pack up and leave her mam, her dad, her sisters and everyone she had around her, to come to a country where she was going to start with nothing. Absolutely nothing. And be isolated. She couldn't speak English. People think refugees are coming here by choice, but these people have no option.

The saddest part was that my mam never got to go home before her mam and dad died. Within six years of being in Ireland, her mam died. She was trying to get home, but within the next year, her dad died too. She never got to say goodbye to them and that still eats at her to this day. People don't want to leave their homes, but if there is a civil war, people are going to leave. They'll look at their kids and they'll pack up and leave. Parents will do anything to save their children. That's what my mam and dad did. They gave up everything.

My grandad was a driver in the Congo. He drove Mercedes cars for the president. My mam went to private school; my dad didn't. Dad comes from a family of 18, so he was like "the poor guy", but he had the intelligence to make money. He would go off and catch fish and sell it in the streets and many people were buying the fish from him, so he impressed my mam. She lived in a gated community, but she had to leave because there was war coming. She gave up a lot.

I feel for people coming to Ireland now, because it's hard. I know what it's like. You come with nothing and people think that you're getting everything for free. My dad worked in factories. He would work any hour and every hour for lower pay than other people were getting, because it was for his family. People always wonder how I afford things and the genuine truth is that it's work. Hard work. I get out and I work for what I have. You put the hard work in behind the scenes to get to where you are. My dad always says, "We came from nothing. I brought you here to give you a better life. Educate yourselves. Go to school. Do the jobs nobody wants to do. Get educated."

I think Dad feels bad for me, because I didn't get to live like a teenager. I was the eldest, so the responsibility was always on me. I'd look out the window at all the kids playing, but I'd be inside babysitting, because Mam and Dad were working. When everyone was going to teenage discos, I would be home minding the kids. My mam and dad had to work hard and educate themselves, so they could earn the same wage as an Irish person.

I have people ask me where I'm from and when I say Dublin, they'll say, "Where are you really from?" I hate that one. Sometimes I follow up with "I'm from Ireland" and they'll say, "No, where are your parents from? There's no way you're of Irish descent." Sometimes, I'll tell people I'm a refugee and they can't believe it. I always explain that we came here on humanitarian grounds. Ireland is open enough and it is becoming more multicultural, but I do feel like I have to work harder than the next person in everything I do. The acceptance is there and at the same time, it isn't. When I was a kid, I would be on my own in the schoolyard. There was a girl in my school from the Traveller community who was left on her own too. She had nobody and I had nobody, so I thought, I can be her friend.

I feel accepted in certain situations because when I speak, I have the Dublin accent and they think, oh she's one of us. But if I didn't have the accent, would they be saying that to me now? I don't think so. I do wonder, do you have to be white to be accepted? Is that what it is? Even with the industry I'm in now, doing television work, I find there are very few black people and it's sad. What gets me is when people say to me "the blacks" are doing this or that, "But I don't mean you!" and I'm trying to explain that I'm also black and that's also my community. They'll say, "Ah I know yeah, but you're different." But why? Why?

My mam and dad are still here in Ireland and are still together. They had two more kids when they came here, so there's five kids now and eight grandkids. Mam works in An Post and Dad now works installing security for banks, after working for Cuisine de France for years. People would have said we were only here for free housing but my family has worked their whole lives.

Dad told us to take every opportunity we could, get stuck into school, do your exams, study. He always said education is key. He also always kept us in sports. I was in track and field for years and I eventually got a scholarship to America. By the time I was 16, I had met my now husband, Gary. At that time, I wanted to be an air hostess, but I also wanted to take up the scholarship. I planned to go to America and then I found out I was pregnant. I told my parents and Dad didn't take it well, because he wanted better for me. He eventually sat down with me and encouraged me to go on to college to become an air hostess. He and Mam fully supported me. They helped me to balance having a baby and going to college. I passed and went on to work in Dublin airport. After a good few years there, I realised I wanted to change my career path; the shift work in the airport and the long hours are not great with a baby.

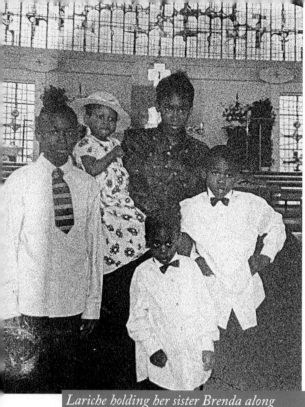

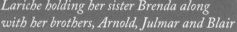
Lariche holding her sister Brenda along with her brothers, Arnold, Julmar and Blair

A young Lariche

I went back to study and ended up working for SUSI, the student grant scheme in Ireland, for a number of years. I liked it, but I always wanted to better myself, so I was thinking, right, where can I go from here? Gary got a job in An Post when I was pregnant and I thought that would also be a good fit for me. I still work there today and I'm also the union representative. My dad always told me that you start from the bottom and you work yourself up. So I went and did just that.

I always wanted to do television. They were looking for contestants on *Ireland's Fittest Family* and my family is very competitive. If someone can do 20 volleys, one of us wants to do 30. I said to Gary that I wouldn't mind applying. When I watch TV here, I've always noticed that there were few black people represented and I wanted to change that. So I went to Dad and said, "Why don't we be that representation?" And Dad said, "Yeah, go ahead!" He always wanted us to show Irish people that we're not here to be lazy and take from the system. We're here to work and to contribute. Our application was accepted, but just before we were meant to go on the show, Dad got injured. We needed to have a parent with us and we were devastated. My mam turned around and said, "I'll do it!" We couldn't believe it. We absolutely love her for that, because she's not into fitness. She did it for us. Afterwards, I asked her why she said she would do it and she said, "I thought you would all tell me 'Ah no, it's grand Mam!' But

Lariche's first year in secondary school

it's not grand to miss out." Throughout the whole show, she struggled but my brothers and I would lift her up and stay by her side and help her through. We stayed as a unit. We've always had to be a unit.

Being in the public eye is mad. There's almost a stigma to being on television. There were a lot of racist comments that followed. A few comments saying that RTE should be ashamed for putting us on it, because we're not Irish, or comments saying, "Africa's fittest family". But we decided that we were going to be resilient and that we would stand together as a family. The overall reaction was positive, but you still look at the negative comments and they affect you. It just snowballed from there. Gary and I then ended up on *Gogglebox Ireland*. Dad encouraged us to do it, so that Ireland could see a white Irish man and a black woman together and see that it is normal.

We have three kids now, 17, 14 and 10. My youngest daughter came into the house crying last week because one of the kids told her that she's a half-caste, saying, "Your mam is like a chocolate bar." It's really down to education and people making sure that they're educated. I had to try to explain the Dublin riots to my children and why people were out vandalising in protest over immigration. I did an ad for the *Irish Independent* and was in it for probably just four seconds. The comments that came in underneath the video were horrific, even giving out my home address. The *Independent* rang me, very apologetic, and asked if I wanted the ad to be withdrawn. They didn't think it would attract that much hatred. I said I would think it over. I then spoke to Gary and he said, "If you take down the ad, you've let them win." When the *Independent* rang me back, I told them, "Leave it up."

I chose to share my story because of the misinformation out there. I want people to know that although yes, I am Irish, I'm not actually from here. Here is my background story. Now, does that change anything? Some people will say things like, "Get all the immigrants out" right in front of me, not realising I am an immigrant. My friends have seen me grow, go to school, have a family and get to where I have by working for it. So are you going to understand that immigrants do come here and do good? Because here I am. There's a stereotype that we're here to take, take, take, but all I do is give, give, give. It's sad.

That's why I'm so stuck on doing television and putting myself out there. I want to be out there for every single black person so they can look at me and say, "This girl has come from a civil war and now she's here. I can do what she can do. I can climb the ladder she has climbed." People think I just love being on television, they don't know the background behind it or understand why I'm doing it. I need to show my kids that I will push for them to have a platform to stand on, so they can be treated like everyone else around them. My parents fought for me and I'll fight for my kids. That's why I keep doing it.

More about
Congo:

142

> **"TO STAND IN SOLIDARITY WITH REFUGEES IS TO STAND FOR HUMAN RIGHTS, FOR JUSTICE, AND FOR THE BETTERMENT OF OUR WORLD."**

KOFI ANNAN

At the age of 14, Nonso, after living in Ireland for 11 years, found out that his family's asylum application had been denied, resulting in the threat of deportation.

His classmates initiated the "Save Nonso" campaign, delivering a petition with 22,000 signatures to Justice Minister Charlie Flanagan, appealing for the family's right to remain in Ireland.

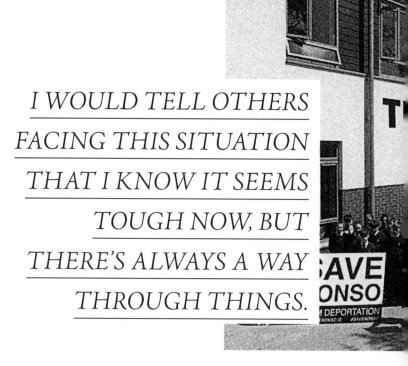

> *I WOULD TELL OTHERS FACING THIS SITUATION THAT I KNOW IT SEEMS TOUGH NOW, BUT THERE'S ALWAYS A WAY THROUGH THINGS.*

NONSO

My real name is Chukwunonso, but people call me Nonso. I was born in Nigeria and I came to Ireland when I was two. After my father died, we left to start a new life. I don't remember anything from Nigeria; I only know Ireland. I met all my friends here; I grew up here. I used to live in Athlone and then I moved to Tullamore when I was about five and started secondary school there. Nearly all of my friends and the people I know are from Tullamore. I'm not sure how to describe myself, but I'm sure I had a good effect on some people, which is why they made such a big effort to get behind me.

There is a lot to say about my mam. She has always done a great job in being a mother. It's just her and two kids. I can only imagine it must have been extremely difficult having to look after two children all by herself. We didn't have much money. I don't know how she did it. There's one day I remember so clearly. We were in a shop and my mam only had this bag of coins. She was trying to use the coins to pay for what we were getting. I remember looking around and seeing people giggling and sniggering. I was upset, because I knew she was trying so hard and people just didn't understand. They were laughing at her.

(offalyexpress.ie)

There's a lot of things my mam did. When we were younger, I wanted to play sports, but we didn't have the money to sign up for anything. When I was about 10 or 11, I was able to play soccer for Tullamore. We couldn't afford it, but she made it happen, because she knew I wanted to play. It made me realise she's put a lot of effort into making sure we could live a normal life.

It was a struggle sometimes, but I'm sure that whatever I was struggling with wasn't as bad as what she was going through. Some days, I would see her crying and it was really upsetting. I don't think any mother – or anybody – should have to go through that. All the burden is on her, because we have no dad to help us out; it has just been her doing everything herself.

I am very thankful for my mother. If I had a second chance, I wouldn't choose anybody else, she's made me who I am today. She has made me very empathetic. I always try to understand others' feelings before I judge, because I know how it feels. I've seen first-hand what it is like to be judged. My mother has struggled and still made it through. She has been such a rock and a hero in my life. I couldn't have asked for a better mother. I think people forget that everyone only has one life and your parents are going through it for the first time too. It's incredible that she's done such a great job for how little we had.

I remember my mam was crying about something one day and she was talking to my brother about it. I was quite young, around 14 at the time, in second year. I never fully understood what our family situation was; my mam never told me. I did know that we were immigrants. I found out later that my family was facing deportation to Nigeria, a country I left when I was just two years old. We had come to Ireland in 2007 and applied for asylum, but 10 years later, our application for humanitarian leave to remain in Ireland was refused.

When I heard the word "deportation", I knew it meant we wouldn't be able to live in Ireland anymore. I guess I was really scared and upset. Can you imagine one day being told to pack your bags and go to a random country? My ethnic background is Nigerian, but I have no memory of Nigeria; I know nothing about Nigeria. I thought, all my friends will be gone, what am I going to do? This life that I wanted for myself is going to be taken away from me. I was distraught.

My mam and my brother went to the art teacher in our school, Joe Caslin. Together they spoke to the principal, Mr McEvoy, and the guidance counsellor, Ms McNamara, to fill them in on our situation. They made a plan to launch a massive campaign for me and my family to remain in Ireland. They hoped to gather petition signatures and as much attention as possible from media outlets and TDs. They did so much. It took me by surprise, because I knew less about what was really happening than my mam and others. They basically said to me that I was the youngest, so I should be the face of the campaign. I didn't really have an option, but it was my family, so I was like, "Okay, sure, grand."

One day out of nowhere, I was chilling at home, when I saw loads of Snapchat stories about this petition, with the hashtag #savenonso. I didn't know that was happening and it took me by surprise. I thought, Wow, this is a lot! At one point, the number of signatures was rapidly growing and it got to over 20,000, which is more than the population of Tullamore! Obviously, I was happy that people cared and wanted us to stay, but at the same time, I felt vulnerable and exposed. I was so young then, and now my face was everywhere; everyone knew who I was and about my situation. Everywhere I went, people saw me and thought, oh that's that kid. It was a lot to handle, but at the same time, it was for the greater good. The school did a lot and I am so very thankful for them. Honest to God, if it wasn't for them, we wouldn't be here.

We held a protest in Dublin outside the Four Courts. Some reporters picked it up and it ended up on the news. We even had a whole day where my friends and I were taken out of class to film for RTÉ. As helpful as it was, I didn't know if I could handle all the pressure and attention. My friends did make it a lot easier, to be fair. I'm very thankful for them; it was just a lot for someone my age. I got to meet the Minister for Justice at the time, Charlie Flanagan. I can't even remember what we spoke about. Fast forward to a while later and we got the news that we could remain in Ireland.

I haven't always had the best mental health, so it did take a toll on me a little bit. All I could do was push through it, especially for my family. At that point, I realised that I wasn't like everyone else. My struggles weren't the same as everyone else's. I realised I wasn't as "normal" as I thought I was. I felt that I had to try a lot harder to prove myself, because of all the efforts of the people around me.

When I look back on it, there are times I wish that it hadn't been my face and my name that was everywhere. You probably wouldn't know my brother or my mam's name. I still struggle with my mental health sometimes. Partly because I feel people still know me as the kid who almost got deported. I remember at the time looking at comments on Twitter and it was so demeaning what some people would say. You get the good comments too, but at 14, some of them were really upsetting; there was no need to make them. As much as I know it's in the past, it still affects me. I'm thankful that it did happen. I just wish it didn't have to happen like that.

I think what I went through has made me more determined about what I want to do with my life. Since we were hit with the whole deportation thing, I feel that you can't take anything for granted. I want to get into a good engineering job or start my own business. I know things won't be handed to me; I have to work hard for them myself.

I'm doing well now. I'm in college studying general engineering and I'm hoping to get into mechanical engineering. I feel like I can start being my own person again. I've met some incredible people in college. Not many of them know about the campaign and it feels good to make friends who just know me for me. My brother graduated two years ago and he's working with a product design company in Dublin. My mam still stays in contact with my teachers, who helped us.

I think the hatred we see in Ireland today is extremely hypocritical. People want to say Ireland isn't a racist country and, on the outside, you would think it wasn't, but there are just so many inner racial prejudices that you don't see in yourself. I remember when an immigrant attacked a young girl and it caused the Dublin riots, but it was also an immigrant who helped her. I think people just want a reason to hate, even if it's something small. A lot of Irish people went to America during the Famine and made new lives there. We don't really have the right to treat foreign people badly, when a lot of Irish heritage is about being the foreigner in another country. It's very sad to see the way the course of our history is changing towards minorities. It's upsetting. I don't want to have to be afraid in the country that I grew up in, my country. I don't want to walk through Dublin and be in fear that someone might attack me, because of the colour of my skin or my ethnic background.

It's not that I feel afraid now, it's that there's a certain level of anxiousness. Where I am now is a very safe area. Nothing has happened to me and hopefully it never will. I'm afraid for the people who are in places of risk. Dublin can be quite a scary place. A lot of my friends who are black or mixed race are in Dublin and they told me that they stayed home during the riots, because they didn't want anything happening to them. It's scary to have to hear that. They fear for their own lives, because of all this hate that's going around.

I would tell others facing this situation that I know it seems tough now, but there's always a way through things. Something I live by is that "Tomorrow will come." No matter what, time will keep moving on. No matter what, tomorrow is going to come.

More about
Nigeria:

148

"REFUGEES ARE YOU AND I WITH DIFFERENT CIRCUMSTANCES."

ELISA JOHNSTON

Fleeing from war and searching for a better life, Salah supports his family at home in Sudan and is still campaigning for the rights of people in his country. Salah has embraced the local community he lives in and gets involved in all aspects of his local football club.

I FEEL MORE ACCEPTED IN IRELAND THAN I FELT IN MY OWN COUNTRY. I WISH WE HAD PEACE IN SUDAN, BUT WE DON'T.

SALAH

I come from Darfur, West Sudan. It borders Congo. I lived in a small town where we didn't have technology, hospitals or any of those things. It was an easy life farming animals. I was educated there and then I moved to a big city to get my secondary education. On the holidays, I would come back and visit my family and the farm. In the summertime, we farmed tomatoes and potatoes. Life was good. I have 14 siblings and I am the second child. My parents have over 100 grandchildren! Everybody used animals to pay for things. If you wanted to buy sugar or tea, you could pay with money or with gold, cows or lambs. It was traditional bartering. We had food and everything we needed. Life was easy. I had a great life as a teenager. We owned the land between six or seven African tribes, small tribes. There was no problem going onto the land of a different tribe.

The war started in 1989 when I was only 17. Omar al-Bashir and his forces came to power through a coup. The villages began to be burned and looted. The cows were being stolen; they even looted the trees and cut the mangoes from them. People were forced to move from their homes. The people who began the war had weapons; we had none. They killed everyone and everything. There was the rape of women and children. Sharia Law was imposed and under Sharia Law, people had their hands and feet cut off. There was a lot of killing on one side; it wasn't from both sides. A lot of the forces came from Libya and Morocco. It was a campaign of occupation. People were moved into camps. My family were moved into a camp of over 300,000.

The population of Darfur was roughly 7 million. In Darfur, there is no peace, they will just kill you on the streets. They don't care. It is genocide. If you are African or a woman, you don't equal anything. People were taken and used as slaves. Even today, they continue to kill women and children and take whatever they have.

People then wanted to defend themselves and started organising militant groups and buying weapons. In 2002, South Sudan took independence and removed themselves completely. Today, there are multiple militant groups fighting in Sudan.

Because of the genocide, the UN intervened, but they couldn't defend the people. The biggest population of UN workers is in Sudan. But they are only peacekeepers. There is no safety, even in the UN camps. I just wanted to get out of there.

I had a friend from America, who convinced me to leave. I had saved money from doing some business and I came here in 2003. Life in Ireland has been very good. I had never had this kind of life before. I didn't know the language when I first arrived, so it was difficult, but I began to meet people and to learn about the country. I was in a hotel, because I came through the asylum process. I was lucky, because in 2004, I got a letter from the Sudanese government to give to the Minister for Justice, which helped me to receive my refugee status. I stayed in Gardiner Street Hotel with two other people in my room. I was there for about two weeks and then I stayed for five months in Killarney before they moved me to Waterford and then eventually to Dublin.

I am 50 years old now and I feel more accepted in Ireland than I felt in my own country.

I wish we had peace in Sudan, but we don't. I worked in Ireland for seven years before retraining. I also volunteer in a local football club. I'm now a computer technician. I studied IT at Technological University Dublin at Tallaght, but I have had computer qualifications since 1995. I've done a few courses in Ireland and a lot of jobs. I've worked in radio, cleaning and construction. However, my favourite thing in Ireland is having access to technology and computers.

It was very difficult to leave my family. I didn't have a choice, but I will never forget them. My sister's son, my nephew, was brain damaged through the conflict and his father was killed. My nephew is on special medicine. I send him money to buy it because there is no proper health care system over there. There is also now a famine in Sudan. I have no family here and no children, so I send money back home to help my family. My father was killed in 2002. He doesn't have a grave – there are only mass graves there because of all the killings. I have lost a lot of people in my family. In Darfur now, most people believe that they would be better off dead. When you lose a part of your family, it is so hard for those who are left alive.

My people don't have anything, they have no power. If you disagree with the government, they will kill you. Even now, there is no solution. My sister still lives there and I worry about her. For her now, it is just daily life. Every time I call her, someone else has died. Whenever they call me, I know it is because someone has been killed. My family have some access to phones, but the government can cut the internet whenever they want. We can only contact each other through WhatsApp and internet. You cannot call a phone directly. When I get a phone call from them, I know it is always bad news.

I go to demonstrations for my country and try to campaign for peace in Darfur. I met with some people from the International Criminal Court and gave presentations. I go to meetings along O'Connell Street to try to fight for my people. I have met a lot of good people trying to make a change. I have even met people on both sides of the conflict in Sudan, who are working for peace. My hope for Sudan is for it to be a democratic country with no war.

More about Sudan:

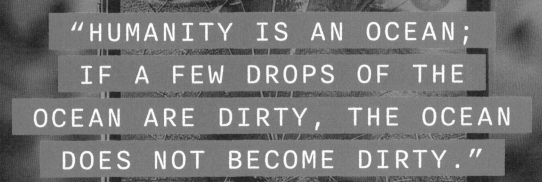

> "HUMANITY IS AN OCEAN; IF A FEW DROPS OF THE OCEAN ARE DIRTY, THE OCEAN DOES NOT BECOME DIRTY."

MAHATMA GANDHI

Mpho's journey from Lesotho to Ireland is a testament to her resilience and determination. Formerly a lecturer in Lesotho, Mpho now works as a Community Integration Officer with Dublin South City Partnership and is an activist and writer in her spare time.

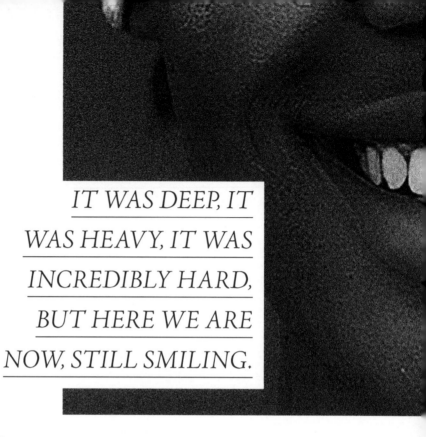

> *IT WAS DEEP, IT WAS HEAVY, IT WAS INCREDIBLY HARD, BUT HERE WE ARE NOW, STILL SMILING.*

MPHO

My name is Mpho and I was born in a small village in Lesotho. I am the youngest of four siblings. My childhood was filled with the joys and challenges of small community life, not too far from the city. I pursued my education diligently, starting with a degree in Development Studies and History from the National University of Lesotho. I advanced my studies in South Africa, where I completed the Master in Town and Regional Planning at the University of Natal, now University of KwaZulu-Natal.

During my high school years, I met the love of my life. We grew up together, our paths intertwining from a young age. We supported each other through the ups and downs of teenage life and beyond. He was with me throughout my studies. When I was 21, we married and were blessed with two wonderful children: a son, now 24, and a daughter, 17.

My husband came from an affluent family, while I hailed from humble beginnings. When you move from one social class to another, there can be a sense of ownership and control from those who feel they helped you rise. This

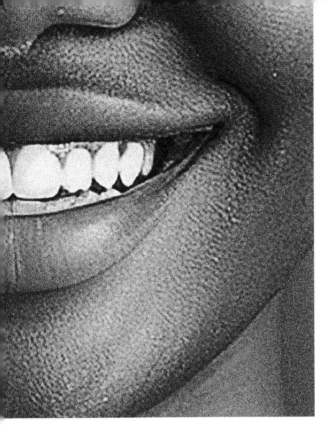

creates a dynamic where your achievements are seen as favours granted to you rather than the result of your own hard work and merit.

In time, tensions arose. My desire to be an independent, educated woman clashed with traditional expectations. Most affluent families prefer women to either assist in the family business or enjoy their social status, without pursuing their own careers. I aspired to break those norms. I wanted to be a provider and a role model for my children. I remained steadfast in my goals. I had to resist the pressure to make me into a dependent wife.

This created a lot of tension and conflict with my husband. I endured significant abuse from him, physical and emotional, and he was frequently promiscuous. In our culture, there is a belief that all men cheat and that you cannot find one who does not. I refused to accept that.

Gender-based violence and abuse are taboo subjects in our culture. Although laws exist to encourage speaking up, it is not acceptable to discuss these topics openly. If you do speak up, you are seen as disgracing your family, or people will ask you, "What did you do to provoke it? There must be a reason why it's happening." These dynamics take a mental toll. It is as if you slowly die inside.

Eventually, I became very ill. I developed several illnesses that may well be due to my abusive situation. I am not saying the abuse directly caused these, but the stress certainly contributed. Now, I live with three chronic illnesses: hypothyroidism, fibromyalgia and chronic migraines. The last could be linked to the constant bashings my head suffered, during which my husband would say, "I want to finish off this sick head" or words to that effect. I also have three herniated discs, which I sustained during one of these episodes. On one occasion, I was violently pushed and my mouth hit something hard. As a result, I have a crown on one of my front teeth. When asked how it happened, I told the dentist, "I don't know. It just broke."

I was physically unwell and constantly sick. It was then that I was diagnosed with hypothyroidism, which I learned can be triggered by high levels of stress. This condition affects the entire immune system and, combined with my spinal injury, forced me to leave my lecturing position. This created a dependency I did not want, which only added to my stress. Eventually, I reached a point where I became suicidal, which led to my decision in March 2019 to seek a divorce. Ultimately, I realised that the abuse did not just impact me, it was affecting my children. That was the wake-up call I needed.

My decision came as a shock to many. There was the belief that certain classes of people do not get divorced. There were also concerns about how I would survive. I was repeatedly asked, "What are you going to do, now that you're not working?" There were a lot of issues to contend with, but I knew it was the right decision.

My spouse refused to agree to a divorce, citing reasons that included claims of love and a desire to work things out. That was not entirely true. There was also a lot at stake – finances, assets and the estate. However, I suspect my husband's main motivation was to maintain control. He and his family, and society as a whole, believed that I did not deserve anything. "She comes from that side, you know! We made her. She came to us with nothing!" They saw me as being from a lesser background, forgetting that I was educated and, for most of my marriage, a contributing partner to our finances.

One fateful Thursday evening, I was getting ready for bed. I remember it clearly. It was just after I had turned off the TV and tidied up the living room. As I was telling my daughter it was time for bed, an SMS popped up on my phone. The message told me to get away from this place, that I was treading on dangerous ground and that I needed to protect myself, because my death was imminent.

I'm thinking, Is this a joke? It seemed too serious to be a prank, but it was hard to tell. So I decided to call the person back. My phone displayed the caller ID, a male, so when he answered, I called him by name. I think this surprised him because he did not expect me to know who he was. The conversation was not at all pleasant. By his voice, I guessed he was in his mid-twenties or early thirties. He was extremely agitated, cursing and making comments like, "Now I understand why you need to die!" and "You think you're so smart!"

He continued like this for a while and I finally told him, "You know what? I'm going to report this to the police."

That only made him angrier, like he could have killed me with his hands if he was in the room with me. "That would be the biggest mistake of your life!" he said. Then he hung up.

I was left thinking, what's happening? Is this a joke? Is this real? The next morning, I was still trying to make sense of it. I called my aunt and told her what had happened. At that time, there was a high-profile case in the media, where a similar threat had been made and the person involved lost her life. The incident happened close to where I lived and I knew the victim personally. My aunt reminded me of this case and urged me not to take the threat lightly, "You need to go to the police."

Unfortunately, the police did not take the threat seriously either. They told me, "If someone really wanted to harm you, they wouldn't call you and use their normal phone." I mentioned the case of the woman who had been murdered, hoping it would underscore the seriousness of my situation. The officer relented and said he would call this person and ask him to report to the station. He made the call while I was there, using the contact information I provided. He put the conversation on loudspeaker.

After being told to report to the station on Monday morning at 9 am, the guy replied, "No, I won't be available. I'm working out of town."

"If you don't show up, we'll know where to find you."

"All right. I'll see if I can make it and call you back."

The conversation was surprisingly polite. After hanging up, the officer assured me that the man would not bother me again, because he now knew I had reported him.

However, from the moment I left the station, I started receiving threatening messages non-stop. They were even more terrifying than before. "So, you actually went ahead? I'm going to kill you. But before I kill you, I'm going to rape you, and they'll never find your body." He went on to say, "I know where you live. I know your kids and I know your every move."

It felt as if this person really did know me. For instance, he mentioned how I drove my domestic worker home at odd hours, indicating he had specific knowledge about my life. I called the police to report what was happening, but they told me to come back on Monday for further action. I also reached out to my aunt, who advised me to stay home and not venture out until then, because the caller seemed unhinged. I followed her advice to cancel all my weekend plans and switch off my phones.

On Monday, I went to the police at 9 am, but this time I was not alone. My aunt, my cousins and I all went together However, the caller did not show up and had turned off his phone.

My aunt, who is an activist with connections in the police, due to her work with prisons and giving motivational talks, decided to take the situation further. She reached out to one of her police contacts, who advised us to go to police headquarters in the city centre. There, we spoke with several high-ranking officials. They too were concerned and reassured us that we had done the right thing. After taking the caller's details and promising to investigate, they asked if there was somewhere safe I could stay. However, I insisted on going home. I felt safest there and decided to stay put as advised.

I reached out to a friend who works with the national identification service. Using the caller's details that I had, he managed to obtain a picture of him. Sometimes, the people involved in violence and crime look completely unassuming. Unfortunately, this person looked just as menacing as the things he had been saying.

The following Thursday morning, I was awoken by a call from police headquarters. They informed me that they had located the caller, using the phone network and towers, and it turned out he was in my locality. He was wanted on multiple criminal charges and was connected to a dangerous organisation who were involved in numerous murders and violent incidents across the country. What's more, he appeared to have vanished. Given that we had contacted the police the previous Friday, he could have already fled the country or he might have simply changed location. Being part of a larger network, even if he had moved on, his task might have been assigned to someone else. It was also possible that he had been merely carrying out orders to intimidate me, but now saw me as a target, because I had exposed him. This made the situation even more precarious and personal, as I was navigating a complex and potentially dangerous network.

There was no concrete evidence linking my husband or his family to the phone calls, although they had the motive. From local knowledge, it could have been anyone, even some woman who would view my wealthy husband as a prize. Whoever was behind the threats, it had become increasingly clear that I was in grave danger and possibly also my children. Consequently, I decided I had no choice but to leave the country. It was incredible and overwhelming. I was lost, scared, worried, in denial and feeling broken, a mix of emotions that is hard to put into words.

I was out of the country by the following Tuesday. So, in less than a week, I'd had to make life-changing decisions. Packing everything up in such a short time is incredibly difficult when you are trying not to alarm people. As I did not know if it was my husband trying to hurt me or someone else, I could not tell anyone. The only people who knew what I was going through were the ones helping me to leave. None of the people around me had any idea.

Trust was scarce. My family were worried about me after learning everything, but they did not know I was planning to leave. They were calling me and visiting the house, trying to reach out, and I was doing my best to talk to them normally, while knowing I was leaving. I looked into their eyes, especially my son's, and I could not bring myself to tell them the truth.

It's an indescribable feeling, a whirlwind of emotions hitting you all at once, with no time to process. You have no idea where you're going or what to expect. The fear of possibly never returning home looms over you and you wonder how you could possibly leave everything behind. I didn't even know whether my escape would succeed. But I didn't want to die. Everyone is terrified of these people who kill indiscriminately. No one wants to be a part of that.

Over and above all of this, however, was what to do about my children. My son was almost 19, close to being an adult. He was already living his own life and had some independence. However, my daughter was only 12 and still dependent on me for everything. I couldn't possibly leave her. I'm the kind of mother who is always present and involved. Not being there for her was unthinkable. She and I are extremely close. She says I'm her best friend and I remind her, "No, I'm your mother." But she insists, "You're my mother and my best friend." Both my children were like that, but as my son grew older, he started to build his own life. As for my daughter, I knew I'd rather die there than leave her behind.

Organising the paperwork to leave was incredibly challenging. One of the people who helped to plan my exit had been exiled due to political issues back home. They had family in Ireland and one of their relatives had studied and married there. That's how Ireland became part of my plan. Since Ireland is an English-speaking country, it seemed like a viable option. I have heard stories of people being sent back from Ireland, which added to the uncertainty. However, when you're in a crisis and have such a short window of time, you're just searching for any place that offers safety.

The only person in my family who knew I was leaving was my dad. He was about to turn 80 and was already very ill. He had worked in an asbestos mine as a young man, which led to several cases of tuberculosis and ultimately destroyed his lungs. He was relying on oxygen to get by, so it was clear he was not going to be with us for much longer. I could not live with the thought of him finding out about my disappearance after I was already gone, so I needed to prepare him for that reality.

I made the tough decision to see him on the Monday, just a few hours before I left, and I told him everything. He already knew about my failing relationship and the abuse. When I told him about the threats and my decision to leave, he cried like a baby. Then, he held my hands and said, "You know what?" He called me by my clan name, which is like a totem name in my culture. In most southern African countries, families are associated with totems. When people are talking about serious matters, they usually use those names.

He looked at me. "Go with God. If I die, we will never meet again, but don't risk coming back. Don't feel bad, because whether you're here or not, I'll still be dead. Nothing will change."

I then went home to organise my departure. Leaving was very difficult, as it had to be kept a secret, even from my children. I packed my bags and said to my daughter, "Do you want to go on a holiday with me?" As it was close to my 40th, I explained, "It's a girls' getaway … for my birthday. Do you want to come along?"

"Where are we going?" she asked.

"It's a surprise."

"Okay. I love surprises."

Being young, she didn't care much about the destination. She just asked, "Is there a beach or a pool where we're going?" I said yes. She then took out her swimwear, sunscreen, a cap, sunglasses and swimming goggles. She neatly packed everything in her backpack and said, "Okay, I'm set. As long as there's a pool or a beach there, I'm Gucci!"

"Don't tell anyone," I warned. "It's a secret. If you tell anyone, you might not be able to go."

The next morning, she went to school as usual and I was to pick her up later. The hardest part was having to leave my son, without letting him know we were going. To complicate the situation, he woke up with tonsillitis. Usually, he never missed school, but that day he came to my bedroom and said, "Mom, I feel really sick. I'm not going to school."

My housekeeper, who had been with us for 20 years, turned up to the house to start her workday. She was more like family than an employee. When she arrived, I was going through my closet.

"Would you like some shoes, like sneakers and flats?" I asked, as she was the same size as me.

"Yeah," she said.

"Take whatever you want."

"Why?" she asked, puzzled.

"I'm spring cleaning. I need to buy new shoes." I went to the closet and looked at my jackets. "Do you want any of these?"

I used to give her clothes sometimes, but not like this. She sensed something was off.

"What's happening?" she asked.

"Nothing," I lied. "I'm just buying new clothes and need to create some space."

I packed a 23-kilogramme suitcase for myself and another for my daughter, but I left plenty behind. God willing, I will sell the rest someday if I ever have access to them again, and donate the money to a worthy cause.

Despite the chaos and the knowledge that everything was about to change, I managed to keep up the pretence that everything was normal. When it was time for me to leave, I asked my brother to drive me and my daughter to the border gate. When he asked why, I said, "I'm meeting some friends for my 40th." As he knew my birthday was coming up on Thursday, he agreed.

During the drive, I was struggling to hold back tears. My brother must have wondered why I was crying on my birthday trip. It was such an odd, sad feeling. At the border gate, I hugged him and said, "See you later."

"Okay, sister. Call me when you come back and I'll pick you up."

Those helping me had arranged for transportation to Johannesburg, from where we would fly to Ireland via Dubai. However, the journey was not without hassle. In Dubai, my daughter and I were stopped as we tried to board. We were held back until the last call for the plane. They were not rude to us or outright mean, but they appeared to be looking for reasons to delay us.

They asked questions about my travel, such as, "If you're going on holiday, why aren't you travelling with the rest of your family? Why just this one?" It felt like they were unnecessarily probing into our family setup. I sensed racism was behind it, as we were the only black passengers going in business class.

When we ultimately landed at Dublin Airport, I sought asylum. There were a lot of things to address. The staff wrote down an address and told us to go there. While at the airport, I decided it was time to tell my daughter that this was not a birthday trip and that we were not going back home. Her response was surprisingly upbeat. She asked if there was a beach here and I told her yes.

"Is there crime here?" she asked.

"I don't think so."

She seemed reassured. "Oh, in that case, I'm fine." Her excitement about the new adventure was palpable, which was a small comfort amid the chaos.

At the International Protection Office, the first person we met was arrogant and rude. The man looked at me and said, "You don't look like someone seeking asylum. You look very fresh." I couldn't help but wonder, what was I supposed to look like? He started asking me questions, making assumptions. "What are you doing here? Taking some chances, aren't you?" He kept going on and on and I just looked at him without responding. Because of my silence, he must have thought I didn't understand English. "There are so many countries in the world," he mumbled, "and you're coming here to ruin ours." He then called out to a colleague, "She can't even speak English," he told her. "I don't know how we can help."

All the while, my daughter was watching this, confused about why I wasn't talking. The man's colleague, a kind lady, then came over and greeted us.

"Hi," I responded.

Surprised, the rude man said, "You can speak?"

I ignored him and spoke with the woman instead. She was nice and understanding. We went through our first interview and spent the whole day there. I tried to use my bank card, but it didn't work. We were starving and I had no cash to buy food. Later, we were given the address for the Ballsbridge Hotel. The nice lady told us which stop to go to and the bus number. When we boarded the bus, I told the driver I didn't have any cash. He let us on and asked where we were going.

When we arrived at the hotel, dinner was almost over. It usually started around five and ended by seven. It was almost seven by the time we got there, so there was not much food left. At the time, the hotel was still fully operational, offering a restaurant, bar and accommodation, all open to the public. Asylum seekers were housed on the first three floors. I explained our situation to the restaurant staff, saying, "I'm not sure if my card will work, but we're hungry and need to eat. Can I tap it first to see if it will go through?"

Instead of helping, he came back with another person, who told us we weren't allowed in the restaurant. I was shocked. "We're not allowed in here?"

"No, your people eat somewhere else," they said, dismissing us.

"But we're going to pay," I insisted.

"No, you're not allowed to be in here," they repeated.

Defeated, we left and went back to where "our people" were supposed to eat. There was hardly any food left, just scraps, but we had no choice.

When we first arrived, a kind girl had showed us to our room. She was from Zimbabwe and became our main contact, helping us to navigate the place. The next day, she guided us through what we needed to do, offering a glimmer of hope in an otherwise difficult situation. She showed us how to get our PPS numbers, find a school and navigate the new system. Her support was a beacon of hope in an overwhelming situation. Sadly, I have since lost contact with her.

———————————

I arrived in Ireland on 21 August and the very next day was my birthday. That morning, my son called to wish me a happy birthday. As we chatted, he asked when I would be coming home. I paused for a moment, before telling him that I wasn't coming back. There was a silence on the other end of the line and then he hung up, confused. Although that moment was difficult, we have managed to remain a part of each other's lives.

Two weeks later, my dad died. It was a Saturday morning when I got the call. I broke down and cried, the weight of grief crashing over me. My daughter woke up, alarmed. "Mommy, why are you crying?" she asked, her eyes wide with worry.

I told her the news and she started crying too. I had to pull myself together to console her, putting her needs above my pain. From that day on, I was never able to truly mourn my dad. I couldn't allow myself to break down in front of my daughter. I had to be strong for her, so I buried my grief and pretended to be okay.

I was still struggling with being an asylum seeker, experiencing a level of degradation and judgement I had never faced before. In the hotel, I was often treated poorly, denied access to certain areas and looked down on. On top of my father's death, it was like a double dose of grief.

When I shared the news with my family that I was in Ireland, they were terrified for me. They worried about my safety, fearing that I might be abused or face other dangers, the sort of stories you hear about asylum seekers. When confronted with their fears and anxieties, I had to stay strong. I didn't let myself cry whenever they called. They had to see that I was okay, or at least that I was trying to be.

Going from a life with dreams and stability to this uncertainty was overwhelming. The stories I had heard about asylum seekers, people going mad, never getting their papers, or even dying, added to my fears. Sometimes, I wondered if staying home would have been better, despite the danger. At the hotel, almost everyone had someone they could relate to. They either spoke the same language or came from similar backgrounds, providing some sense of solidarity and shared experience amid the hardship. As there was no one from my country, I had no one to talk to, other than my daughter.

When I said I was from Lesotho, people often asked, "Where's that?" An Intreo worker, who had been in the field for 20 years, told me, "I've never heard of anyone from Lesotho before." It was disheartening to hear how little was known about my country or the struggles we face. This makes it hard when applying for asylum here.

On the morning I received the news about my dad, I didn't go for breakfast. I was too overwhelmed with grief. By lunchtime, I was starving and so was my daughter. We needed to go downstairs for food. As soon as we stepped into the lift, a woman greeted me with a simple "How are you?" That triggered something and I suddenly broke down. She asked if I was all right. "My dad just died," I told her. She was sympathetic and asked if there was someone she could call for me. I explained that I didn't know anyone here. She was genuinely concerned and kept saying, "I am so sorry."

When we reached the dining hall, I realised I couldn't eat, because I was still crying. I went to the bathroom, washed my face and then returned to my room. Later, the same woman came to my room, though I'm not sure how she found it. She introduced me to a group called Movement of Asylum Seekers in Ireland (MASI). Although she was not a member herself, she thought they might be of help. She mentioned that they support people in distress and offered to put me in touch with them. This nice lady's name was Agnes and she and her family have become my closest friends to this day.

She left and soon after, there was a knock on my door. Someone on the phone wanted to speak to me. It was Lucky Khambule, the co-founder of MASI. He introduced himself and expressed his condolences. He wanted to extend his respects and offer support, which was a hugely comforting gesture during such a painful time, especially coming from a stranger.

The previous day, a Friday, my daughter and I had gone into town to buy her schoolbooks, as she was starting school on the following Monday. We took photos of her with her new books, trying to focus on something positive. Little did I know, my daughter had posted a WhatsApp status with a picture showing a Dublin bus, with its logo visible. This seemingly small gesture ended up revealing our location. Her dad saw the status and learned that we were in Ireland.

This news quickly reached his sister. At the time, she was a diplomat, and her family had been posted to Ireland a few months earlier, although I had no idea they were there until our location had been revealed. On the Monday, she sent me an urgent text message, filled with concern.

"Hello, my sister. Where are you? Are you in Dublin?" she asked.

I was surprised and shocked that she knew. "Yes, I'm in Dublin," I replied. "Why?"

"I need to see you. Now."

I was trying to figure out how they had found me and, in my confusion, I forgot to be discreet about my whereabouts. I sent her my location, and she replied, "You're just ten minutes away from me. I'm on my way."

This is how I learned about the photo that had given our location away. When she arrived, she was eager to know what was happening, but I brushed off her questions with a laugh, trying to lighten the mood. In the beginning, she offered me a place to stay, but I refused to leave direct provision, because I was uncertain about how it would impact my case. Although I had known her for 19 years, I did not know who I could trust. I began to open up, realising she truly meant well. She became a friend, a supporter and everything I needed. She and her family have since left Ireland. Although we don't share blood, she has remained loyal to me to this day, despite our family separation.

A few days later, I met Lucky in person for the first time. From that day forward, Lucky has been a constant presence in my life. He would regularly check up on me, especially since I suffered from chronic migraines. He would often bring me medicine and offer support. He became my "next of kin" in Ireland, offering a sense of connection in a strange land.

I've since started writing a book titled *Next of Kin*, reflecting on my experiences, although it's still a work in progress. Writing has been my outlet, and I also keep a blog and contribute to newspapers and magazines back home.

I was added to the MASI WhatsApp group. One day, Lucky posted a message inviting residents to the launch of MASI's first journal. I was determined to go, as I felt a deep sense of indebtedness to him. It was not only a welcome chance to eat something different, but to show my appreciation and be part of something meaningful. When I went, I was immediately hooked. The experience was transformative and I found myself drawn into the MASI community.

Since then, I have been an active MASI member. In a way, I believe my dad's passing led me to this newfound family. At the time, I felt incredibly alone and overwhelmed by sadness and grief, to the point where dying seemed like an easier option. But through Lucky and MASI, I found a sense of belonging and support that I desperately needed.

The emotions I had experienced since coming to Ireland had been overwhelming. For the first time in my life, I was made to feel worthless. The way people spoke to me and looked at me, it was as if I didn't matter. I remember walking down a corridor and being asked if I was selling sex or if I wanted drugs, something I had never encountered before. This was also the first time I could not afford the things I wanted or the food I preferred to eat. My daughter, who had come from a wealthy background, was experiencing poverty for the first time. I was grappling with the reality of sending her to a public school, when she had always gone to private schools. I came to learn, however, that the national schools here are very good.

I kept asking myself, what did I do to deserve this? It felt like the universe was conspiring against me. On top of everything, my father was dead and I didn't know if I would ever see my son again. The weight of it all was crushing – it was deep, it was heavy, it was incredibly hard, but here we are now, still smiling.

After meeting Lucky and engaging with MASI, my enthusiasm must have been evident. He noticed my eagerness to learn and explore and we started discussing my background. He advised me to empower myself by going back to school and staying busy. There was an open day at An Cosán Virtual Community College and I decided to attend. I made it my mission to stay active and engaged, rather than succumb to depression. I told myself that when my daughter went out the door to school, I would use that time to explore and network.

At the open day, I attended a session given by a woman who worked as the manager of a lifelong learning team. Being my inquisitive self, I asked many questions and we talked after the session. I mentioned that I was in direct provision, not realising that people often kept that information private. She gave me her business card and when I returned to the hotel, I sent her a thank-you email.

Her response was warm and inviting. She asked if I would like to meet for coffee sometime. I eagerly agreed. I brought my CV to our meeting as requested. She reviewed it and pointed out I needed to streamline it more, to suit the Irish market. She told me about unaccredited courses she was running and I decided to make the most of this opportunity by taking some of them.

However, just as I was getting started on my studies, Covid hit and I was moved to Mosney Accommodation Centre in Co. Meath. I called the lady from the open day to let her know my situation. She understood and, despite the challenges, she supported me. Knowing that my internet access was poor, she arranged for a device to boost my connectivity. With this new equipment, I was able to continue my classes online from Mosney.

Before the pandemic, I had applied to study property management at Ballsbridge College of Further Education, as it aligned with my town planning experience, and my application was accepted. I managed to juggle this with my other courses at An Cosán. I would set up my phone and laptop side by side, simultaneously attending all classes. It was intense, but I managed to graduate at the top of my class in property management.

During the Covid lockdown, things were tough. My daughter and I used the internet for our studies. She was doing her schoolwork online and I was trying to keep up with my own classes. She had an iPad for her lessons, thanks to her school, and when we moved to Mosney, the centre provided her with a desk and chair for studying in her bedroom. I asked for one for myself too, so we each had our own space to study. She'd be in her room doing her work and I'd be in mine. We made the most of our limited resources during those challenging times.

When it came time to advance to Level 6 of property management, which required a two-year internship, I faced a new challenge. I was the only student who struggled to secure a placement. I was called for interviews, but the opportunities seemed to dry up once the interviewers saw my race/face. Despite having the relevant background, extensive experience and passing well in Level 5, I failed to secure an offer.

The final blow came from an interview that was particularly disheartening. I made sure to present myself well – full makeup, professional attire. As the interview commenced, they never asked me a single question about my work experience. Instead, they grilled me about my personal life and my reasons for being in Ireland. I was vague in my responses, not wanting to divulge too much, but also trying not to be rude.

Almost 40 minutes into this interrogation, the interviewer finally said, "Okay, I'm very sorry, but you are not what we are looking for." He then added, "It was lovely meeting you," which felt utterly insincere. Then he asked if I had any questions.

"Yes," I said. "What exactly are you looking for?"

"Why would you ask me that?" he asked, bewildered.

"You just told me I'm not what you're looking for. So, I'm trying to understand. You didn't ask me anything about my skills. If I were an employer looking at a CV like mine, I'd be impressed. I'm mature, with over 15 years of experience in town planning. I graduated at the top of my class and hold qualifications in grant proposal writing and community development, to name a few. If I were hiring for an internship and saw this CV, I'd hire the person to maximise on their skillset. But you have just said I am not what you are looking for. I hope that getting clarity on where I fell short will help me with my future interviews. Hence my question."

The interviewer said he was not going to answer that, so I simply thanked them and left. However, I decided I was done with this search for an internship and I was done with property management. I had been humiliated enough. This was my fifteenth interview and I was exhausted.

At the time, I was also involved in various activities, including volunteering. During Covid, an international human rights organisation reached out to me after they saw me speak at an event. They invited me to work with an activist group on a project called "End Direct Provision". I collaborated with brilliant minds on various campaigns with this group and it was an inspiring and productive experience. However, when I was about to go for my next asylum interview, I requested a reference letter from the human rights organisation to confirm my volunteer work. They refused, citing that they did not wish to influence the decision, even though I clarified that I was asking only to confirm my volunteer status, not advocate for my case.

The situation became even more frustrating when it was later revealed that an Irish colleague from the group, who had made the same request, received their letter without issue the same day. It strongly appeared that I was being discriminated against by a human rights organisation, on a platform set up to advocate for international protection applicants' rights. The world is full of surprises!

It is worth noting that after the activists I worked with learned about the rejection, they brought pressure to bear on the organisation and I was finally given the reference letter. Due to this incident and my frustration with the internship interview mentioned earlier, I decided that I wanted to work in a space with like-minded people and serve those facing similar challenges in the future. During an internet search, I came across a master's programme in Refugee Integration at Dublin City University and I immediately applied. Thanks to the support from MASI, I was able to pursue this new path.

As I neared the end of the programme, the woman I met at the open day at An Cosán sent me an email about a job opening that seemed like a perfect fit for my skills. So, I applied. Before sending the cover letter, I asked if she could review it. With her feedback, I submitted my application and, as they say, the rest is history!

To conclude my story, I always leave people with this question: If you were forced to flee your home or country, how would you wish to be treated by your hosts?

I was once a guest speaker representing MASI in Trinity College Dublin, at an event discussing direct provision. When concluding my talk, I posed that question as food for thought for the attendees to take away with them. However, a young man in the audience responded by saying that "we" (people from the first world) are unlikely to face wars or be forced to flee, because such occurrences mainly happen in "third world" countries. He attributed that to lack of order, corruption, poor service delivery and poverty.

The following year, in February 2022, just after war broke out in Ukraine, I was invited back to Trinity as a MASI member. This time I was there to talk about the formation of social movements, which also happened to be the focus of my thesis at Dublin City University. When I entered the classroom and introduced myself, one of the students recognised me. He was that same young man.

"I know you from a talk you gave last year," he said. "When I saw you walk in today, everything you said came back to me. I'm sorry for what I said then. Now I understand better." It turned out that he was a Ukrainian living in Ireland. I reassured him that he didn't need to apologise. I encouraged him to use this experience as a learning opportunity. Regardless of our circumstances, we can never predict what the future holds.

The key is to maintain humanity and respect in our interactions, hoping that if circumstances change for anyone in the future, they will be treated with the same respect and dignity.

In my current job, which I love, the support I receive is immense and I do not feel singled out as the only black person in the office. Despite the long commute – nearly six hours each day on public transport – I feel valued and respected. I worry about whether I would find the same supportive environment if I were to switch jobs. For now, I am grateful for the flexibility and understanding I receive in my current role, which allows me to balance my professional and personal life effectively.

Reflecting on my own experience, I note that Ireland was once a poor country, with many forced to emigrate, yet in Ireland today, there is much anti-immigrant feeling. Imagine if Ireland today faced a crisis that forced its residents to flee, how would they want to be treated by others? This perspective is crucial as it fosters empathy and reminds us that anyone could find themselves in a vulnerable situation. This reflection is a powerful reminder of the importance of compassion and understanding in addressing the needs of those seeking safety and protection.

More about
Lesotho:

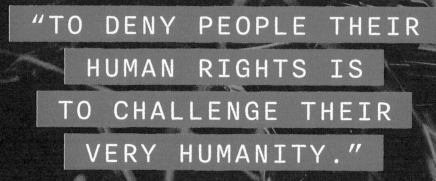

"TO DENY PEOPLE THEIR
HUMAN RIGHTS IS
TO CHALLENGE THEIR
VERY HUMANITY."

NELSON MANDELA

Berhane was born and raised in Eritrea. He is a former journalist, who came to Ireland in 2002 to escape media persecution by the Eritrean government. In Ireland, he obtained a degree in Science and Pharmaceutical Healthcare and a diploma in Pharmaceutical Technology, and he now works in the industry. He is a proud husband and father to five children.

> *IN ERITREA, I HAD A GOOD JOB AND I WAS RESPECTED. I DIDN'T COME HERE FOR MONEY. I CAME HERE TO BE SAFE AND TO LIVE IN PEACE.*

BERHANE

Eritrea is a small country that only became independent in 1991. We were under Ethiopian rule for over 30 years. We fought for independence through an armed struggle from 1961 to 1991. Before that, we were under British administration for 10 years, and before that it was an Italian colony for 60 years. When we became independent, nobody expected anything to go wrong, but our leader quickly became a dictator. That meant we fought another war after independence.

My dad was killed during the Ethiopian civil war, when I was still young. So I grew up with a single mother and my brother. We lived in Asmara, the capital of Eritrea, a beautiful city with a lot of Italian architecture. Many of its buildings are under UNESCO heritage protection. Life was always associated with war. Growing up, you see a lot of things, but after independence, we thought that after so much loss of life, we would finally have a peaceful country. From 1992 to 1996, we were so hopeful. The country was picking up and the whole world wanted the best for Eritrea, but it didn't work out like that.

My life was good and I had a good job working in television. When I was young, I always loved to watch TV, sometimes all night. While I was studying journalism at university, a new television station was being set up in the city and they were looking for staff. They approached our college and invited us to apply. I attended an interview and got the job! That was in 1992. I worked for the national broadcaster, Eritrea TV. My face was always on television, so I was really well known, mainly as a sports broadcaster.

However, during the war, I was on the frontlines like everybody else. Young people, men and women, have no choice; they must join the army. For two years, I had to serve at the front lines. If you watch war movies, it's just like that. Everybody is in the trenches. Life was tough, but I was lucky, because they eventually set up a media group for the frontlines. I was about 26 at the time. You get used to bullets flying around and you grow immune to it. War is something that you wouldn't even wish on your enemies. Our country created wars with the nations around us to deflect from what was going on with the government.

My brother was also on the frontline and it was very hard for my mother. After a while, my brother deserted the army and went home to work. They caught him and put him in prison for three years. This kind of thing is normal. When I reflect on it, I wonder how we survived. I remember the moment I realised I had to get out. A colleague of mine, an ex-fighter who had lost a leg in in the war, didn't agree with something the minister said and they put him in jail. A colleague and I went to visit him and when we were there, we found the jail to be full of journalists, most of whom I knew. I was unsure whether to say hello to them or stay quiet. If I said hello, what would the guards do? I didn't know what to say, so I said nothing. My colleagues just looked at me. There was about 18 of them and they were never seen again.

It was clear that journalists were being purposely targeted. First, they started shutting down the newspapers and in the months that followed, they started to shut down all the private media. Fortunately, I had managed to avoid any direct confrontation. I was also able to travel because of my job, being one of very few people allowed to leave Eritrea for work reasons. I eventually told my mam and grandmother that if a situation arose where I could leave the country again, I might not be back. It was certainly not an easy decision to make, especially as I was married by then and my wife was pregnant. Soon, the opportunity did arise. In March 2002, there was an athletics competition in Dublin, the World Cross Country Championships. There were journalists covering the event from all over the world and I was sent there on a job assignment. I had a visa to stay for two weeks, but I had no intention of going back.

The first night I stayed in Ireland, in Gardiner Street, I hardly had any money, only about 100 euros. Back then there was a reception centre on St Margaret's Road in Finglas. I went there and applied for asylum. They interviewed me and I filled out all my documents. They sent me to a direct provision centre in Galway, where I lived for about six or seven months. I really enjoyed Galway. It was a confusing time, but it was okay. I was with people who were in the same situation as me. However, when you have a family at home, you must provide for them. When I was in Galway awaiting my refugee status, I got a job for a week at the Galway Festival and I also worked as a kitchen porter. It was so difficult to go from being a journalist to doing these jobs, because I wasn't used to it. I went from everybody knowing me to knowing nobody.

I was able to buy a mobile phone with some money a friend of mine and my sister-in-law sent me. It was the only means I had for people to reach me. I didn't even have an address yet. Because I came here legally, I had no issues with my application and I had explained my situation clearly. They gave me refugee status and I was able to restart my life. I was lucky that it only took about six months. Some people are left in direct provision for years.

Galway was really beautiful but it was hard at that time to get a job, so I decided to go back to Dublin. One person I was staying with in Galway had friends in Dublin, who were looking for a roommate, so I moved to a house in Mulhuddart. I remember the night when I fully realised I was never going home. I was in bed and, out of nowhere, I just cried and cried and cried, alone in my bed. Can you imagine? I was a grown man, 30 years old and all those emotions came out of nowhere. After that, I said, "That's it!" I accepted that things had changed and I started my life from there.

It was really difficult and often lonely. I got a job in a company called National Linen. The people I lived with worked there too, so if we were working the same hours, I got a lift with them. Other times I would catch the bus into town and then a bus to Bluebell. I would get up at 5.30 am to make my way there. National Linen is where I met Noeleen, my best friend. She got me a room to rent that was only a 15-minute walk from work, so I didn't have to make the long journeys. I then ended up in an apartment in Rathmines.

When I didn't return home from Ireland, it was all over the news in Eritrea. Everyone knew I had fled the country. I can't imagine how my mam or wife were feeling. My mam was living in government housing and they kicked her out because of it. She lived in fear for a very long time, because the government often came after family members of people who fled.

My wife and I had met on a night out through a mutual friend. I was married only six months when I left and she was pregnant at the time. I came to Ireland in March 2002 and my son was born in July. I would go to internet cafes to call her, because we had no video calls back then. People were afraid to talk to me at home, because the government listens to what is said. The internet is limited and there is only one telecommunication network controlled by the government. My wife was living with her mam after I left. I had applied for family reunification in Ireland and it was approved. However, as she was the wife of someone who had fled the country, they would not let her leave Eritrea. Eventually, she had to smuggle herself and our child out of the country and into Sudan. This happened in 2005.

The day she decided to leave, I couldn't sleep at all. A lot of people are shot and killed crossing the border or jailed for who knows how many years. Even when they make it past the border, people can die of dehydration and are eaten by hyenas. She had to walk three days and three nights through the desert with a child on her back. During the day, she hid from the army by crouching under bushes, and move during the night. It was such a brave thing to do.

Once they arrived in Sudan, I had all the paperwork completed for her to come here, so she was able to fly straight from Sudan to Ireland. We were back together after three years apart! Seeing my son for the first time was unreal. Unbelievable! You don't think these things will ever happen and somehow it did. Three years was a long time but a lot of people are in this situation; they marry and become separated. We were lucky really, and I have my family.

The apartment in Rathmines was very nice, but also expensive. We lived in Rathmines briefly and then my friend Noeleen said, "Why don't you get a flat in Dolphin House?" I had no idea what Dolphin House was, but Noeleen had grown up there. Her sister Carol still lived there and was on the housing committee and they both spoke to the manager. I was asked to apply to Dublin City Council and we got a flat. We were the only foreign people there, but personally, it didn't feel like it, because Noeleen's sisters, Tara, Linda, Carol and Barbara, looked out for us. They were our community and family. It was difficult at times, but we were okay.

It was tough for my wife when she got here, because everything was different. We didn't have an Eritrean community here and she barely spoke English. I had no problem, because I had travelled and could speak English fluently. We had learned English in school, but she never spoke it, so it was a new language for her. That can be very isolating. I would be out working among people and she would be at home alone with the baby.

After a few years of having my wife and child here, I went back to college and retrained. I did a degree in Science and Pharmaceutical Healthcare at the Technological University Dublin and then I did a diploma in Pharmaceutical Technology. I work at Baxtor Healthcare now, where I've been for nine years. We make chemotherapy drugs, antibiotics and penicillin.

I gradually forgot my old life, but I have been contributing online to Eritrean websites. I was trying to create motivation for people to come together and solve problems at home, because in Eritrea, people have no voice; they are silenced. There is only one radio station and one television station and they belong to the government. Other than about 15 minutes of news a day, it is total darkness in terms of information. Everyone's mind is under complete control via government propaganda.

Personally, my experience in Ireland has been all good and all positive. I didn't see the hardship that my wife did before she left the country. Our life here is better. Irish people are so nice. They know charity, they know struggle, they know starvation and they know their history very well. They understand and they try to help. There is no country in the world as charitable as the Irish.

My brother made it out of jail, got to Ethiopia and is now living in San Diego. It cost about three and a half thousand euros to be smuggled out. He is trying to get my mam to America. At least we have video calls now and I call her every week. She is much better and is out of Eritrea now, but still lives in fear.

If I were ever to go back to Eritrea, they would shoot me and I'd never be seen again. There is no court, no judge. It's hard to explain the situation to people who are used to normalcy. Eritrea is a very old culture, we once had plenty of rights – rights for women, rights for land, a very communal and advanced society. The civilisation of Eritrea was similar to ancient Greece or Egypt and there is a lot of important archaeology there. The people now in control have no heart and no connection with their culture, history or society. They are destroying the social fabric – the culture, community, respect for the elderly, respect for women. I'm not sure what type of society they are trying to build. People are fleeing and many end up perishing in the Mediterranean.

Change is inevitable. The president of 33 years is now in his 80s and cannot remain in power for much longer. However, I cannot see anyone worse than him coming to power. I do not know how or when, but change will come. I miss my country, but I am used to it now. For my kids, Ireland is their home.

We moved out of Dolphin House after about five years and we continued to grow our family. We now have five children. We all have each other, so my children will at least feel like they have family here. My eldest son trades online. My daughter just turned 18 and she is going into her second year in Dublin City University, studying chemical science. My other three children are still in school. My wife works in home care now and her English is really good. She looks after people and they love her. She went on holidays recently and everyone was asking when she would be back. There are so many elderly people trapped at home all day with no family and my wife is sometimes the only person they will see in their day.

Life in Ireland has meant everything to me. I am living in peace and my family is together. We try to share whenever we can. There are a lot of people in Eritrea who have nothing to eat, so we help friends at home and elderly people. We are blessed and I am really thankful for Ireland. In Eritrea, I had a good job and I was respected. I didn't come here for money. I came here to be safe and to live in peace.

More about Eritrea:

"IT IS NOT OUR DIFFERENCES THAT DIVIDE US. IT IS OUR INABILITY TO RECOGNISE, ACCEPT, AND CELEBRATE THOSE DIFFERENCES."

AUDRE LORDE

Kelvin is a global youth educator, youth worker, facilitator, trainer, dancer and spoken word artist, dedicated to promoting human rights, inclusion and minority integration.

MY IRISH IDENTITY WAS NOT SHAPED SOLELY BY THE COUNTRY ITSELF, BUT RATHER BY THE IRISH PEOPLE WHO PROVIDED ME WITH SPACE AND RECOGNITION.

KELVIN

My name is Kelvin and my story finds its true beginning in Ghana. When I was five, my parents moved from Africa to Europe. However, because I was turned down for a visa, they were unable to take me with them. This move meant that for almost eight years, my parents and I lived apart. Yet despite their physical absence, I always knew my parents cared deeply about me. Their move was driven by a desire to seek better opportunities, not because Ghana was unbearable, but because opportunities were scarce. However, this search for a better life came at a cost.

During their absence, I was raised by my aunt, whom I consider my second mother, and my grandmother. Growing up, I was surrounded by the nurturing presence of these two powerful women. Inevitably, I formed deeper emotional bonds with my aunt and grandmother than with my biological parents. When my biological mother visited, my friends often mistook her for another auntie. Introducing my real mother as "Mum" felt strange to me, partly because she looked so young, having had me at twenty.

Left to right: Kelvin's mother, auntie, grandmother and family friend. Kelvin is in white with arms crossed.

Although my father was absent for much of my childhood, he has been a significant influence on me, especially as I get older. His journey, from humble beginnings fixing shoes in Ghana to pursuing higher education and becoming an accountant in Ireland, resonates with me. Even before leaving Ghana, he was deeply committed to youth development, actively engaging with issues affecting the young . In 2006, he ran as an MP in his local area and almost won. Our shared commitment to these causes has naturally brought our beliefs and values together as one.

Ghana was truly a wonderful place to grow up, despite my parents not being around. I learned to dance and to delve deep into the values of humanity and respect. I also forged a strong connection with God. As a child, life in Ghana was beautiful. We played football, often barefoot, and the sense of community was strong. My aunt would go to work, leaving me alone at home, but I was never really alone. Our neighbours always looked out for me. Even though life seemed harsh and difficult at times, there was always joy. One incredible memory I have is of playing games in the moonlight, because we had no electricity, and all the kids would gather in the streets. We did different activities, with boys on one side and girls on the other, singing songs to pick our partners. These moments created bonds that lasted a lifetime and people still remember me when I visit Ghana. The community work done by my grandmother and second mother, along with our involvement in the church, also played a significant role.

I was the only child in my family that was born in Ghana. My brothers and sisters were born while my parents were in Europe, some in the UK and some in Ireland. While my parents were working, they sent my siblings back to Ghana to be raised by my auntie. After two years, my parents came to bring them back to Europe, but I remained in Ghana. Years passed, and my parents tried multiple times to have me join them. At one point, Ireland relaxed its restrictions on migrants, providing an opportunity for my family to move there and to send for me. It was at last our chance to reunite.

Life was a series of transitions and adjustments while my parents sought stability in Ireland. Sadly, one of my sisters passed away while living in Ghana, and her passing pushed my parents to try harder to get me to join them. My second mother and grandmother were relentless in their efforts, but we constantly faced issues with visas and passports. I remember a pivotal day when my parents said, "We are going to try one more time. If you are denied, we cannot bring you to Europe. But we will do our best to make your life in Ghana feel like Europe." I had become accustomed to rejection, so when my parents said this, I accepted it.

By around age 11 or 12, I had almost given up hope. Then one day, instead of going to church, our family went to pray in the mountains, as Jesus had done. While there, my second mother told me to pray only about making it to Europe. I followed her advice and later, I had a dream of a star coming towards me. Shortly after, my auntie came to me all excited, "Kelvin, run and get a passport photo!" She believed this time it would work and miraculously it did! I got my passport and my visa!

I remember it was an ordinary day like any other. I was playing with my friends, unaware of the life-changing journey on which I was about to embark. Suddenly, someone called out to me, "Kelvin, you are going to Europe now! Go home and change." My mother had come to take me with her.

My bags were already packed. We quickly hopped into a car and immediately headed to the airport. It all happened so fast! Before I knew it, I was on a plane and then I arrived in Ireland.

At thirteen, the idea of Europe was a dream come true. I wanted to be a football player and experience snow and Santa, like I had seen in the photos my parents had been sending me. The urgency of our departure meant that I didn't have time to reflect on leaving Ghana. However, once I settled in Ireland, the reality hit me and I missed my country more and more, especially as I did not know when I could return. I had to start school afresh and adapt to a new culture.

I understood what was happening around me and how to navigate life's challenges, though I did not always know the best way to handle them. This new feeling of being in Ireland was strange. However, the knowledge that my mother and second mother wanted me to come here gave me comfort.

My auntie frequently called and would always ask, "Kelvin, how are you? I hope you're being a good boy."

And I would reassure her. "Yes, I'm being a good boy."

When I first arrived in Ireland, stepping off the plane was a whole new experience. I had been nervous during the flight, especially when there was turbulence, and my mother would hold my hand to comfort me. After passing through the checkpoints at the different airports, I kept asking, "Are we there yet? Are we safe yet? Am I safe? Am I in Europe yet?" Every time we moved from one stage to another, through security and onto the next, my anxiety was palpable.

Even when we arrived in Ireland, my mam kept reassuring me, "Not yet, not yet. We are almost there." I did not have a European passport, so they had to scrutinise my visa and all my documents. Finally, we were told, "Okay, now you can go through."

When I finally emerged from the passport checking area, I saw so many white people! I had never seen that many in my life before. In Ghana, seeing white people was a rarity. I only had one white friend, a girl from the US. Her family were friends with some of my aunties. One day, they came by and we kids started talking and playing. I used to boast about it to my friends, saying, "Yo! I got white friends!" Which was a big deal, because not everyone had white friends. Now, in Ireland, I felt like a minority for the first time.

We went to live in Buncrana, which is in the north of Ireland. My first culture shock was the weather, which was unlike anything I had ever experienced. I went to school there and I think that's when life in Europe started to feel more real. It was going to be very different, because I was also taking care of my brothers and sisters. My father was living in Co. Louth for work, so, as the big brother, I helped my mother with the siblings. She was pregnant with our youngest at the time.

Kelvin and his sister, Golden

School was different. Even though I loved football, which was my escape, and everyone at school, including the PE teachers, appreciated my passion for the game, it did not change the challenges I faced.

This is when I first experienced racism. Back in Africa, I never encountered it and didn't even know what racism meant. In Ireland, some kids laughed at me, calling me names like "bastard". I didn't understand why they acted this way. While some kids were friendly, there were always groups that targeted me, as my brother and I were the only black students at the school. I told my mother about the name-calling and bullying, which upset her, but most of the time, I just tried to ignore it.

Kelvin at 14, six months after arriving in Ireland

Unfortunately, the situation sometimes got worse. My little brother, Chris, who is the second oldest, was also being bullied. There was a time he had a fight with a guy who had been picking on him. Later that day, my brother's teacher had to leave early, so his class joined my class for the afternoon. This meant my brother and I were in the same classroom. The boy who fought with my brother raised his hand. In front of everyone, he asked the teacher, "Miss, do you have a banana?"

"Why?" the teacher asked.

Kelvin graduating in 2023 as a Global Youth Educator from Maynooth University

"Because there are too many monkeys in the class."

The teacher and I exchanged a glance, staring at each other. Inside, I felt like crying, but I could not let it show. I held back the tears and decided to show strength. The teacher said nothing, just told the boy to sit down.

I used to feel scared all the time about school, but it was the only time I could play football, one of the few opportunities to enjoy myself. Some of my friends asked questions that might seem racist, but they were just being curious.

"Is it true that you guys sleep in trees?"

"No, where did you hear that? I sleep in a nice house."

Their reactions were different from how other kids reacted to me. It made me realise that they wanted to learn. I knew them and appreciated how well they treated me. Their questions helped me to understand other perspectives.

We lived in Buncrana for about three months, before joining my father in Co. Louth, where it was more diverse. We were not the only black people in the school, which made me feel more integrated into the community. I was eager to learn and even picked up a bit of Irish. It felt like a weight had been lifted. I joined a Gaelic sports team at school and became part of the club, where people embraced me and I found happiness and acceptance. Transitioning to secondary school was a mixed experience, but just as I was settling in, my mother announced we were relocating to Dublin. I remember grappling with conflicting emotions, including having to leave a girl I had developed a crush on. However, Dublin beckoned with its own allure.

The move to Lucan in south Dublin gave me a whole different perspective on society and what life could be like. I was excelling in school, but at the same time, my passion for dance was growing. I began teaching dance at church. In Africa, our church experience was vastly different from Ireland, where I found the services to be slower paced, with less energy and fewer attendees. I had taken charge of the church Sunday school. However, I felt compelled by a higher calling, drawing from my experiences in Ghana. Each session lasted about an hour and a half. So, for about an hour, with around 14 young children, I focused on teaching about God. Then, in the last 30 minutes, I shifted gears to teach dance and choreography.

Soon, word began to spread. Parents started hearing their kids express a desire to attend "Kelvin's church". This led more children and their parents to our church, drawn by the opportunity to learn to dance. Sometimes, we'd even showcase our routines for the adults.

———————————

Around this time, I was asked to participate in a programme in Adamstown that aimed to engage young people in community activities, targeting kids aged 11 to 15. Being almost 17, I felt unsure if I belonged. My mother, with whom I had grown close after rebuilding our relationship, encouraged me to go. So, I agreed, thinking I'd only stay for a week. Yet, I found myself enjoying it, despite being the oldest participant. One day, the director, Tony Fagan, from Tallaght Community Arts, mentioned that they were looking for young people to join a project in the UK. He expressed an interest in me and offered me one of the spots, which I accepted. Unfortunately, my plans were thwarted when the UK denied me a visa.

Despite the disappointment, this setback led me to cross paths with two remarkable individuals, who have since become mentors and dear to me. They are Jennifer Webster and Jenny McDonald, whom I affectionately refer to as my "white aunties". They have consistently stood by me, offering advice even to this day. They assured me, "Kelvin, for the next project, we will make sure you definitely go."

About a month later, another opportunity arose, this time in Portugal. My "white aunties" endeavoured to secure my participation. They made calls to the Portuguese embassy, but the responses were not promising. They advised me to go with my mother to the embassy, urging us not to leave until we secured the visa. They had already booked my flight, which was only three days away. "Kelvin, we don't mind losing the money if they still won't grant you the visa, but just go to the embassy, please." So we went, prayed and hoped for the best.

To our surprise, we met the ambassador. Initially, he said it was too late. Then, quite unexpectedly, he asked, "What do you want to do in Portugal?" We found ourselves discussing Portugal, without even mentioning the visa issue. Eventually, as his time was running short, he said, "Promise me, when you come back, tell me all about Portugal and what you enjoyed the most." I promised eagerly.

I got the visa. That opened a new chapter for me – my first journey outside of Ireland since arriving in Europe seven years earlier. The trip took me to a different country, where I connected with young people from all around the world.

When I returned to Ireland, my first project focused on using dance to address racism. This marked the beginning of my journey into activism, engaging with social issues and connecting with diverse communities across Ireland.

In 2014, I obtained my Irish citizenship, a moment that filled me with immense excitement. At the time, I didn't see myself as Irish, even though I'd been in Ireland for many years. When I walked on the street, I would still hear hurtful remarks like "Go back to your country" and even racial slurs like the N-word. It made me realise that without the official recognition of citizenship, I wasn't perceived as Irish.

Receiving my passport marked a significant milestone, yet the prejudice did not disappear. This prompted me to deeply ponder the meaning of being Irish and the essence of citizenship. Despite being called a citizen and actively participating in Irish culture, like speaking the language, supporting local sports teams and even singing the national anthem, I continued to encounter rejection and bigotry.

Nevertheless, that period in 2014 was a turning point, as it granted me the chance I had long awaited. My mentors, the two Jennies, were working with the National Youth Council of Ireland (NYCI) at the time. The Council was involved in a project related to Europe's No Hate Speech movement, for which the NYCI took on a coordinating role. They organised various activities, including training courses, to engage young people in addressing societal issues. There were opportunities in countries like Greece and Serbia for young dancers, photographers and others. Jenny MacDonald informed me about a specific opportunity in Serbia. She thought I would be a good fit and encouraged me to apply. To my surprise, I was accepted. For the first time, I travelled using my Irish passport, without experiencing the usual scrutiny or segregation.

Interestingly, before embarking on this European journey, I had been tasked to interview a woman named Aiste, a person who would profoundly impact my life. Aiste, originally from Lithuania, was associated with the NYCI and had her own organisation, Eurobug. After the interview, we decided to travel to Serbia together.

In Serbia, I encountered a diverse group of young people who used art to confront social issues. While I initially focused on dance, I found myself drawn into the world of rap, which Serbian youth were heavily into. I also met Milan, an incredible individual, with whom I was to explore several artistic endeavours. Milan suggested to me, "Kelvin, why don't we write something deeply personal about ourselves? Something intimate, not just anything, but something truly personal, such as our own personal journey." The only thing that came to mind was my journey from Africa to Europe and I had never written about that before. So I thought, yes, why not?

Having been drawn to rap, I transitioned instead to spoken word, because I found rap too focused on themes I did not resonate with, especially the portrayal of women. My initial attraction to rap stemmed from artists like Tupac, who used their platform to address social and racial injustice. However, as the scene shifted towards sexualisation, I felt disconnected from the direction in which it was heading.

I was searching for a different means of expression, one that allowed me to discuss social issues through poetry, whether it be rap or another form. When I returned to Ireland, I started writing more, not only about racism but also delving into my personal life, social inclusion, women's empowerment and generally exploring my creativity. Consequently, I became deeply involved in the poetry scene.

Around this time, Aiste invited me to join her Eurobug association. This opportunity opened the door for me to participate in numerous youth exchanges after finishing university. Initially, I had planned to become an accountant, following in my father's footsteps, but he wisely advised me against it, knowing the challenges I might face as a black person in that field. He encouraged me to pursue what truly made me happy. This shifted my focus towards art. I initially aimed for animation, but ended up applying for and studying graphic design.

After university, I began integrating my skills and knowledge from graphic design into poetry and dance. During a youth exchange in Lithuania, someone asked me if I would teach poetry writing. Despite feeling unsure, I shared my writing process. To my surprise, the young participants were deeply moved, some even crying as they wrote. They began confiding their personal stories to me and, at just 21 or 22 years old, I struggled to find the right words to comfort them, often just listening and offering sympathy.

Gradually, I continued my journey with Tallaght Community Arts. From being a participant, I rose to become the artistic director. We were deeply involved in teaching and performing, as the group evolved with a growing number of African youths. We had the honour of performing twice for Michael D Higgins. During this time, I was also teaching dance to the African community and crafting artistic pieces. One notable work was a dance piece titled "We Are Here". Inspired by my experiences and a poem I wrote in Serbia about my own journey, this piece explored why migrants leave their homelands for new shores.

My mindset began to shift beyond advocating for change to actively telling the story of my community – being Black, African, migrant and more. Despite my contributions to Ireland, I had not embraced my Irish identity. When asked about my background, I began introducing myself as Afro-Irish. This term has become integral to how I define myself, even today. My Irish identity was not shaped solely by the country itself, but rather by the Irish people who provided me with space and recognition.

During this time, I created another significant piece that resonated widely in Ireland, addressing themes of racism through dance performances. The young kids I was working with at the time had told me of an incident at their school involving a teacher. They reported the incident to the principal as racist. The principal refused to acknowledge the incident as racism and instructed the students to apologise to the teacher through an essay!

Based on this incident, we combined poetry and dance to craft their narrative, aiming to convey their story on stage. Being a group of black kids addressing racism in Ireland, they were very anxious prior to the performance about how it would be received. I reassured them (and myself), urging them to trust in their message. Their performance received a standing ovation and widespread acclaim.

I embarked on my first personal project, supported by the South Dublin County Council, which I called "Calling Back History: Africa". I wanted to educate others about African history, especially since I had noticed that the African history taught in schools lacked a positive perspective. Having experienced the Irish education system from the age of 13, I noticed that discussions about Africa often commence with slavery and the subsequent European colonisation, shaping a narrative that portrays Africa and Africans in a limited light. When we depict one race as powerful and dominant over another in history, it leaves a young person thinking that, because their ancestors conquered and took control of the lands of others, they were the superior race and the colonised race was inferior. But that's not the full story. The rich and diverse history of Africa and all its positive aspects are often neglected in our education system.

That is why I created "Calling Back History: Africa", to highlight African history in its entirety. It's about celebrating African achievements, understanding why Africans moved from one place to another, both within the continent and beyond, and expressing these stories through poetry and dance.

I had travelled to Lebanon in 2016 through the Irish Refugee Council, where I met someone and fell in love. She was from Syria and works with refugee children. This visit was for a project that lasted about eight to ten days. However, the next time I stayed for almost a month. While I wanted to spend time with my girlfriend, I also wanted to help the community.

I had some friends working in the Palestinian refugee camps, so I visited two of these: the Shatila camp and one other. I helped out by teaching football and dance. For three weeks, I dedicated my time to these activities. That period also changed my perspective on life, especially my experiences with the young kids there. They loved me and the community welcomed me warmly. People on the street would offer me coffee and ask where I was from – mainly whether I was from the UK or US. They'd ask if I danced and then show me their own dances. When I bought fruit, they'd often give me extra for free. In contrast to Europe, the people who had the least were the ones showing the most love.

Initially, due to the media coverage, especially about ISIS and the prevailing religious stereotypes, I had a huge fear of Muslims. Although I had Muslim friends, I was always cautious, afraid that I might unintentionally offend someone and get into an altercation. However, my experiences in the camps helped me to overcome this fear and reshaped my understanding and appreciation of the Muslim community.

I was initially nervous about their rules and religious customs. One day, I was asked to teach a class of girls. When I arrived, I remembered that part of Islamic law prohibits girls from hugging strangers. However, the kids seemed to forget about this rule, because as soon as I walked in, they hugged me and eagerly showed me the dance they had been working on, building on our previous lessons. I let go of my fears and hugged them back, embracing the moment. It was a profound experience and I even wrote a poem about it.

I'm sharing this story because it plays a significant role in what I am about to discuss. This was around 2020. When I returned, my girlfriend and I broke up, though we remained friends. Around the same time, Aiste asked if I wanted to turn "Calling Back History: Africa" into a European project. I was surprised by the suggestion and sceptical at first, but after some discussion, I agreed.

My aunt had recently passed, and my grandmother was severely ill. She called, expressing her wish to see me before she died, a desire she had held for a long time. This and the breakup with my girlfriend all happened around the same period and weighed heavily on me.

But there was worse to come.

Around this time, I was to experience one of the darkest episodes of my life. I was heading to Georgia to work on a project about labels and labelling people. As part of the project, I was also going to teach a flash mob dance to be performed in public. It marked the first time our organisation was taking young people from Ireland, all of whom were African or black. I brought along a Bluetooth speaker that I'd been using for three years, as part of my teaching. Everything seemed fine and it passed through Irish security without any issues. We then arrived in Germany, stayed overnight in Berlin and played music with the same Bluetooth speaker.

When we got to the airport and went through security, they stopped us. They asked, "Whose Bluetooth is this?" I said it was mine. They asked what was inside and I replied that I didn't know. They let the younger people go, but instructed me to stay and asked me to sit down. Then I noticed about five or six officers examining the Bluetooth speaker, trying to scan what was inside. Then suddenly, they took me to a back room to interrogate me. I thought maybe they suspected I had drugs.

Our flight was about to depart, so Aiste told the rest of the group to go ahead and take the flight. The group did not want to leave, but she insisted they go to Georgia. She would stay with me and we would catch up later. We thought the situation would be resolved quickly. However, it was another two hours before they sent for an interpreter or even asked if I needed one. Aiste came to check on me and gave me water to drink. After a while, they sent her away and said they would continue questioning me in a few hours. Then without warning, they shut down that entire section of the airport. I looked out the window into the main terminal and saw many police officers surrounding a man in a bomb suit.

The bomb squad had arrived to inspect the Bluetooth speaker, what they thought was a bomb. They evacuated me and everyone else from that area of the building.

They took the item to another building for inspection and then returned to discuss their findings. As the inspector was leaving, the interpreter asked him, "Can I ask if you found anything?" The inspector replied that, personally, he would release me immediately, but ultimately, the decision rested with the police. It was at this moment that the detectives realised their accusation had been a mistake.

However, it was not over. When they scrutinised my passport, they noted my trips to Lebanon. They began questioning me about these visits, asking what my purpose had been. I explained my reasons, but nevertheless, they kept up their accusations and then started changing the narrative. Their new angle was that I had attempted to conceal something resembling a bomb inside the Bluetooth speaker, with the intent to cause chaos on the plane. They led me to a room where they subjected me to a humiliating strip search, completely removing all my clothing, apparently looking for any signs of concealed wires or devices. They gave me no food, no water, nothing.

Aiste contacted the Irish embassy, but they explained that they could not intervene, as I was only being detained and not yet formally arrested. Eventually, a different team of inspectors took over and they decided to let me go, but they kept all my stuff. As a result, I lost all my client contacts. I was told it would be returned within three weeks to three months.

Through the interpreter, they asked if I had anything else to tell them. I said that I wanted to thank them for making me believe in the work that I am doing, because the work I'm doing is making sure that people feel safe and that people feel they can express themselves in an inclusive world. With that, we parted ways. About three months later, they returned everything to me, including the item they had suspected was a bomb. In their letter, they stated I would not receive any compensation, except for my Bluetooth speaker, which they valued at €25. They provided a claim form, but I decided it was too much hassle.

My passion lies in youth work and empowering others to thrive in an inclusive world. Yet, I was labelled a potential terrorist and faced restrictions throughout the investigation. They did not simply take my belongings; I was effectively blacklisted in Berlin and viewed as a threat. After they released me and I had to catch my flight to Georgia, I faced repeated police searches at every step, even though I had already been thoroughly searched. I would be double-checked right before boarding the plane, with police waiting to search me again at the end of the flight.

By the time I returned to Ireland, it had all left a lasting impression. During that period, everything seemed like a whirlwind – being labelled a terrorist, losing my second mother and going through a breakup. It was not just a rough patch; the circumstances were overwhelming. That phase was undoubtedly the darkest in my life.

Then Aiste intervened. She urged me to shift my focus and suggested it was time to leave Ireland for a while, to get away from familiar but difficult surroundings. However, I had withdrawn into myself, barely eating and expressing a deep disillusionment with life. I didn't want to die, but I just didn't want to be in this world. What pulled me out of that abyss was a Palestinian friend I had met in Lebanon. She reminded me that the love I possess is a gift meant to be shared. "Kelvin, if you say that you don't want to be in this world, think about it. God has given the love you have to give it to somebody in this world. If you say you're not going to be here, then you are preventing somebody in this world from receiving your love."

This message really opened my mind. She challenged me to think about the impact my absence would have on those who need my love. I then went to Reggio Calabra, Italy, where I met new people and really started connecting with myself again. I finally got myself back together.

Before the trip to Georgia, I had travelled to Ghana to lay my second mother to rest. During my stay, my grandmother, already in a fragile state due to dehydration and the recent passing of her daughter, was unresponsive. During the burial ceremony, she had to be taken to hospital. Despite their efforts to rehydrate her, she remained unresponsive until they mentioned my name. I was an hour and forty-five minutes away by bus, when I received the urgent call to come immediately.

I had not seen my grandmother in ten years, not since leaving Ghana. When I arrived, she started speaking and responding, displaying remarkable energy.

"Have you gotten married yet?"

"I'm trying," I replied. "I'm trying." She then urged me to marry my childhood crush!

A week after I returned to Ireland, my grandmother passed away. Although this news was deeply saddening, I found solace in knowing that her wish to see me one last time was fulfilled. I cherish the memory of getting to say goodbye to my grandmother, even though I could not be present for her burial. This final visit held immense significance for me, marking a poignant chapter in my life.

Returning from that journey, I felt re-energised. I was ready to resume work on my project, even though it had shifted focus to Europe. Initially hesitant, I confided in my boss that I was not enthusiastic about the new direction. Her response was reassuring – pursue it with an open mind and the outcome would guide our next steps. She came up with the idea of building bridges instead of walls.

So, the "Bridges, Not Walls" project was formed and, to my surprise, accepted. It was my first ever international project. It was a huge success and the young people involved were eager to continue. At their suggestion, we came together and wrote "Bridges, Not Walls: Part Two". Its success was mainly due to the participants' enthusiasm.

Then Covid struck. However, after the pandemic, we successfully organised the third and fourth editions of "Bridges, Not Walls". This project grew into a global community, primarily in Europe, connecting many young people who now know each other through their involvement.

Last year, this project brought me back to Germany. I wanted to go, because I had previously received a letter stating that the investigation was over and everything was clear. I wanted to see if I was still blacklisted. Thankfully, I wasn't. In Germany, we focused on dance, film and music. We created a 40-minute show and performed it in three different cities, effectively creating a mini-tour.

In Ireland, I was not seen as a youth worker but rather as a youth leader. To be a youth worker, you need a degree. The NYCI provided me with an opportunity to take a course at Maynooth. After completing the course, I transitioned to becoming a youth worker. The NYCI played a significant role in my journey. In 2019, they selected me to represent Ireland at the European Youth Conference. Out of 250 young people, I was one of only two black participants, which highlighted the ongoing issue of inclusion in Europe. I addressed this during the conference, questioning the lack of diversity.

I've gained a lot from moving to Ireland. However, my work with the European project precipitated a move to Spain and I was there during the pandemic. I had also noticed significant diversity issues in Spain and across Europe, prompting my desire to establish an organisation to address these gaps.

Bridges Not Walls in Lithuania – Project focus on migration

2019 European Youth Conference in Romania as a Youth Delegate for Ireland

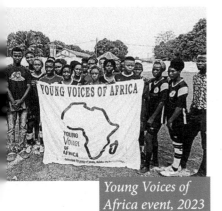

Young Voices of Africa event, 2023

So, I founded an organisation in Spain to provide opportunities for young migrants and artists to showcase their talents and connect with peers across Europe. This experience shaped me into a global youth worker.

In 2022, I began focusing more on Africa, realising the need to contribute to my homeland. I participated in an NYCI event, discussing African representation and advocating for direct involvement of African youth. We organised workshops and included young Africans in the event to showcase their perspectives and talents. I feel like African youth voices are not being adequately heard, especially those on the African continent. So, this led to the formation of Young Voices of Africa, aiming to amplify African youth voices globally.

In 2023, we held our annual general conference in Sierra Leone during a period of political unrest, marked by a failed coup attempt, a government on high alert and a curfew in place. With the support of a police ambassador from our Young Voices of Africa group, we liaised directly with the police to ensure everything proceeded smoothly. We also approached the local chief, a significant figure in African communities, akin to a king, and he was impressed that young people were organising an event independently. With his approval, what was initially planned for 50 attendees saw over 500 participants.

All the logistics and finances were managed through my personal efforts, where income from my work funded the event. Due to technology limitations in the country, my youth ambassadors and I communicated through WhatsApp calls. I trusted them with funds to organise the event, which turned out to be a significant success. The entire women's community forum participated and we even had a grand parade with bands and the Young Voices of Africa flag. This event was transformative for African youth, gaining recognition and invitations to community meetings. It sparked a ripple effect across other African countries.

Inspired by this success, we decided to replicate this model in Europe, akin to the European Youth Goals. After researching, we found no equivalent for African youth, so we initiated the African Youth Goals. Our completed goals were showcased to 22 organisations at a workshop hosted by the NYCI. They found the goals beneficial and endorsed them. However, our main objective is to advocate for their adoption by the African Union. These 15 goals represent the aspirations of African youth, both on the continent and in the diaspora, aiming for impactful change in African policies and politics.

This year, our primary focus is female empowerment, reflecting our commitment to addressing historical and current inequalities faced by women in Africa. We have undertaken numerous projects to achieve this goal, because we believe women's inclusion is crucial for African and youth development. Young Voices of Africa is dedicated to this cause. Meanwhile in Spain, our group creates opportunities for young artists, migrants and minorities to explore the world.

I believe in positivity, where the more love you give, the more you receive in return. My journey from Ghana to Ireland has been filled with hope, resilience and a deep sense of family and faith.

More about Kelvin and Ghana:

> "THE GREATNESS OF HUMANITY IS NOT IN BEING HUMAN, BUT IN BEING HUMANE."

MAHATMA GANDHI

Fatima has been actively involved in human rights, political and youth causes since she was 13, advocating for climate action and against gender-based discrimination. She is involved in campaigns for diverse communities and advocates for meaningful dialogue among people of different backgrounds. Recently, she has been advocating for her family and community and those affected by the war in Sudan.

I HAVE THE OPPORTUNITY TO ECHO THE VOICES OF THOSE WHO CANNOT SPEAK OUT THEMSELVES.

FATIMA

I was born in Khartoum in Sudan and I now live in Ireland. To truly understand the journey that led me and my family to this point, let me take you back to the early years of my life.

When I was just five, my family decided to move to Jordan so my mother could pursue her postgraduate studies. We lived there for about five years before returning to Sudan. Moving to Jordan exposed me to a world of racism I had never encountered before. It's startling to think that a five-year-old could vividly recall such experiences, but I remember them clearly.

Teachers often singled me out for punishment, when I had done nothing wrong, making racial taunts. On one occasion, a teacher took away my colouring pencils, saying they were "too extravagant for me", and redistributed them among the class. I remember being blamed for noise in the classroom, which I myself was not making, and the teacher hit me on the head with a book. The pain was sharp, but what hurt more was the humiliation.

Students would ask me, "Why are you so burnt?" They would call me crazy names and say hurtful things. It made me question where these thoughts came from, because children are not born with such ideas. At least, that's what I believe. These thoughts must come from somewhere – their homes, the TV and films they watch, or the environment they grow up in. Those moments, filled with racial taunts and prejudiced assumptions, were confusing and isolating. I found myself grappling with a sense of exclusion that was both profound and formative.

These early experiences shaped the type of work I do now. In Ireland, I work on anti-racism efforts and different projects that address this issue. After those formative years in Jordan, we returned to Sudan. Despite the challenges, life there was filled with vibrant memories. In Sudanese and Middle Eastern cultures, you're often surrounded by many people. In our house, we had different floors for different family members. For example, the ground floor was my granny's, the first floor was ours, the second floor was my uncle's, and the third was for another uncle. So, there was always a lot of people around. Growing up, I was surrounded by family. We often had relatives visiting and a typical day involved waking up to have breakfast with a house full of people – cousins, uncles, aunties, other grandparents and extended family members.

I really appreciated this aspect of our culture, though I didn't realise how much until I left. Our school was close to our house, so we would walk there. I loved school; it was one of my favourite places. I enjoyed spending time with friends, liked my teachers and participated in sports and activities. Because of the hot weather, most activities in Sudan happen in the evenings. We lived in Khartoum and one of my favourite memories is going to the Nile River to drink hibiscus tea and gather with family and friends. These gatherings, usually at night, are some of my most cherished memories.

There was no significant violence before the recent war broke. Sudan was peaceful then and we were happy. The economy was not great and occasionally, the water or electricity was cut off, but people managed. Violence itself was uncommon. Now, instead of the peaceful place of joy and happiness from my memories, Sudan is bleeding. Even though I am far from home, the pain is deeply felt.

Securing a quality education in Sudan was extremely difficult. Despite being fortunate enough to attend private English schools and being raised in that curriculum, we knew it was not enough for us to achieve our full potential. The desire for a better education and more opportunities in life were the primary reasons we left Sudan. However, this came at a price – a life without our extended family or the familiarity of home. We then relocated to Ireland when I was 13, where I've lived for almost seven years. Our move to Ireland was influenced by my mother's ties to the country. She was born in Ireland and spent her earliest years there, while my grandfather was completing his postgraduate studies at Trinity College Dublin.

Moving from Sudan to Jordan was challenging enough, but maintaining family connections was far more difficult when we moved to Ireland. Sometimes, I felt like "that cousin" who lives abroad, which is a strange dilemma, as if this is your family, but you're so far away from them.

The only other family member my mum was allowed to bring with us to Ireland was my grandma. Moving to Ireland brought many opportunities, but it also felt isolated, especially during celebrations. In Sudan, during religious celebrations like Eid, we would spend the whole day visiting family, driving from house to house. While there is a Muslim community in Ireland, which helps to recreate some of the sense of togetherness we had back home, it's not quite the same.

Despite the difficulties of distance, I stayed connected with my family in Sudan. However, everything changed when war broke out in 2023. This conflict has truly torn our family apart, leading to heartbreaking losses. Some family members have died in the war, while others have been scattered across the globe – to Egypt, Saudi Arabia, the UAE and more recently, Uganda.

From watching global news, I thought I understood what war might be like, but witnessing my own family's ordeal in a full-scale war made me realise how wrong I was. It's in these moments that you truly grasp how unsafe the world really is. While many people across the globe remain unaware of the war in Sudan, I feel compelled to raise awareness about the continuing crisis.

Since gaining independence in 1956, Sudan has endured three civil wars, the latest being the most devastating. The conflict erupted between two groups: the Sudanese Army, led by Abdel Fattah al-Burhan, and the Rapid Support Forces (RSF), led by Mohamed Hamdan Dagalo, also known as Hemedti. In 2019, an RSF military coup removed the president, Omar al-Bashir, after months of demonstrations against his 30-year rule. Both the army and the RSF were running the country together until relations broke down on 15 April 2023.

My cousin told me that when the war broke out, she was in school, sitting an exam, when suddenly the building started shaking. Gunfire and explosions could be heard, fighter jets were seen around the city and military tanks were everywhere. It sounded like a movie, but it was all too real.

The scariest part of the war was when we heard that large groups of RSF soldiers had entered our home in Sudan. They held my family at gunpoint, accusing them of weapons possession. The RSF has informants in different cities and these informants reported our family for having military connections in the past. Some of this information was correct, as my grandfather, whom Omar al-Bashir is believed to have assassinated in a plane crash in 2001, held the position of Commander of the Military Corps and also served as a consultant orthopaedic surgeon.

However, my family did not possess any weaponry and the RSF did not believe them until they saw evidence that our claims were true. When they found nothing, they resorted to stealing all our cars and money. The worst part is that there were children in the house. Is there any justification for a child to witness this? The RSF has used civilians as hostages and human shields and that could have easily happened to my family.

Throughout this war, we've lost many friends and family members. Civilians are often caught in the crossfire, becoming collateral damage. Many sought refuge in rural areas, but the RSF's reach extended there as well. Recently, a family

Fatima's family home in Khartoum after the missile attack

member was attacked and killed in his own home by the RSF and his son was critically injured. This war isn't just a power struggle between two leaders; it's a deliberate strategy to terrorise innocent civilians, instill fear and gain control.

The UN has called Sudan the "world's worst displacement crisis," with over 10,130,400 displaced as of July this year. Many are spending their life savings seeking shelter, but with almost no job opportunities available, escape remains challenging. In the backdrop of war, a silent genocide in the Darfur region is also taking place. Systemic murder, the burning of entire villages, rape and mass displacement are a few of the human rights violations.

When I asked my family how they cope with the ongoing hardship, they told me, "People harden with time." Yet, they find hope and resilience, believing that the "glass is always half full." Despite the less-than-ideal situation, they are grateful to be alive. In moments of struggle and difficulty, clichés seem to make perfect sense; they help make a complicated situation feel more manageable.

Unfortunately, the situation is only getting worse and many people are losing hope. One day, my uncle was using the stairs to go outside to his car. Just moments later, our house was hit by a missile. It seemed as if it had been specifically targeted. The missile struck the exact spot on the stairs where my uncle had been. Following this terrifying incident, my family had no choice but to leave and make their way out of the country.

We found out about the attack through pictures of our house being shared on social media. We couldn't contact our family and didn't know if they were alive or not. For weeks, we had no information. When they finally reached a safe place and were able to contact us, we were relieved.

(Sudanese Documents Library, Newspaper Archives, 4 May 2001)

Aftermath of the crash

Fatima's maternal grandfather, General Malik Elagib Haj Elkhider

Their journey out of the country was horrific. They faced numerous problems, including not having anywhere to stay for a while. My younger cousin, who is 14, the same age as my sister, recounted terrifying experiences, like being approached by soldiers or civilians with guns. Hearing these stories horrified me. Experiencing war from afar is different, because while I'm safe, my family is not. It was hard sleeping well, knowing they were still in Sudan, constantly in danger.

Even now that they are living outside of Sudan, they are not entirely safe due to a lawsuit we initiated before the war broke out. My family has persistently sought the truth about the plane crash that caused my grandfather's death, but each attempt was met with harassment and intimidation. For nearly twenty years, the truth has remained hidden, with the case file closed by order of the now ousted president. Due to the war, many government facilities have been destroyed, most likely burning all pertinent documents. In addition to my grandfather, fourteen army leaders were also liquidated in the crash.

My family's struggle for justice and truth has put them in constant jeopardy. They have endured threats and harassment and even now, the threat lingers.

I deeply admire my mother and grandmother for their strength. I once asked my mum how she found out about her dad's death. She was a university student at the time and she heard the news on the radio, while driving with friends. That moment must have been incredibly difficult for her. Even during her university years, she continued to face harassment from journalists and security guards. My grandmother, on the other hand, continued raising her children with resilience and grace. When we moved to Jordan, she came with us for support, ensuring we had the stability and love we needed. Their courage in the

face of adversity inspires me every day and I strive to embody the resilience and compassion they have shown throughout their lives.

This experience has instilled in me a deep appreciation for the privileges I have. Living in a safe environment is a basic human right that many do not enjoy. It motivates me to do good, to strive to do better and to change the lives of those I meet. I have the opportunity to echo the voices of those who cannot speak out themselves. This drive is also why I want to pursue a career in politics, which I will be studying at university.

I am also inspired by my paternal great-grandfather, Ismail al-Azhari, who played a crucial role in securing Sudan's independence from British and Egyptian rule. After Sudan achieved independence in 1956, al-Azhari became the country's first prime minister. His tenure was a formative period for the newly-formed nation, laying the groundwork for its future. He later served as President of Sudan from 1965 to 1969, during a time of significant political and social change.

Having moved around so much, both within Ireland and to different countries, I often reflect on the differences in our lives compared to those of my family back home. We moved here to access better education opportunities. By contrast, my cousins in Sudan have had no access to education for about two years, due to the ongoing situation, at such a crucial time in their development.

In my third year at school in Cork, I made the decision to wear the hijab. I had many concerns about how it would affect my school life. In Ireland, where the majority of people are Catholic, being Muslim can be a challenge. I will never forget the first day I walked into school with my hijab on. I wore a grey hijab,

Fatima with Oliver Ropje, President of the European Economic and Social Committee, at the YEYS event

Fatima speaking at the YEYS event, representing Irish youth and contributing to the European dialogue

the colour allowed by the school, and matched it with a burgundy beanie to go with the school jumper. At the time, my class and maths teacher was Mr Fitton. He was a teacher who instilled a sense of tolerance among students, creating an environment where we felt comfortable asking him anything. When he first saw me wearing my hijab, he said, "How did you manage to beautifully match the scarf with the beanie?" That comment was more than just a compliment; it was a sign that I could be myself and feel accepted in this environment.

Despite receiving some strange looks or being referred to as "a nun" by other students, Mr Fitton's example of genuine tolerance and openness taught me to approach such situations with patience and understanding. Mr Fitton's impact went beyond the classroom; it shaped my approach to inclusivity and dialogue. What I learned from him has stayed with me and still influences how I engage with others in every aspect of my life.

After graduating, I took a gap year to focus on activism and advocacy, travelling to Belgium, Spain, Iceland and America. I was awarded a bursary grant, funded by a local credit union on the theme of "power of education", which provided crucial financial support for various exchange programmes and projects. One of the most memorable experiences was attending an event in Belgium – Your Europe, Your Say (YEYS), the flagship event of the European Economic and Social Committee (EESC). The theme for YEYS 2024 was "Stand up for democracy and speak up for Europe: youth priorities for the next EU Legislative term." The conference focused on encouraging youth participation in elections, particularly the European elections, and motivating young people to make their voices heard. Given that first-time voters were prioritised for the selection process, turning 18 a week before the conference made me eligible to participate. I applied and was nominated by the National Youth Council to represent Ireland. My interest in voting rights had been ignited by meaningful discussions within the EU Youth Dialogue Young Voices Core Group.

My goal is to facilitate conversations about topics where people often don't see eye to eye. It's all about the mindset we bring to difficult conversations. For example, when someone makes an inappropriate or offensive remark, the immediate reaction might be to label them as racist. This quick judgement can close off the chance for a meaningful dialogue about why they said what they did. Instead of saying, "That's racist," we might ask, "Can you explain why you think that?" This approach invites a deeper discussion and offers an opportunity to address and potentially change prejudiced views.

Adopting this mindset, whether dealing with racism or other issues, can lead to more productive conversations and help foster a greater understanding among people. One key hope I have for the future is that everyone can live a safe and fulfilling life, with the opportunity to engage in meaningful dialogue with people from different backgrounds. I also hope that no one has to endure horrific experiences such as racism, war or other forms of suffering.

My family is the foundation of who I am and who I am becoming. My diverse background helps me to engage in conversations with people holding vastly different views. Even when our opinions are at opposite ends of the spectrum, I can sit down and discuss our perspectives, seeking common ground. This ability stems from my family's influence and the support they have given me throughout my life.

One of my hopes is also to build a home that offers my family the same sense of belonging and togetherness we cherished in Sudan. I want to express my gratitude to my family for their support and the sacrifices they have made. Their encouragement has been a constant source of strength, guiding me through every challenge and triumph. Their sacrifices have given me opportunities to pursue my passions and advocate for change.

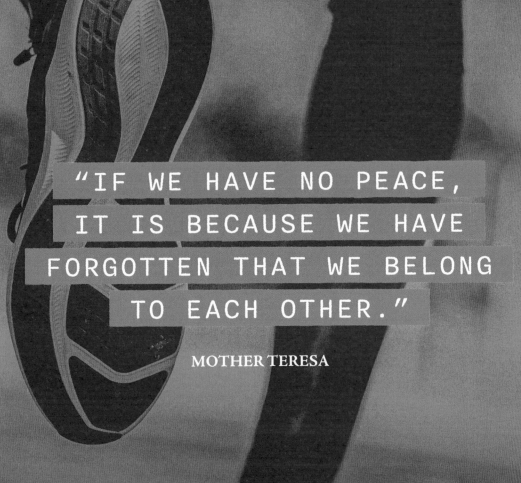

"IF WE HAVE NO PEACE,
IT IS BECAUSE WE HAVE
FORGOTTEN THAT WE BELONG
TO EACH OTHER."

MOTHER TERESA

Sylvester, originally from Zimbabwe, is an accountant who currently works for a charity organisation in Ireland. Driven by his passion and dedication, he excels in everything he sets his sights on. A fitness enthusiast, he has successfully completed three marathons.

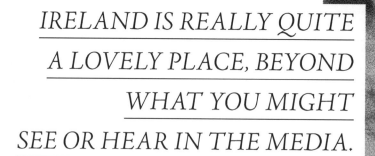

IRELAND IS REALLY QUITE A LOVELY PLACE, BEYOND WHAT YOU MIGHT SEE OR HEAR IN THE MEDIA.

SYLVESTER

I never intended to leave my home country – who does? However, the political imbalances in Zimbabwe were severe. In 2008, I moved to South Africa to finish my ACCA to qualify as a certified accountant, but things did not go as planned. I ended up teaching high school to make ends meet, which I did not enjoy. I stayed in South Africa until 2022. Most people from neighbouring countries move to South Africa due to its stronger economy and better opportunities. However, despite these advantages, the situation for foreigners in terms of acceptance can be daunting.

In 2022, I moved to Ireland, a challenging transition, since it took me even further from home. Although I had visited my brother in Ireland before, moving permanently was a different experience. Suddenly, you find yourself staying at a place where you have to register all your movements – when you leave and when you come back. If you want to stay out overnight, you need to register as well. It's like being treated as if you're a child or in a prison. It's hard for some people to adapt to these kinds of situations. For me, the experience wasn't too bad, because I never had any significant problems with the rules.

Sylvester participating in the Tom Brennan 5K memorial run, Phoenix Park

My first encounter with Sanctuary Runners was in March 2022, during their run at the Sport Island Campus. I had been a runner before meeting them, as I was in the daily habit of running, to combat what had become the monotony of my days. It's not easy for a previously active adult to suddenly have nothing to do. It wears you down. By the end of the first month, it had become really difficult. Running was my mental escape from the repetitive cycle of waking up, eating and sleeping, which was taking a toll on my mental health. To cope, I started running heavily and that's when I met the Sanctuary Runners.

In late June, I suffered an injury and couldn't run for a while. Looking for something to occupy my time, I talked to some other migrants at the hotel in Blanchardstown, where I was staying. They suggested I try Parkrun. I had no idea what Parkrun was, so I decided to check it out. It was a long drive, but Denise, who was a volunteer with the Sanctuary Runners, began collecting me and others from the hotel, ensuring we could always be involved. I registered and did my first parkrun while still injured, which unfortunately made it worse. Right after the run, I could barely walk and had to stay off my feet for about three months. It was a difficult time. Filled with frustration and impatience at losing my only active outlet at the time, I decided to stay involved with Parkrun, sometimes going there to just walk. I became a regular and got involved in various activities. Eventually,

I moved from Blanchardstown to Dublin city centre.

Denise began picking me up from there and she's been doing so ever since. I became one of the lead organisers for the Sanctuary Runners in Poppintree. I then started joining races and have completed many since. I don't think I would have known about those races if I hadn't joined the group. Running brings me happiness and has introduced me to many friends. I look forward to every Saturday with great anticipation. That is why I reached my 50th Parkrun milestone quite quickly and in about three months or so, I'll hit my 50th milestone for volunteering as well. It has become an integral part of my life and community, and I'm proud of it. Every two months, I have the privilege of serving as the Run Director, which is truly an honour to contribute to the community that I've come to enjoy so much. When they reached out looking for new Run Directors, I eagerly volunteered and they welcomed me with open arms.

Living in direct provision, sometimes (if not always) you must adjust. There are some people here in Ireland who are living on the streets, because they don't have anywhere to go. At least, I have somewhere to live and that gives me comfort. There are situations that you simply cannot change. Sometimes, you have the

Sylvester and Denise at the Dublin Marathon 2022

Sylvester and Sue during a Poppintree parkrun

Volunteering with the Sanctuary Runners

choice to either dwell on what's beyond your control or focus on the positives and enjoy the present moment. That's what I do.

One day, Denise said to me, "You're always smiling, even when things aren't going well." I told her that I choose to focus on the positive. I know negativity can be overwhelming, but I try to stay positive. I am around people that are happy, encouraging and supportive. So, whenever I show up, I try to bring a positive attitude as well. That's my approach.

However, someone in my situation cannot always feel positive. I call it a seesaw of emotions, because you don't know when the decision about your future will be made. It can be a week away, one month, three months or a year. I also miss my family. Not long after I arrived here in March 2022, my mum was involved in an accident and broke her leg. I haven't seen her since and I don't know when I will. Sometimes I fear that I might be too late. It's hard, because she's older now and breaking a leg at her age can be devastating. The thought of not being able to see her is just heartbreaking.

Ireland is really quite a lovely place, beyond what you might see or hear in the media. In the two years I have been here, I haven't personally experienced racism. The closest I came was during the riots last November. I mostly stayed indoors, but even when I was out, I didn't encounter any racism myself. When people talk about these issues, I often wonder where and how they're happening.

The riots were a shock, especially because I didn't expect anything like that in Ireland. One of the reasons I left South Africa was to avoid such situations, and here they were happening only about 100 metres away from where I was staying. It made me question whether I'm meant to be here. Despite this, my workplace was incredibly supportive. They encouraged me to stay home if I wasn't feeling safe enough to travel to work, but I chose to go, because staying home was uncomfortable and work actually felt safer. However, catching the bus to work was tense, not knowing what to expect.

Meeting Denise is an example of the kindness I have encountered in Ireland. She is a lovely person and gives her all to assist whenever she can. She is always there for me, even inviting me for Christmas dinner with her family, which was nice.

Another good friend is Deirdre. We do long Sunday runs together and she has also invited me over to her house for lunch. When I suffered an injury in the Phoenix Dublin Half-marathon, she stayed with me until I got home. I can mention a lot of names from Sanctuary Runners who are exceptional people, like Ciara, Sue, Ruthiem, to mention a few. These are the people I see almost every Saturday. Ciara has been a pillar of strength, who is always available to listen and advise, as well as being eager to help, and Sue invited me to her 50th birthday celebration in February in Dunshaughlin.

Currently, I'm still in the asylum process and things are uncertain, but I'm grateful to be back in the accounting profession. I remain hopeful! Ireland has been a great place for me, because I've met so many wonderful people. I haven't encountered any specific hate and most of the people I meet are genuinely good. I'm looking forward to building a future here.

"EACH PERSON MUST LIVE THEIR LIFE AS A MODEL FOR OTHERS."

ROSA PARKS

A teacher, a dad and a loving husband in Somalia, Mo remained the pride of his community, because of his level of education and commitment to empowering others, before tragic circumstances forced him to flee his country in 2023.

NO ONE
SPEAKS OUT.

MO

I have chosen to remain anonymous. This is to protect my identity and, for the purpose of my story, I will be called Mo. I was born in Somalia in 1993, and my father was a veterinarian. In Somalia, around 80% of people are pastoralists. We have a deep connection to animals, particularly camels. After the government fell, my father started his own business, providing veterinary services. This work became our family's source of income and security.

Despite the challenging situation in the country, my father was determined to ensure that his children received an education. He always said, "Even if we don't have a country, even if we're living in difficult conditions, I will take personal responsibility for educating my children." He was committed to this promise and made sure all four of us, two girls and two boys, went to school, even if it meant finding alternatives to public education.

The teaching we received was based on the teachers' personal experiences and cultural knowledge, without a regular programme or set curriculum. They taught us whatever they felt was important. We also learned from our parents at home.

I turned to books for comfort and guidance. My father had a vast collection of books and he allowed me to read them. It felt like he was directly telling me that if things didn't improve, it was not something he could change. I sensed that my father, despite his strength, felt powerless in certain situations.

It became evident that I was a quick learner and I managed to progress through the entire system up to Class 6. When they see that you are a quick learner, your parents might decide to send you to a better school with a more advanced curriculum. But if you're not, you might not be able to continue your education. Instead, you may have to stay home and take care of the animals. Those are the individuals being targeted by extremists, because their knowledge is limited. They are vulnerable to being recruited into extremist activity such as making suicide bombs.

My father had to take me to a private school in the capital city, far from where we lived. The school, called a madrasah, provides an education that includes both Arabic and secular subjects. My father wanted me to gain a broader understanding of Muslim culture, so I went through this system. After finishing high school, I was hired as a teacher at the same school. I taught there for seven years. The curriculum they follow is based on a Middle Eastern educational system. The school is extremely strict and students cannot question the rules or decisions made by the administration. The principal has complete authority to hire or fire staff, as the school is privately owned by wealthy individuals. Up to now, I don't know who owns the school. I started teaching what they call "upper primary", which covers grades 5, 6 and 7, typically children aged 9 to 12. During this time, I developed a passion for education, particularly for teaching girls.

In our culture, women are traditionally expected to stay behind the scenes. The woman's role consists of two main duties. The first is to take care of the house and engage in activities limited to managing the home. The second duty is to take care of her husband. In our culture, women are often discouraged from pursuing higher education or professional careers like medicine, teaching, engineering or law. The expectation is that girls only need to learn basic literacy skills, such as how to write their names. As a teacher, I have a soft spot for girls who show a strong interest in education. I often reach out to them directly and I see their potential. I have always felt inspired to help them achieve this and I always kept a close eye on their progress. However, it's disheartening when they eventually leave school without any explanation.

As I mentioned, you cannot question anyone or anything. You cannot go to the principal and ask why a student has not returned to school. If you ask too many questions, you could get into trouble. So no one speaks out. As more and more girls began disappearing from my class, I decided to investigate on my own. I found out that the girls in question had been married off to much older men, around 60 or 70 years old. Often, these men already have three wives and the young girl becomes the fourth. You can't question anyone and they justify it by saying their religion allows it. But that is not true; no religion permits marriage at the age of 10 or 11. Young girls have limited knowledge and have no real experience of life. How can she now have a husband, especially someone so much older? It just doesn't make sense.

Once, I tried to ask the vice-principal about it, since I couldn't talk to the principal. She told me, "Mo, you don't know what you're asking. Do you want to risk your life? Just be quiet, teach whoever shows up in class and then go home."

I said to myself, "Mo, what can you do to address this situation?" I decided to tackle the problem directly. I realised that to solve this issue, I needed to focus on adult education. Many older men, despite being righteous, are ignorant and lack knowledge. They don't think critically, but believe they have the right to take an 11-year-old girl as a fourth wife, especially if they have become wealthy.

So, I decided to act. I started my own adult education programme. I wanted to show them that this was wrong, but without confronting them directly. My idea was to bring it to their doorstep without them realising my true intentions. I knew that if I stayed in the city, the terrorist organisation, al-Shabaab, would easily find me. So I decided to go back to the large town where I was born and grew up. Everyone there knows me. When I would visit during holidays, people recognised me as a teacher, which is a prestigious title. People called me "Teacher Mo" or just "Teacher". I received a lot of respect from everyone, young and old alike. I thought it would be a good place to start something new.

So I opened a school, renting a large two-room space. The area is mostly under the control of al-Shabaab extremists, but I felt it was important to begin my work there. The extremists respected me at that time, because I was a teacher and the school I had come from was considered a religious school, even though it was integrated. After I opened the school, it took about a month for people to gradually start attending. However, I had to set up two separate classes: one for women and one for men, as intermingling is not allowed.

Women typically handle their family activities early in the day, so I scheduled their classes for the afternoon, while the men attended in the morning. After the first month, I noticed that the men's classes were not as full as I had hoped, but the women's classes were always packed. I was not charging a lot for the classes and I told them they could pay whatever they could afford. If they couldn't pay, it was not a problem. All I asked was that they come and get an education.

As everyone is using phones these days, I would say to the women, "You have a phone, but if you want to call a relative, you have to go into town and find someone who knows how to read and then ask them to dial the number for you." That's the situation many of them were in. I explained that if they learned to read and write, they could call or text anyone they wanted. This especially resonated with them.

They were extremely eager to learn. I had my own savings at the time and I was prepared for the possibility that I might not receive any payments for the first two or three months. However, to my surprise, the women started making contributions within the first month. They even formed a group and offered to pay six months' rent in advance.

I began by teaching them the basics: A, B, C and D, going through it slowly. I didn't push them too hard, even when it came to writing. I showed them the correct way to hold a pen, starting from scratch, because they had never learned before. I moved at a pace that suited them. As a teacher, you can't just impart knowledge without context. It's important to use examples they are familiar with to help them understand. But what I really wanted to address was the issue of young girls who don't fully understand their own bodies and are being exploited.

This is where I gradually introduced the "campaign". The first issue I raised was about self-awareness and body respect among young girls. These small children don't even know their own body and they are being misused, especially through forced child marriage. The second issue was Female Genital Mutilation (FGM), because in Somalia it's 100% practised. It's expected that every girl will undergo FGM by the age of 13 or 14. Nobody thinks this is wrong. However, witnessing my own sister going through this, seeing the group of young girls crying with her during their so-called "parties", where multiple girls are brought together to undergo the surgery at the same time, I understood that this was not right. Men face challenges too with circumcision but for the women, FGM a significant burden.

When talking to the men, I would say to them, "Look, I'm a young man and sometimes I joke and say you're like a father to me – you know more than I do. What about a child who is 11 or 12 years old?" I would bring this up and then move on to another topic. I used this as a rhetorical question to get them thinking, without asking for, or needing, an answer. My goal was to plant the idea in their minds, to make them question what they were doing. The aim was to get them to think critically about the actions and "norms" in our society.

After two months, I received a text message: "We know you and have respected you, but now what you are doing is against our religion. Talking about child marriage and FGM, all of that – we are doing things according to our traditions." Although they did not explicitly identify themselves, it was clear that the message came from the extremist group that controls the region where I lived. They warned that I had better stop what I was doing and if I didn't comply, there would be consequences. They initially permitted my activities, because they thought I was only running a religious school. However, they now saw my work as promoting Western culture.

Despite their threats, I continued with my efforts. I was not too concerned, because I am well known in the area. However, a second message arrived three months later. This time, they did not target only me: "We know you are married and have a daughter. If you care about your family, then this is what you need to consider." They gave me one month to cease my activities or my wife and daughter would be killed in front of me.

At that time, the two classrooms were overcrowded, with many eager students standing outside or peeking through the windows to get a glimpse. Meanwhile, I heard rumours that some women had formed their own group. They were advocating against FGM, stating that it is wrong to mutilate a part of a person's body and that they would not allow their daughters to undergo this practice. They started discussing this, because in my lessons we would address it. For example, I sometimes joked by asking, "Imagine seeing a woman with one of her ears chopped off. How would she look?" They usually laughed but they understood my meaning – that FGM is like having a part of your body amputated, such as an ear, an eye, a leg or a hand. They were also teaching their husbands at home that this practice was wrong. I also covered topics like hygiene and menstrual care. In Somalia, many people don't have access to sanitary products, so they use makeshift alternatives, like cloths with padding sewn in as improvised sanitary pads. I discussed these hygiene practices and body care with them.

I dismissed the second threatening message just like the first one, thinking they wouldn't take any action. However, they proved true to their word. As a Muslim, I follow five daily prayers and the first prayer is at dawn, around 5 am. One morning, I stepped out of my house to go to the mosque a little earlier than usual. As I reached the mosque, I heard an explosion and saw dust rising. However, such explosions were common, so I was not unduly concerned. I knew to stay calm and seek shelter. I entered the mosque and joined the congregation for our morning prayer, which lasted about ten minutes. Then some of my students arrived at the mosque and were startled to see me there. They told me the explosion was at my house and they assumed I had been at home! They instructed me not to return to the house, to stay silent and not speak. They then brought me to one of their homes, instructing me to stay hidden and not say a word.

For two days, I stayed in hiding, while al-Shabaab searched for me everywhere. During this time, I was informed that they had killed my daughter and my wife had been taken away. They then blew up the house, believing that I was hiding somewhere inside. I don't know what happened to my wife and to this day, I still don't know where she is. Three years have passed and I still have no information about her. I have searched for her everywhere, but to no avail.

Those students helped me to get to the capital city, but they didn't just leave me there. They raised money, by reaching out to their relatives around the world. This provided me with crucial financial support. One of them introduced me to a group that assists people in escaping to safe countries. They assured me, "Don't worry. We'll get you to safety. Staying here is too dangerous."

This was in January of last year (2023). However, even in the capital city, I was not safe. I was told they were looking for me there. I don't know how they found out where I was, but I was terrified. In this chaos, the person who promised to help me escape disappeared. Despite the significant financial contributions from my students, their relatives and even my own mother (who had sold some of our assets to fund this effort), I found myself isolated and vulnerable. I was then introduced to a man who was involved in trafficking people. I had never met him before, but I had to trust him, as I was now completely reliant on these traffickers for protection. They provided me with a passport from another country, but the fear and uncertainty about my future was overwhelming.

All I could think about was if I would be alive to see the next morning. I was just waiting, wondering, "When will it be over?" I was merely going through the motions. I was just surviving, eating and drinking without truly understanding what was happening to me. I couldn't accurately describe how I felt because, to be honest, I didn't even know myself. I just assumed I was done for.

The traffickers assured me that they would help me and told me not to worry. One of them accompanied me when I boarded my first flight ever, filled with fear but also a glimmer of hope. That was the moment I started to realise what was really happening. We landed in Turkey, where we stayed for a while. I was told to wait for another flight, so we spent some time at the airport, before I eventually found myself here.

I flew into Dublin. The person who had been assisting me and had provided the passport guided me through immigration. Once I cleared the checkpoint, he reassured me, saying, "Now you are safe, just be yourself." He handed me 20 euros in cash and called a taxi for me. That's how I ended up in front of the International Protection Office.

After arriving in Ireland, I found that many Somalis had little to no English. While staying at the Balseskin Reception Centre in Dublin, I saw the security staff struggling to communicate with Somali individuals. They would ask, "What do you need?" but many couldn't express basic requests, like asking for a towel. They often resorted to gestures to communicate their needs. Seeing this, I decided to step in. I spoke with the staff and offered to help. I arranged to use a space at the centre where I could teach others, who were struggling with English and with reading and writing. I wanted to make a difference by helping others in similar situations, so I took on this role for seven months, while I was staying there.

Arriving in Ireland, that was when I could finally say, "I am safe." However, having gone through so much, I found myself constantly crying. I was feeling overwhelmed and emotional, but then I found a way to cope. I met a wonderful woman named Ciara. She invited me to attend the Sanctuary Runners, an initiative for refugees, asylum seekers, migrants and Irish people to connect through sport. I went along the first Saturday after I arrived in Ireland. The previous week, I had been unable to sleep due to overwhelming thoughts and images. I went and did their regular 5K run, wearing some runners she had given me. After the run, I was supposed to have lunch, but instead I slept like a baby. Although I was exhausted, the experience was incredibly uplifting. I slept deeply that night, which was a relief after a week of sleeplessness and stress.

Running became a form of therapy for me, helping me regain my mental clarity and balance. I became heavily involved in running and began encouraging my students to join me. That's how it all started. I adapted to my new environment, and the people here appreciated my efforts. Even the locals were impressed, saying, "Wow, he's doing great."

In Balseskin, I met Somali individuals with disabilities. One of these was a 17-year-old boy in a wheelchair. I suggested that he join the Sanctuary Runners with me for the next 5K run, offering to push his wheelchair. By involving him in the group, I helped him to feel included and he gained a sense of satisfaction from participating. For the first time in his life he saw people appreciating him. In Somalia, individuals with disabilities are often kept hidden due to societal stigma. In many cases, their families will lock them in a room and only bring food through a small opening, preventing them from seeing sunlight or participating in daily life. At first, the boy had refused my offer, but I told him, "This is not Somalia." That day, he saw how people appreciated and clapped for him as he approached the finish line. Now, that boy never misses his Saturday "run".

Another Somali person I met in Balseskin is visually impaired. I suggested to him that we run and walk together. I started accompanying him to the Sanctuary Runners events and, for the first two months, we completed the 5K together. Towards the end of his first run, he could hear the cheering and asked me if we were nearing the finish line. When I told him yes, he cried for joy. It was a completely new experience for him. At first, he was walking the 5K in about an hour and ten minutes. Seven months later, he completed the race in just 29 minutes. This was remarkable. He even joined in the one-mile run, which was a new challenge for him.

When I was transferred to Cork, many of the Sanctuary Runners at the centre were in tears, because they had come to see me as a father figure. I had been helping them to learn English so that they could better connect with the community. Every Saturday, I still call them and ask the 17-year-old, "How did you complete the run today?" One person from the wheelchair association told me that they would be sponsoring him for the Paralympics.

They believe in themselves now, even without me. They can live on their own. That's the real pleasure for me. I often remind myself that I succeeded because they are managing on their own without me. My visually impaired Somali friend has now joined the Visionary Care School and is studying in Dublin. He navigates the city on his own now and no longer feels confined to one room or limited by his past experiences in Somalia.

I got my refugee status this year, my dad often shared a lesson from my childhood that really stuck with me. He used to say, "Look at the animals in the world – elephants, giraffes, lions. The elephant is much stronger than the lion, maybe 20 or 30 times stronger. But despite its strength, the lion can still defeat the elephant." I would ask why. He explained that, when a lion sees an elephant, it doesn't think about the elephant's strength; it sees food. The lion's mentality is one of determination and belief in its ability to succeed, even if it lacks the strength of the elephant.

My dad would then tell me, "You're a smart boy. Whatever you set your mind to, know that you can achieve it." He reminded me that the only true power comes from God. He said, "Don't fear anyone in the world. Trust your own judgement. If something seems right, do it. If something seems wrong, stand up and address it."

I was transferred to temporary tent accommodation at the Central Mental Hospital in Dundrum. There were about 50 people in total at this temporary accommodation centre and I think around 20 of them were Somali, many of whom are around 60 years old. There were also some teenagers, aged about 17 or 18. When we arrived, people were queuing up, but I told the other Somalis to sit down instead and stay quiet. Once the queue was gone, I planned to speak to the management myself.

The security staff initially thought we wanted to protest or cause trouble. I explained that I was representing the group and needed to speak with the management. I introduced myself to the manager and explained that all the people with me were Somali. I told him that these people didn't speak English, which would make it difficult for them to communicate and express themselves. They couldn't live comfortably with others, because of the language barrier. I asked if they could be accommodated together in a single area, as it would be challenging for them to integrate without being able to communicate. I explained that if we can't understand each other, it would be hard to coexist. The manager thought this was a good idea and decided to clear three tents to accommodate them. I also offered to help with communication by acting as an intermediary, saying they could call me if they needed to pass on any information to the group.

The conditions we were living in were challenging. The beds were like folding stretchers that you'd find in ambulances. It was winter and we had elderly men who could hardly sleep, because the beds were so narrow, you couldn't turn over. If you tried to move, it felt like the whole thing would collapse. It was very cold and sometimes the wind would blow so hard that it felt like the tents might be blown away, especially when it rained. We often had to huddle together in a corner for warmth and safety. Despite these challenges, we managed. The staff helped us a lot by providing portable heaters. For the months of September, October, November and December, I ensured that the whole group travelled every Saturday to the Sanctuary Runners. We would get the Luas to town and then a bus.

From December last year, I was moved to Cork. Upon arriving, I quickly settled in and even joined the local Sanctuary Runners group, which I found was just a five-minute walk away. I went there wearing the Sanctuary Runners T-shirt and when I arrived, I saw five people already there with the same shirt. It made integrating into the group very easy, as we were all established members. We started running together, exchanged contact information and continued to run as a group. I even participated in a half-marathon with them.

Meeting Ciara at the Sanctuary Runners was special. She's like a sister or even a mother to me. When I found out she had come all the way to Cork from Dublin to take part in the half-marathon, I felt so proud of her. I told her I would run the entire way with her, side by side. From the start to the finish line, we held hands and crossed the line together. We stayed together throughout the race; whenever she slowed down, I slowed down with her. She told me she had never run a half-marathon before and was a bit scared, so I reassured her that we would do it together. It was a great experience.

I really believe that things are going to get better. Even those who have been oppressed or felt dehumanised will one day enjoy their life again. I truly feel that there is no such thing as a superhuman. Everyone, regardless of their beliefs, interests or feelings, is just as human as anyone else. We all have blood running through our veins and it doesn't differentiate based on whether you're a man or a woman, black or white. What matters is how you treat people, how you coexist with others and how you show respect. Everything else is secondary.

When I left Somalia, I knew I could not contact people back in my community, because many don't have phones or don't know how to use them. There's no free education, decent roads or proper infrastructure. Back in my hometown, we don't have electricity and rely on pressure lamps. Only the wealthy have generators for their homes and trucks. The streets are dangerous, as you can be easily attacked and robbed. You must be careful, because people don't always trust one another. Weapons are not well-regulated and anyone can have a gun. Hospitals are available, but they're often inadequate, relying on trial and error or traditional methods, due to a lack of qualified doctors. Many women give birth at home, because there are no reliable hospitals or health care facilities.

This is the harsh reality of life in my country. I really wanted to experience for myself what good governance feels like. When I came here, I felt the sweetness of effective government. We lost our government during the civil war in 1992, the year before I was born. My father often told me about the time when we had functioning hospitals and other essential services, but now there's nothing like that.

Even though I could see and read about the quality of life in other countries like Ireland, where people protest for their rights, it felt distant from my reality. People have the right to express their concerns, but back home, we are more focused on basic safety. All that matters in my life is, am I safe? Am I in a safe country? That is my priority.

The more I talk about it, the more I feel relieved and adjust to my new life. This is just the beginning for me and I believe that eventually, there will be times when people might need my help in some way. There may be someone out there who will find inspiration in my story and understand the challenges people face. It's important for others to know why people come to new countries and what they endure. Many people might not understand why we flee our homes. Sharing our stories helps to provide that understanding.

For me, it's important to be there for others, even in small ways. I always try to bring a smile to someone's face. I feel grateful for the second chance I've been given in life. As fate would have it, just by leaving my house a few minutes earlier than usual on that terrible morning, I am here now and I believe part of that purpose is to spread positivity and kindness to others. In my mother tongue, we have a saying: "A thorn cannot remove itself, just as a person cannot help themselves alone."

"THE LIFE OF A SINGLE HUMAN BEING IS WORTH A MILLION TIMES MORE THAN ALL THE PROPERTY OF THE RICHEST MAN ON EARTH."

CHE GUEVARA

Ciara has been actively involved with the Sanctuary Runners since 2019. A proud mum, she understands the importance of community, acceptance and above all else, compassion. Ciara is the glue that keeps so many of the Poppintree Sanctuary Runners connected, both past and present.

IT IS ABOUT DOING SOMETHING WITH, RATHER THAN FOR, PEOPLE.

CIARA

I dedicate my Saturdays to the Sanctuary Runners, because it profoundly impacts my perspective on life. It feels like my eyes have been opened to a new understanding of the world and this drives me to continue. Even though it can be emotionally demanding at times, the sense of purpose and connection I gain is incredibly fulfilling.

Prior to joining the Sanctuary Runners, I had never been involved with any groups or projects that focus on the inclusiveness of migrants, refugees or people seeking international protection. However, I would regularly attend the Poppintree Parkrun on Saturday mornings. One day, back in September 2019, I noticed a couple running ahead of me, wearing these vibrant blue T-shirts with the words "Solidarity, Friendship, Respect" on the back. That is how I came to learn about the Sanctuary Runners. The media that same week had been full of protests that were happening in Oughterard over the opening of a direct provision centre. While I've never been any sort of activist, the tone of the protests was bothering me. So wearing one of those vibrant blue T-shirts seemed like a simple show of solidarity.

My first interactions with the Sanctuary Runners were with Anna and Maria (who were among the longest standing Poppintree volunteers). Anna mentioned that they sometimes needed people to offer lifts to participants from the Balseskin Centre. I hesitated at first, thinking I wouldn't know what to say to someone who was newly arrived in the country. But I need not have worried; the first person I met in Poppintree was Noel from Ghana and we chatted about the fact that my mother-in-law had lived in Ghana in her twenties and still cooks her curry with a Ghanaian twist! So, the following Saturday I volunteered to give people lifts and that's how I got started with the Sanctuary Runners.

There was, and still is, a great group of volunteers looking after the Poppintree team and providing lifts to the park – Maria, Phil, Susan, Ruth, Paul, Anna and Sorcha. So I thought my contribution to the group could be to bring along some tea and cake to share in the park afterwards. Since then, the "tea and cake" time has provided a lovely opportunity for people to take time to chat after their run. Our group was quite small at first, with Balseskin being the only centre we were connected with. The group from Balseskin included Noel, who now serves as the group's Liaison Officer for Dublin. Another member, Chawa from Zimbabwe, started around the same time I did. For years, I watched Chawa go through the highs and lows of the IPO system, but now she lives in her own apartment, has just finished a master's degree, is due to become an Irish Citizen next month and remains very much a part of my life and that of my family.

By early 2020, the Poppintree Sanctuary Runners group was starting to grow nicely. We started picking up participants every Saturday from various hotels in the area. By March 2020, our group had blossomed, attracting a diverse range of ages and backgrounds.

Covid brought a lot of challenges. As people could no longer meet to run, we became very conscious that people were living in very difficult communal settings and worried that their mental health, in particular, could suffer. We had to find new ways to support and encourage each other from a distance. We started setting up "virtual" runs and challenges. We encouraged people to organise their own 5Ks and post photos to our WhatsApp group. We even arranged a virtual inter-county challenge that had Sanctuary Runner groups compete against each other for the longest collective distance (Cork won). It was about finding different ways to keep people motivated, exercising and most importantly, connected.

Eventually, some Covid restrictions were lifted and we could meet up, but we could not offer people lifts. So people would walk from Balseskin to Poppintree, where we organised our own version of the parkrun! It was really uplifting to see the amazing collection of volunteers who keep the Poppintree group ticking over, return to the park in those early post-Covid days.

Since then, we have secured funding for a double-decker bus that transports the people to and from the centre. We also now have around 40 groups across the country. So, when someone is transferred away from Dublin, they can rejoin another group immediately without missing a Saturday session. It's wonderful to be there to welcome new people and give them a positive first impression. They often leave Dublin with the expectation that the warmth and friendliness they experience in Poppintree will be reflected throughout the country when they move on … and it is.

Being involved with the Sanctuary Runners has shifted my entire perspective on life. Each week, people teach me about resilience and what's truly important. That's what brings me back week after week. At a workshop in 2022, the Irish-born participants in the group concluded that it was "the opportunity to be continually inspired by those we meet" that encapsulates the essence of what we gain from the Sanctuary Runners.

Sometimes I'll receive texts from newcomers before the Saturday parkrun. For instance, Mo from Somalia reached out to me with a few texts before we met. It's remarkable how you can start to form an instant connection with someone in this way! When Mo arrived at the park the first morning, it felt like we had known each other forever. He was incredibly warm and genuine. I never ask people about their personal stories or why they're here. I prefer to let our interactions speak for themselves. From the moment he arrived, Mo seamlessly integrated into the group. Everything about him, from his smile to his eye contact, made it clear he was a genuinely warm and sincere person. At first, he preferred to run alongside others and was modest about his abilities. I kept telling him I thought he was a strong runner and would eventually break free and show his true potential. He never sought to draw attention to himself; he was always understated. Despite this, he excelled at encouraging others to join and participate.

In March, a month after Mo joined us, Mustafa came along to the group. Mustafa is visually impaired and Mo had taken him under his wing, looking after him with great care. Then Mo mentioned that he also had a Somalian friend who was wheelchair-reliant and asked if we could accommodate him. It was something I hadn't considered before, but after a quick check on bus accessibility and the park's wheelchair facilities, we were good to go! When Liibaan joined us, he was in a very basic wheelchair. Mo would run the 5K route around the park while pushing him and it was incredibly challenging work. Despite how easy it might look, pushing a wheelchair is tough!

Mo had a natural ability to gently motivate others to join in. Mo, Mustafa and Liibaan are all from Somalia originally and I often feel there are similarities between Somali and Irish people in their sense of community and strong sense of clannishness. Mo fostered a sense of unity, making everyone feel included and part of a community. He effectively opened up the group to the idea that we were all in this together – whether running or just coming along to have a coffee. His natural leadership and diplomacy made a significant difference, helping to bridge gaps and build connections.

When Mo was moved to temporary accommodation in Dundrum, his leadership skills really came to the fore. The situation there was quite challenging. He noted that it was the first time he had seen so many grown men crying together, especially that first night, which was horrific. He understood that collective action would be more effective in addressing the issues they faced. From then on, everyone started to turn to Mo. He became the key person in Dundrum, handling management issues and addressing all concerns. In the early days, they faced challenges like living in tents in freezing conditions, sleeping on tiny camp beds with no mattresses, running out of food and each tent having only one electrical socket. Mo took on a lot of responsibility, ensuring everything ran smoothly. Even after they moved to Dundrum, Mo continued to coordinate getting people to Parnell Square by bus, and then from there to Poppintree, so they could run on a Saturday morning. He felt it important to get people out of the tents for a few hours, to experience a sense of normality and even have a little fun.

I invited Mo to the Dunshaughlin 10K in June 2023, knowing he had never been outside of Dublin. He was excited about the opportunity and was thrilled by the new experience of running through the lush green fields and scenic backroads. He was captivated by the beauty. After the race, my mother invited everyone to her home for refreshments. Mo later told me how he couldn't believe he was sitting in my mum's house having a cup of tea! It felt so different from where his life had been just six months earlier.

Later that summer, we attended an event called the "Run'n'Roll" at St Anne's Park, organised by the Irish Wheelchair Association. I thought Liibaan would really enjoy it, so we went along. Mo and Mustafa joined us as well, running the 5K alongside Liibaan. The day was made all the more wonderful when Liibaan was the first wheelchair athlete home!

Knowing what Mo went through before his arrival in Ireland is a profound reminder of how perspective can shape our appreciation for what we have. Even when Mo was living in the tents, enduring storms and rain, he would still say, "But, Ciara, we must be grateful. We are safe where we are. It might not be ideal, but we are safe." His perspective was truly remarkable. He has an ability to inspire, uplift and connect with others.

Morton Games 2023, to support a fellow Somali, Mahad

Sanctuary Runners is quite unique in what it does. It is about doing something with, rather than for, people. The only interactions new arrivals have with Irish individuals might be in formal settings, like centre managers, doctors or immigration officials. The opportunity to engage with others in a more casual, communal environment helps break down barriers. That's also why the T-shirts are so significant. When you come to the park, the focus is on being a Sanctuary Runner, not on your background or status. The idea is that everyone, regardless of their personal history, is on the same level. For that time in the park, the label you wear is simply that of a "Sanctuary Runner."

Dunshaughlin 10K … in my mum's garden, pre-race!

Sanctuary Runners is crucial for educating people and bridging gaps within the community. They create a space where individuals can come together around a neutral activity, like running or walking, and connect on a personal level. By running side by side, people from different backgrounds can build understanding and camaraderie.

Run 'n' Roll 2023, St Anne's Park

Cork Half-Marathon 2024

> "WHERE, AFTER ALL,
> DO UNIVERSAL HUMAN RIGHTS
> BEGIN? IN SMALL PLACES,
> CLOSE TO HOME."

ELEANOR ROOSEVELT

At the young age of 21, Mustafa has garnered the respect of the Somalian community in Ireland. Among other notable achievements, he was responsible for establishing the first ever mosque in his direct provision centre in Dublin. He is a highly intelligent scholar and leader, who speaks three languages, all the while showing resilience in the face of his visual impairment.

HIS DEDICATION INSPIRED ME TO BELIEVE THAT I COULD RUN AND THAT I COULD IMPROVE MY RUNNING OVER TIME.

MUSTAFA

My name is Mustafa and I am currently living in direct provision, where I have been since September 2022, when I first arrived in Ireland. I came directly to this centre as a refugee seeking asylum.

I was born in Somalia's capital, Mogadishu, in 2003. Although growing up in Somalia was challenging from the start, I come from a supportive family. My mother worked tirelessly to educate and care for us, despite facing many hardships. My father was deeply passionate about encouraging us to pursue an education. Whether it was Islamic studies, English, science or any other subject, he believed in the importance of learning and supported whatever we wished to study.

Even though I was visually impaired, my father ensured that I could access an education. He arranged and paid for a private taxi to take me to and from school, which was quite far from where I lived. I learned uncontracted Braille and studied for about six years, before moving on to other educational pursuits. It was very hard for me to learn but I would memorise everything by heart. When I was seven, I began studying the Quran at an Islamic school, where it took me three years to complete my studies.

Being blind in Somalia is a significant challenge and it was even harder for me, because I lived in the capital city. While one might expect that living in a capital city would offer more resources and accessibility for the disabled, the reality was quite the opposite. Despite the large population, Mogadishu does not have adequate facilities to support people like me. In fact, navigating the city can be more challenging than living in a small village, where there are fewer obstacles. Overall, however, Somalia's educational, professional and social environments are not accommodating for individuals with vision impairment. However, I believe that in the last five years, there has been significant improvement.

In Somalia, having a disability is not universally accepted. Some parts of society do not fully understand or accept individuals with disabilities. Assistance largely depends on family support or the kindness of others, but this help is often limited and inconsistent. Those without strong family networks may not have access to the same opportunities or comprehensive support that I had. Some people even exploit individuals with disabilities, using them as a way to make money through begging, often keeping the money for themselves.

However, my disability was not my greatest challenge. Somalia has been suffering from internal conflict since 1991. There has been ongoing warfare between various clan groups, who disagree on leadership and governance. In 2008, when I was five, a group called al-Shabaab emerged. They claim to represent Islam and to be upholding its principles, but their actions are starkly different from true Islamic teaching. Their activities have affected the entire country with their acts of terror and violence, causing the deaths of thousands of innocent civilians and causing great suffering among the Somalian community. Al-Shabaab encourages children and young people to carry out attacks against the government and anyone who opposes them.

In 2019, when I was 16, I was studying at an Islamic school that was officially recognised by the government and was part of the education system. One day, my class was taken on a trip outside of Mogadishu. The headmaster took me separately in his car, as he told me that he wanted to discuss something important. During the trip, he revealed that the entire school staff, including himself, had become members of al-Shabaab. This news came as a shock, as the teachers had always been good to me and taught me so many valuable lessons. At the time, I was old enough to understand that what they were doing was wrong, as I had witnessed the impact of al-Shabaab's actions from a young age. Many of my friends had died as a result of their terror attacks.

The headmaster told me that he wanted to reward me for being a good student. Then he revealed his true intentions – they wanted me to participate in a suicide bombing mission, which meant sacrificing my life to kill others! I was stunned. Initially, I refused, but realising there was no way out, I pleaded for a chance to return home and say goodbye to my friends and family. He agreed and I was given a week to prepare.

When I arrived home, I was in deep despair. I broke the news to my mother, as my father had recently passed away. The gravity of the situation was overwhelming. After a very intense discussion, we understood that our only option was to escape the country. This was a scary and painful time. How could the people that educated me condone this? Our religion and its beautiful teachings emphasise the importance of accepting and respecting one another. The Quran includes a verse that states killing an innocent person is akin to killing all of humanity. This principle is profound and underscores the gravity of taking an innocent life. Whether one kills one person or a hundred thousand, the act of killing an innocent individual is equally condemned by Allah. There is no justification for taking innocent lives, and such acts are never permissible.

It was a very difficult time for our entire family, as we did not know the best way to handle the situation. However, one of my uncles stepped in to help. He is a kind and supportive man, who does a lot to assist others. He was also actively working against al-Shabaab. He agreed with my mother that the best course of action was for me to leave the country immediately. He helped us to arrange for a smuggler to get me out of the country. I was to fly from Somalia to an Arab country, where I could begin my journey from there. It all happened so quickly and I didn't know how it would end – whether I would make it through my journey or be stopped along the way. Despite my fear, I was reassured by all the support I received.

Someone well known to my uncle accompanied me out of the country. This was my second time on a plane. I had flown once before when I was young, travelling to Mecca in Saudi Arabia to complete Hajj (pilgrimage). As previously arranged,

I connected with others in Dubai, who helped me to continue my journey. From the beginning, I didn't fully trust anyone or believe that I would be able to escape. Even when I arrived at my final destination, I was still in shock.

It has been a long and difficult journey. I suffered for a long time afterward, and it felt like an ongoing struggle. However, I managed to cope. Ireland has been very good to me, helping me through my difficulties and allowing me to build a better life. I'm very grateful for the support I have received. Despite this, I still worry about my mother and brother, as al-Shabaab also came for them. My mother, who had a small shop in Mogadishu, was given two days to either hand over her shop or face consequences. She was strongly against doing so, but had no choice but to comply. She also managed to leave the country and she is now living in Kenya.

I didn't expect Ireland to be as positive as it turned out to be. Despite the suffering, the stress and the difficulties I faced, I was fortunate to meet supportive people. Upon arriving in Ireland, I first went through security procedures and once that was settled, I began connecting with people from various backgrounds. I spent about seven months searching for a school and ended up on a five-month waiting list for an English class. I spent more than eight months just sitting in my direct provision centre, rarely going outside, and it was quite difficult.

I had mentioned to my social worker that I was interested in sports, particularly running, and he connected me with a person who introduced me to Ciara. She is an amazing woman who connected me with Ireland and showed me its positive aspects. From the beginning, she was very supportive and helped me to get involved with her running group. I didn't believe I could ever run or achieve anything in this area, but thanks to her help, I've made progress. At that time, there weren't many people coming to the group from my reception centre, so Ciara would give me a lift in her car, sometimes with her husband. They were very supportive, helping me get to the park and other places.

One friend I made was Mo, whom I met within his first week at the centre. We became best friends in a short time, but it felt like we had known each other since childhood. Mo was very proficient in English and I noticed he listened to a lot of English audiobooks and news. We developed a friendship and I learned a lot about English from him. I told him that I was going to start running every Saturday and he joined me. From the beginning, I noticed he was very dedicated and gifted, completing the 5K Saturday run in about 27 minutes! Initially, I had restricted myself to walking, but we began running together. From the start, his dedication inspired me to believe that I could run and that I could improve my running over time. Sometimes, I couldn't even finish a run, but his support motivated me to keep going. One kilometre felt like twenty! But we began training in the centre during the week, preparing for our Saturday runs. My running improved and gave me something to work towards.

I also started English classes with him. He was an excellent teacher, guiding me to useful websites and helping me with different assignments in both English and Somali. Thanks to his friendship, I have recently completed my Level Four English course.

One of the hardest things about my time in Ireland has been meeting so many wonderful and diverse people, only to eventually part ways, because they were transferred to different parts of the country. However, I still stay in contact with Mo and most of the people I have met.

I was very worried when I first arrived in the centre, because there was no nearby mosque where we could pray five times a day. After seven months, I mentioned an idea to the manager, Martin. I explained that, since most of us were from various Islamic countries, it would be beneficial to have a meeting room or a small mosque where we could pray. Martin was very welcoming to the idea and shortly before Ramadan 2023, we started using the social room for prayers. This initiative allowed us to pray five times a day during Ramadan.

I hope to pursue higher education and complete my studies. In the future, I aspire to become a teacher. I hope everyone in this country will be able to live well together, in peace and love. I hope that people with disabilities will have their situations improved, through understanding and support, moving from suffering to enjoying a good life. I hope we can change the current situation in Somalia for the better. My biggest hope, however, is for my family to be able to join me in Ireland, such a beautiful country!

"YOU MATTER BECAUSE YOU ARE YOU, AND YOU MATTER TO THE LAST MOMENT OF YOUR LIFE."

CICELY SAUNDERS

Only 17 years old, Liibaan epitomises
what strength and bravery look like.

> *WHEN I GOT MY POWER WHEELCHAIR, IT WAS A MOMENT OF GREAT HAPPINESS FOR ME. I COULDN'T BELIEVE THAT ONE DAY I WOULD BE ABLE TO DRIVE IT MYSELF.*

LIIBAAN

My name is Liibaan and I am from Somalia. I am 17 years old. I was born in the countryside and I lived as part of a clan. From the beginning of my childhood, life was not good and I did not have the opportunity to study. In our village, al-Shabaab had a strong presence and life there was very difficult, especially for people with disabilities. I got my first proper wheelchair only after I came to Ireland. With no access to a wheelchair and not being able to walk, I had to move around using my hands.

It was difficult. Life is hard, but it's much harder when you depend so much on others. I wanted my life to be like other people's lives, but I had to struggle just to manage on my own. If I wanted to join others, go outside and spend time with people my age, I didn't have much opportunity to do so. Most of the time, I stayed at home and didn't go out much. However, when I did want to go somewhere, my father would carry me. He could do this easily when I was small, but as I got older it became harder. From the beginning, it was difficult for both my parents and me. We have all suffered a lot and faced many challenges, as my parents' resources were limited.

When the sun was beating down in the afternoon and the weather was cooling off, I would occasionally go outside on my hands to get some fresh air and enjoy

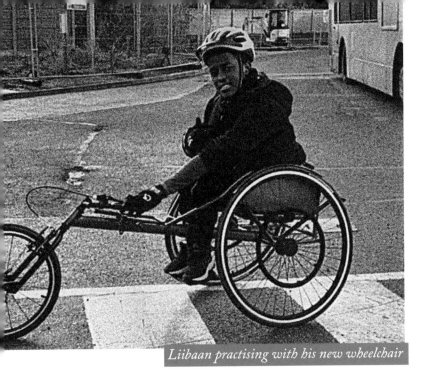
Liibaan practising with his new wheelchair

the change in temperature. The people in my village would turn away from me, avoiding me; it felt like they were scared. I could see their panic, as if I were a threat. Their reactions made the situation even more challenging, because they didn't understand my circumstances. People didn't recognise me, or if they did, they could not accept the way I was. I started going outside less and less, because I did not wish to keep facing this situation. Most of the time, I stayed in my home.

My dad and mum owned and managed some small shops. So they were kept very busy. I am also the first of ten children. What was heartbreaking for me was wanting to help my parents and do things with them, but not being able to. I wanted to get involved in many different activities, but I couldn't contribute as much as I wanted to.

In our village, al-Shabaab were in full control. Because my parents were shop owners, the authorities began demanding taxes from them. My parents refused to comply with these demands. They explained that they couldn't pay any taxes, because they didn't have enough to get by and support their family. They could only manage with what they had for our own survival. Because of their refusal, life became even more difficult and the situation rapidly worsened.

The authorities came to the shops and threatened to kill them if they didn't comply. They first went to where my mother was working and started threatening her. This made it impossible for her to continue running the business or selling goods in the shops. Eventually, she had to leave the village. They then came to my father, demanding to know where my mother was. They told him that he and my mother must pay the taxes and that they were getting their last chance to comply. They insisted that, if my parents refused, there would be severe consequences. They threatened to kill him if he didn't obey their demands. My father did not give them a clear answer, either yes or no. One day, they came to our house looking for my parents. I was there alone, so they talked to me. They insisted that unless my parents returned immediately and paid what they owed, the men were going to come back and take me.

That evening, when my dad came home, I told him what had happened. He reassured me. "Don't worry. We'll figure this out together, whether we can handle it or not." Very early the next morning, we were awakened by a phone call. It was the same group who had visited the previous day. They warned my dad that today was the final day to meet their demands and if we failed to comply, our family would be in serious danger. My dad then made plans for us to escape. For me, the situation was far more difficult, as I was unable to go anywhere on my own. However, he was determined to keep us all safe.

My aunt took me to her house in Mogadishu, while my dad and siblings escaped to a nearby village. However, she soon received a phone call from al-Shabaab. "We know where you are," they told her. "No matter where you go in the country, or even if you leave the country, we know exactly where you are living. We also know that you have your brother's son with you. If you don't comply with our demands, you'll see what happens."

The situation was extremely difficult. My aunt had her own family and children to think of and she was terrified for their safety. Fearing that they might be harmed, she found some people smugglers to help me escape. She also managed to buy an old wheelchair for me, which helped me to navigate through the airports. Although the wheelchair was not ideal – it was quite large and difficult for me to manage by myself – it was still helpful for getting around. The smugglers took me from Somalia to neighbouring Ethiopia. From there, I was able to get to Italy and finally to Ireland. When you have to split from your family and leave your country, it's very hard. For me, it was terrifying! I was not only scared for myself, but also for my family. My parents also feared for their lives and for the safety of their children. The whole experience was deeply frightening for all of us.

When I arrived in Ireland, I was warmly welcomed and informed about a special group called the Child and Family Agency (Tusla), which works with children and young people. I went to their office, where they conducted an interview. When I arrived, it was the Friday of a bank holiday weekend. They sent me to Citywest and on the Tuesday, I went to the IPO.

They informed me that the Child and Family Agency was not yet ready to accommodate me, because my room needed to be accessible for people with disabilities. This was upsetting, as the situation at Citywest had been chaotic, with people staying up all night, fighting and causing trouble. Through an interpreter, I shared how challenging it was and expressed my concerns. The staff were very understanding and I had several meetings with them, repeatedly explaining the difficulties I was facing. They were responsive and tried to address the situation, but it took time.

In addition to being in a wheelchair, the fact that I was an unaccompanied minor posed further problems, as parental consent was needed for health screening and other tests. However, thanks to a chance meeting with an HSE staff member, who was originally from Somalia, the HSE head office was informed of my situation.

The following Friday, staff from Citywest told me that a taxi would be coming to pick me up. The taxi took me to another centre. That was in February 2023. Being in a new country that I didn't know much about was challenging. I was unfamiliar with the culture and the way people communicate here. Not speaking the language only adds to the difficulty, because you don't understand what people are saying. It was also very difficult for me to accept being so far from my family, especially in the beginning. However, when I arrived at the new centre, I met many young people from my country, who were also living there. They were very helpful, assisting me with integrating into the community, translating for me and supporting me. We also had a lot of good times together.

At the centre, I met with health care professionals and doctors who wanted to assess my situation and understand what had happened to me. One lady, whose name I cannot remember, put me in touch with a group known as the Irish Wheelchair Association (IWA). They provided me with a smaller wheelchair and told me that they were requesting a power wheelchair for me, which would be much more suitable for my needs. In Ireland, I first learned about the nature of my medical condition and they assisted me in getting the accessibility support I needed. Once my age was verified and I received my refugee status, it made a significant difference, both practically and psychologically. I felt a huge sense of relief and was able to relax. Additionally, with refugee status, I gained access to various other forms of assistance and additional rights.

Taking part in the Sanctuary Runners 5K

Liberty IWA Run'n'Roll 2023

When I got my power wheelchair, it was a moment of great happiness for me. I couldn't believe that one day I would be able to drive it myself! At first, it felt almost impossible to imagine, but with time and practice, my confidence grew. I practised both inside and outside, and gradually improved my skills, learning to increase my speed and manoeuvre more effectively. Now, I'm proud to say that I can drive it with ease.

I hear from my father about once a month, or whenever he has the chance, depending on the availability and the situation, which is always challenging. The family are in a better situation now, because they are living in a small village outside the capital. They are currently in an area where al-Shabaab does not have much control. However, they are attempting to regain control and my parents' village is caught up in the fighting between al-Shabaab and the government.

After a while, I joined the Sanctuary Runners. In the beginning, I wasn't very fast, because I didn't yet have the sports wheelchair. Ciara was incredibly helpful in getting me this wheelchair, so I could "run". When I was pushing myself in the old wheelchair, it often left me exhausted. Mo was a great support during this time; he encouraged me and even helped to push me when I was too tired to push myself. He also translated for me and communicated my needs to Ciara, who was instrumental in encouraging me to keep going.

Thanks to their support, I was able to participate in the park runs. After getting the new wheelchair, my situation improved, and I felt more empowered. Ciara has even helped me to get involved in the Liberty IWA Run'n'Roll 2023, which is very exciting.

I hope that I can start school soon and learn English. I want to become proficient with computers, because I aspire to work in an office. My hope is that one day in the future, I will be able to compete in the Paralympics and go far!

More about
Somalia:

Unaccompanied minors arriving in Ireland seeking international protection face numerous challenges that significantly impact their wellbeing and development, having endured perilous journeys, separation from family and sometimes exposure to violence. Upon arrival, they must navigate a complex asylum process, language barriers and cultural differences. Isolation and vulnerability can make them susceptible to exploitation. The psychological toll of their experiences, coupled with the uncertainty of their legal status, exacerbates mental health issues, requiring comprehensive support systems.

According to the *International Protection Act 2015*, any child under the age of 18, arriving at a port of entry or at the International Protection Office (IPO) and who is not in the custody of an adult, will be referred to the Child and Family Agency (Tusla). The Agency may then decide that an application for international protection should be made on behalf of the minor. The IPO, in conjunction with Tusla, will then make specific arrangements for the processing of their application. Tusla will support the minor throughout the process, including attendance at interviews, and the IPO has specially trained caseworkers to process such applications.

In cases where the child is without documentation, e.g. a passport or birth certificate, an age assessment interview is conducted to establish some basic facts: parents' whereabouts, education standard and level of maturity. With the assistance of Tusla, the case officer will then decide whether they consider the person to be under the age of 18.

Recent Developments

In May 2024, the Minister for Children, Roderic O'Gorman, reported that there were 34 missing children under the care of Tusla, 23 of whom were unaccompanied minors seeking international protection. Tusla is currently conducting a review into concerns of sexual exploitation in residential care 'following the 2023 publication, *Protecting Against Predators*, by researchers at the Sexual Exploitation and Research Programme at University College Dublin. The study revealed that children and young people, particularly girls, in residential care or those who go missing while in State care are being systematically targeted for sexual exploitation by organised predator networks.

In 2024, Tusla informed the *Irish Examiner* (28 May) that 50 reports of young people suspected of being at risk of sexual exploitation while in State care were notified to Gardaí and the agency in 2023, up from 22 the previous year.

Facts and Statistics on Unaccompanied Minors

In 2022, across the EU and associated European countries:

- 42,000 applications for asylum were lodged by unaccompanied minors

- About 1 in 7 asylum applicants from Afghanistan and 1 in 8 applicants from Somalia were unaccompanied minors

- Of all unaccompanied minor applicants, over 93% were 14 to 17 years old and less than 7% were younger than 14 (European Union Agency for Asylum).

The rights of people with disabilities have received growing recognition, understanding and protection over recent decades. However, significant challenges persist in achieving global equality and inclusion. According to the World Health Organisation, "An estimated 1.3 billion people experience significant disability. This represents 16% of the world's population, or 1 in 6."

Despite these international guidelines, the enforcement of disability rights differs greatly from one region to another. Some of the core challenges and barriers center around societal attitudes and accessibility. Physical, information and communication barriers remain widespread. Many public and private spaces are not fully accessible, limiting the ability of persons with disabilities to participate equally in society. Societal attitudes towards disability often result in stigma and discrimination, restricting access to education, employment and social inclusion opportunities. Women with disabilities are recognised to be doubly disadvantaged, experiencing exclusion on account of both their gender and their disability (*Disabled World*).

Education and Employment

Access to quality education and employment opportunities remains a significant challenge. Ninety per cent of children with disabilities in developing countries do not attend school (UNESCO). The global literacy rate for adults with disabilities is as low as 3%, and 1% for women (United Nations Development Programme study, 1998). Many persons with disabilities face high unemployment rates and limited career advancement, due to discriminatory practices and inadequate accommodation.

Health Care

Persons with disabilities often encounter difficulties accessing adequate health care services, which can exacerbate existing conditions and lead to poorer health outcomes.

Laws and policies may deny people with disabilities the right to make their own decisions and may allow a range of harmful practices in the health sector, such as forced sterilisation, involuntary admission and treatment and even institutionalisation (WHO).

Incorporating disability inclusion is essential for attaining the UN Sustainable Development Goals and ensuring comprehensive global health, aiming to achieve health equality for everyone. There are five key approaches to take moving forward:

1. Develop and enforce legal frameworks that protect and care for the needs of people with disabilities.

2. Launch public awareness campaigns and education programmes to change societal attitudes and promote inclusion and respect for diversity.

3. Invest in making environments, services and technologies accessible, thereby removing physical, information and communication barriers.

4. Develop inclusive education systems and promote equal employment opportunities with supportive policies and practices.

5. Foster collaboration between countries, international organisations and NGOs to provide the necessary support and resources to advance disability rights globally.

SANCTUARY RUNNERS

Sanctuary Runners is a solidarity-through-sport initiative that unites asylum seekers, refugees, migrants and Irish residents through running, jogging and walking. With groups across Ireland and expanding internationally, its model promotes community integration, encourages mutual understanding and enhances physical and mental health.

Engaging in sports activities allows asylum seekers to connect with local residents, breaking down cultural and social barriers and promoting understanding and empathy. This interaction not only helps to build friendships and support networks, but also aids in the mental and physical wellbeing of participants, offering a positive outlet for stress and anxiety.

As a non-political organisation focused on positive action, Sanctuary Runners adheres to the principles of solidarity, friendship and respect. Its goal is not to be the fastest running team in the world ... but certainly the friendliest!

The prevailing happenings were threatening.
So horrendous, affinity with fugitivity was embraced.
In a hurry, I scurried to a haven.
The haven looked cucumber.
Alas! At a close proximity, it was never green.

Life in obscurity is not a walk in the park.
The vilifying ditty resounds from a minuscule
of misanthropes who finagle their way into a sub
of the society.

There they are at every turn,
ferociously chanting, ranting hate.
They dispense calumny, vehemently abrasive.
Their voices reverberate across the Island.
Their ignorance of humanity forestall solidarity.

I summoned myself to a rendezvous.
Go home, I muttered!
You're better off among your own,
where the shade of your exterior
will not matter or be denigrated.

The cost of hiding is no less than
the pain of separation.
Home is gravely sick, with no cure in view.
The new haven is fortified with scotoma sufferers.

When it feels cloudy and dingy,
empathy seems downtrodden,
compassion on a ride into extinction,
common sense slipping into rarity.
Then there appears from the horizon
a pocket of rainbow sprinklers.

They shine their lights in my direction,
making sure my dimmed light
does not get smothered,
courageously enflamed in their hands.

Again, I invite myself to a meeting
with the whole of me.
Remind myself how far I have come
and that the greater one is in me.
The one I journey to is the one I journey with.
He is with me all the way.

I know how it feels to be looked down upon,
So, when I arrive at the beautiful gate,
I shall prioritise humanity over fraternity.
I shan't look down on any human.
Comfort others with the comfort I have received.
I will not let freedom die in my hand.

Sumbo Akanbi

You can see more about the countries, creatives and social justice, music, poetry and documentaries by scanning the QR code:

AFTERWORD

In creating *Are We Human?* one undeniable truth has surfaced: our humanity is defined not by our birthplace or circumstances but by how we respond to those fleeing persecution, violence, hardship, poverty and war.

This book forced us to confront our own privilege, a privilege granted solely by the accident of our birth. Our lives hold no more intrinsic value because of where we were born, yet we live in a world where some lives are reduced to mere statistics – numbers in death tolls from wars or disasters. These statistics represent someone's loved one: a son, daughter, spouse, sibling or friend.

Statistics and facts fail to capture the pain of a grieving heart, the cries of the mourning, or the isolation of those starting over in a foreign land. They overlook individual and generational trauma.

Privilege is not something we choose; it's something we have. It's up to us to decide how we use it. Ireland is becoming increasingly divided, fuelled by misdirected hate and misinformation. We have heard concerns about the influx of migrants and refugees, doubts about our country's capacity to cope and worries about vetting processes and tent cities.

The crucial question is: If we were in their situation, wouldn't we do the same? If faced with war, discrimination or persecution, wouldn't we seek a better life for our families? When we acknowledge that we would, how can we judge others or deny anyone a chance at a better life?

We all harbour biases and prejudices. Part of our journey is recognising this. This book has taught us to pause, listen and understand the person before us in their entirety – not just their label as a "refugee" or the simplified news portrayal. It urges us to confront our biases, learn and grow, and keep trying when we get it wrong. Embracing a new perspective is how we can truly make a difference.

While we can't end all of the suffering refugees endure, we can make an impact. As Nobel laureate Malala Yousafzai wisely said:

"When the whole world is silent, even one voice becomes powerful."

Melanie Martin & Leah O'Shaughnessy

Speak Up!

Speak out for those in need, challenge the devaluation of lives, and engage in dialogue to reshape perspectives. Advocate for issues that matter, join marches, and address hate with compassion – because hate is learned and can only be unlearned through love.

When people claim "Ireland is full," remind them:
The 2022 census reports 163,433 vacant homes in Ireland, with 48,000 empty since 2016. As of March 2024, 13,866 people and children are registered as homeless. Ireland isn't full, it's derelict and abandoned. There are more empty homes than homeless people. Homelessness and the refugee crisis are both urgent issues. We don't have to choose one over the other; there is space for all to be sheltered and safe.

When people say "Asylum seekers are unvetted," point out:
All individuals seeking protection in Ireland are photographed, fingerprinted and checked against the EuroDAC system. For more details, visit EuroDAC.

When people argue "They just live off the government and don't want to work," remind them:
Asylum seekers are prohibited from working for the first 6 months after arrival. Yet, over 65% of volunteers with I-Vol in Ireland in 2023 were non-Irish, demonstrating their commitment to integration and community support.

When people claim "They're just let in," highlight:
60% of all asylum applications in 2023 were refused at the initial stage.

When people speak about rising immigration, remind them:
This book and the people we've met show that a refugee could easily be any one of us. Discussions on land, resources and "looking after our own" risk overlooking the intrinsic value of every human life. Are We Human? *reminds us that the worth of a life is not bound by geography; every human life holds equal significance, regardless of birthplace.*

CALLS FOR CHANGE

Throughout our work on this book, we have come across several challenges that deeply concern us and that we believe would benefit from positive change.

Direct Provision

Direct provision refers to the accommodation, food, financial support and medical services provided to individuals while their international protection applications are processed. Originally designed as a temporary solution for asylum seekers, it has become a long-term system where applicants often wait years for decisions. This prolonged limbo fosters a sense of marginalisation and "otherness" among refugees and asylum seekers. The institutionalised conditions erode dignity and further harm those who have already fled vulnerable situations.

In February 2021, Ireland published the *White Paper on Ending Direct Provision*, proposing a new International Protection system focused on accommodation, integration and support. The plan assumed around 3,500 new arrivals per year, but with over 26,900 new applicants in 2022 and 2023 – surpassing the previous eight years combined – a reassessment was required. The rise in asylum applications must be viewed within the broader context of global conflicts, evolving migration routes, poverty, changing EU refugee policies, and the impact of climate change.

In March 2024, the Government approved a Comprehensive Accommodation Strategy (CAS) to address the shortfall in housing and increase capacity. The CAS aims to provide 14,000 state-owned beds by 2028, reducing reliance on private providers while meeting Ireland's international obligations.

The new approach must be implemented fully, signalling a shift towards a more compassionate and humane system for welcoming and accommodating those in need of protection.

The Disputed Minor

We have witnessed the profound impact of a child seeking international protection on their own being classified as a "disputed minor" by the State. When a child's age is called into question, they are often burdened with the task of providing extensive documentation and, in many cases, it seems common sense is overlooked. During our work with an unaccompanied "disputed minor" for this book, it became heartbreakingly clear through our interviews that he was indeed a child – alone, anxious, traumatised and in desperate need of care and support. Yet, due to the uncertainty surrounding his age, Ireland has not recognised him as a child. This means he is denied education, child safeguarding protections and the support every child should receive. Instead of being in the care of Tusla, the child protection agency, he is placed in a direct provision centre with adults, further heightening his vulnerability. We can only imagine how frightening and isolating this must be for him – alone, with limited English, in such an unfamiliar environment. There is a real need to reconsider how unaccompanied minors are treated, to ensure that those who are most vulnerable are given the safety, dignity and opportunity they deserve to start a new life in Ireland.

Community Integration

Becoming part of a community can feel natural for those who have grown up within it, but for refugees, it can be overwhelming. We have witnessed how eager and excited asylum seekers are to volunteer, work and contribute to their new communities. Yet, time and again, we've seen the challenges they face in becoming part of someone else's circle or friend group. This made us reflect on our own lives – how many of us had friends who were refugees or asylum seekers? The answer opened our eyes. It's worth asking yourself the same question: how many refugees or asylum seekers do you talk to? How many are part of your life? Do you know their stories or their struggles?

In speaking with contributors to this book, we've heard them express deep gratitude for the warmth of the Irish people – our friendliness, our famous "hundred thousand welcomes". But can we move beyond surface-level politeness and create deeper, more meaningful connections?

Community integration has the potential to break down barriers and foster open, honest dialogue. We've seen this first-hand through the Sanctuary Runners model of integration. Whether running, walking, laughing, crying, or simply sharing a coffee and conversation, we've formed friendships with the asylum seekers involved. The only shortcoming is that there aren't enough programmes like Sanctuary Runners. When you see the success and values of this charity, it's hard not to wish for more initiatives that offer hope, connection and a sense of belonging – erasing the "them and us" divide.

Resources and Funding

Resources and funding for communities supporting refugees and asylum seekers are essential. Too often, we've seen communities stretched too thin, with inadequate funding to meet the growing demands. A 2024 report from the *Irish Examiner* highlighted this imbalance, noting that Dublin City accommodated 2,896 refugees, while the Dun Laoghaire Rathdown area housed only 691. To prevent communities from being overwhelmed and forced to compete for limited resources, a more even distribution of refugees is necessary. This would help ensure that all communities have the support they need to welcome and integrate those seeking protection.